A Slice of Spice

A Slice of Spice

Travels to the Indonesian Islands

Marika Hanbury Tenison

with decorations by Ruth Tenison

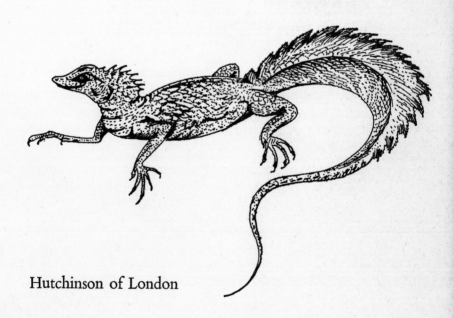

Hutchinson of London

Hutchinson & Co. (Publishers) Ltd
3 Fitzroy Square, London W1

London Melbourne Sydney Auckland
Wellington Johannesburg Cape Town
and agencies throughout the world

First published 1974
© Marika Hanbury Tenison 1974

Set in Monotype Bembo
Printed in Great Britain by The Anchor Press Ltd
and bound by Wm Brendon & Son Ltd
both of Tiptree, Essex

ISBN 0 09 121350 9

Illustrations

Foreword

My husband, Robin, has been travelling and exploring the more remote and little-known areas of the world since the age of fifteen. He is, I maintain, without exaggeration and with only the slightest hint of a boast, one of the most experienced travelling adventurers in the world today.

Until 1971, I was content to stay a homebody, running our Cornish farm, looking after our children and working to build up an unexciting but rewarding reputation as a cookery writer. Then, in January of that year, I cut loose and accompanied him on his travels for the first time in my life.

As a joint venture, our travels in Brazil were a success. Although I was totally inexperienced, ridiculously comfort-orientated and as physically soft as the most pampered of Persian cats, I emerged after three months of South American jungle life, battered but triumphant. (See *For Better, For Worse*, Hutchinson 1972.) I had discovered the fascination this kind of travelling held for Robin and some of it, at least, had rubbed off on me to the extent that I now wanted to travel with him again.

In 1973, Robin chose to go to Indonesia, for a number of reasons. The plight of the vanishing tribes of South America and Africa has always been widely publicized and more work has been done on their behalf than in any other area in the world; both were situations Robin knew well and he felt it was now time to open up new horizons and, although little has been written about Indonesia since the end of the Dutch colonial rule, the islands were probably an even richer source of isolated minority groups than the Americas. His object in going to Indonesia was not to make a definitive report as he had done after the Brazilian expedition, but to make a first survey of the tribal people of the country, to get as wide an overall picture of their way of life as was possible in three months and to see how Indonesia, the fifth largest country in the world and a fast-developing nation, was coping with their problems.

For nine months, he worked hard to arrange the expedition and in March 1973 we left England for Jakarta. His itinerary appeared hopelessly ambitious on paper; it was almost impossible to make any concrete plans in England and, despite his background work, we had little idea what we were getting ourselves into when we left.

I had thought our Brazilian expedition had been gruelling, but from the information we had on Indonesia it looked as though we were in for an even tougher time with erratic and tenuous communications, a political situation which could be tricky and a serious lack of basic information about the country itself. This time too I was no longer a tenderfoot adventurer; in Brazil I had been blooded and now I no longer had the excuse of inexperience to carry me through. On this trip I would have to act in the role of a partner in the expedition rather than just, as my American publisher of *For Better, For Worse* neatly summed it up, *Tagging Along*.

This is the story of our travels in a country with as many contrasts and as many colours as a rainbow in a stormy sky; of three months living a life in which every day brought new excitements, physical hardship and frequent danger and it is the story of the people we met in that vast country, their environment and their way of living.

Our journey would not have been achieved if it had not been for the help, advice and experience of many people we met and whom Robin corresponded with in Indonesia and in other parts of the world. I would like to express my appreciation to them and, above all, to those many hundreds of people who gave us hospitality as we travelled. In this day and

8

age when, in the so-called civilized world, we sometimes scorn to give even our next-door neighbour access to our jealously guarded domains, it is almost overwhelmingly refreshing to journey through a country where hospitality is still a by-word and where a traveller is treated as a treasured guest by both rich and poor. It is this unrestrained hospitality which I shall always remember.

Maidenwell

Dedicated to John and Lecke Hopkinson, my parents, to whom this particular goose has always been a swan.

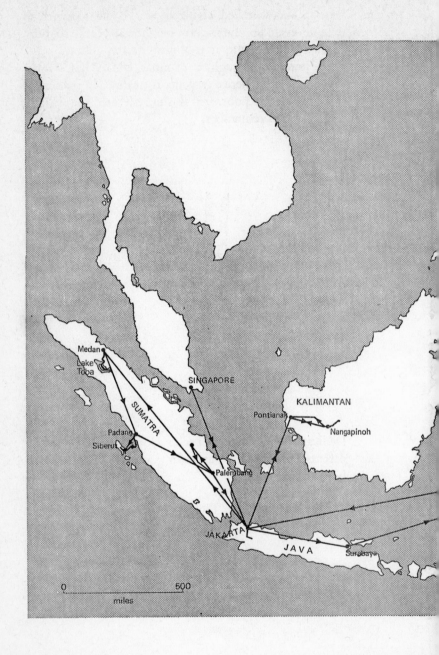

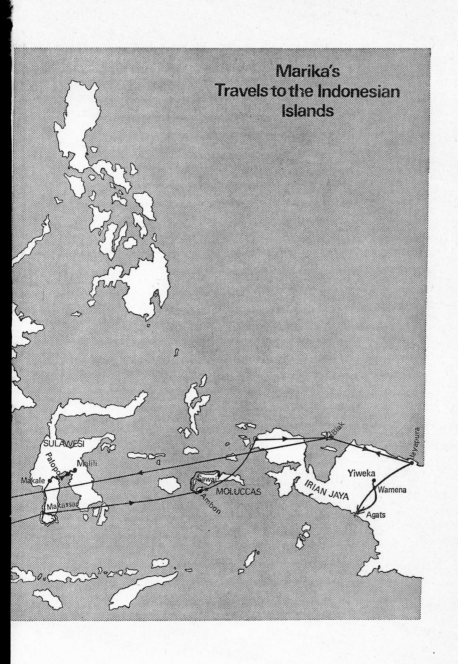

Chapter 1

On the *Anggrek III* it was hellish dark and smelt of cheese. The air was thick, the sky pitch black with the stars obscured; all sight of land was obliterated and the tropical heat was fast giving way to a damp, clammy chill. Under a torn, flapping tarpaulin over the front of the Chinese steamer, the only light came from a thumb-sized bulb swinging on the end of a ragged flex and the occasional sparks as its naked wires hit a metal plate. The smell was overpowering; oil, rust, stale spiced food, rotting fish, damp canvas, the cloying odour of salt, stale vomit and old sandals. The crew were a motley collection of youths in tattered jeans, and old, almost hairless men with sagging bellies and tired eyes.

I was born with a cowl over my head and knew that, according to an old superstition, this meant I could never die by drowning. As the storm continued to build, as the bulb finally smashed, as water poured through the covering above and swept across the deck, taking first my shoes and then a notebook into the blackness below and as the termite-ridden wood of the boat creaked and groaned the knowledge did not mean a thing. I knew we were all going to die that night.

I could clearly see the havoc as the boat smashed into pieces, then hear the silence as the bodies floated on the water before sinking slowly to the bottom of the sea. I could smell my own fear already souring my clothes. Robin, beside me, was curled up, a smile on his face, totally oblivious to the danger, his soaked sleeping bag and the drunken dance our luggage was leading as it rolled crazily across the hold. The children opposite tossed and moaned but he never stirred, blissful and un-aware on a heavy dosage of librium and tuinol. Usually, he is a bad sailor – this time he had been determined to have no trouble. I was not feeling sick – just terrified – but at last I managed to forget the screaming of the *Anggrek*'s timbers, to forget the chaos all around and to be oblivious of the ache of an empty stomach and the pain of spongy swollen legs. With one hand gripped around a rail, I sank into a whirling, spinning doze.

I woke screaming as something wet, spiny and infinitely revolting slapped across my face and over my hair. Still screaming hysterically, I shook Robin, who groaned and tried to turn away. Finally, he located the rubber torch, cursing and swearing as he managed to get it the right way up and slide up the 'on' button. The thing lay between us, gulping and floppy, a spiny fin extended along a shimmering back and a look on its face of even greater terror than there was on mine. Laughing, Robin picked up a small rainbow-coloured flying fish by the tail and flung it into the next wave that smashed across the deck.

Five nightmare hours later, the storm died down and we were still alive. The sky cleared and, in the first silvery, rain-drenched light of the next day, we saw the Mentawai Islands and Siberut as smoky splodges on the horizon.

This was our second week in Indonesia: our husband-and-wife expedition was well under way and the *Anggrek* still miraculously churned crookedly through the water. In the Mentawai Islands, we could meet the first Stone-Age tribes of our journey, and get our first taste of living in the vast jungles. Robin felt that, as Chairman of Survival International (a charitable organization helping remote tribal minority groups), it was time he saw for himself the original peoples of that part of the world and how they were coping with the impending march of civilization.

When we had left the Cornish moors, it had been a day of freak February sunshine. Everything glowed with that strange light which is peculiar to Cornwall; the house and garden looked almost heartbreakingly precious and there was an unfair promise of spring in the air.

In London, we did last-minute shopping and had last-minute jabs. Clothes were a problem. Someone had sent me the Foreign Office manual for wives in Indonesia and from that I gathered life was one round of cocktail dresses, evening dresses, parasols and kid-gloves; I felt I needed something more in the jeans and safari-jacket line. My shopping spree was totally unsuccessful; it was virtually still winter and any hot-weather gear available had been designed for elderly ladies, with forty-inch waistlines, going cruising.

We lunched on our last day with two friends who had lived in Java for three years. They made me more nervous than ever. John Villiers had been with the British Council and he and his wife, Miranda, had travelled extensively around Indonesia during their term there. They were full of enthusiasm about the islands but what they described made even the capital, Jakarta, sound more primitive than a South American shanty town.

'The shops are hopeless,' Miranda warned us. 'You must buy all essentials here or in Singapore. What can be bought in Jakarta is prohibitively expensive and fly spray, torches, batteries, make-up and those boring female requisites all have to be taken with you.' Above all, she impressed, we must not forget to stock up with lavatory paper as Indonesians follow a strange Dutch habit of sloshing themselves with water instead of having a good wipe. Her descriptions of the country's sanitary customs had us all convulsed as we sat in the civilization of London's Fulham Road.

John had serious advice on footwear and health. 'Jungle boots are essential as a precaution against snakes.' Never, he told us, go near a local doctor. Take a well-equipped medicine chest and resign yourselves to the inevitability of getting dysentery, malaria and a few other anti-social diseases. Food, he said, was also a problem in the interior and there would, of course, be no drink as the population was largely Muslim.

After lunch, I staggered round Oxford Street, searching for jungle boots and ending up with a scruffy pair of sneakers reduced in an 'everything must go' sale to 40p. The white canvas, with a sticky, rubberized sole, did not look as if it would offer much protection but, by that time, I was too tired to care.

Zero day came and my prayers for measles, mumps or mastoids failed to bear fruit. Our eight enormous pieces of luggage were packed, strapped and lined up in rows. We had made our final, frenetic telephone call to our tower-of-strength secretary, Shirley, who helps run our lives, and warned her that, inevitably, we had left undone a few thousand things we ought to have done.

At the airport things went smoothly until, just as we were about to board the plane, a delay was announced. Robin went off to see what was happening.

Among our fellow passengers I had noticed a short, dark-haired man with an attractive French accent who, dressed in a neat business suit and velvet-collared overcoat, and carrying an important-looking briefcase, looked expensively out of place among the usual rather motley collection of passengers for a cheap charter flight. On the long journey back to the waiting room he helped me with the heavy bags I was struggling with, and since one of my many hangups is not that of talking to strange men (a habit which Robin tends to deplore) we firmly made straight for the bar.

His name was Francis Lang; he was a director of a merchant bank, and he was setting off on a tour of the major Far Eastern cities. He had seen our name on the passenger list and it turned out we had a number of friends in common. By the time Robin came back and the flight was called once more, we were well into a second drink and knew quite a lot about each other.

From information he had been able to obtain in England, Robin had ringed areas on a large map of Indonesia where isolated tribal minority groups were likely to be found; on the map the islands looked close together but in reality they were ingredients into shallow convex pans over the fires and shouted to each other with high twittering voices.

We chose a variety of dishes from the fresh, raw ingredients – clams, oysters, squid, strange greens and multi-coloured sauces – then sat at one of the tables while an amazing parade of nationalities, colours and races strolled past us – Indians in saris, Malays in sarongs, Europeans in discreet holiday get-ups and Americans in loud-coloured Bermuda shorts and short-sleeved shirts. Bare-footed boys brought steaming hot food (far too much, but at only a few shillings a dish, who cared?) on English Edwardian china, prissily painted with faded pansies and rosebuds. A young Chinese girl, infinitely polite, gave us tall glasses of some fruit juice decorated with shocking-pink ice-cubes, and we gorged ourselves on oyster omelettes, deep fried shrimp, small, succulent dumplings and the sharp, fiery sauces.

Singapore is a city of shoppers and the next day we joined the thousands of other tourists who gazed in wonder at cameras, watches, wirelesses and jewellery which filled the shop windows and, because they bore no purchase tax or duty, looked unbelievably cheap.

In a supermarket, we stocked up with all those items we had been told would be hard to find in Indonesia: lavatory paper, toothpaste, torches, batteries, lilos and plastic sheeting – more weight to add to our grotesque luggage. We had lunch at the famous Raffles Hotel, whose charm was that it had not changed much since the nineteenth century (even the elderly gentlemen playing billiards looked as though they had been standing in the same positions for well over a hundred years).

Back in our hotel the daily papers were stacked in the lobby. To our horror we saw that 'General Strike in Britain in-evitable' was the headline on all the Singapore newspapers. 'The country is in chaos' they screamed out in print. We looked at each other in dismay. What was happening? How would everyone at home cope if there was a General Strike? What the hell were we doing on the other side of the world at a time when we should be 'holding the fort'?

'What should we do?' I asked. 'I feel rather as if we were leaving the sinking ship.' We decided to send Shirley a telegram telling her not to hesitate to recall us if the situation was as bad as it looked in the papers. No response came from Shirley and, in the morning, we left for Jakarta. Our Singapore honeymoon was over.

Singapore had been pleasantly hot; Jakarta was stifling and, despite being dressed in lightweight clothes, we were both sweating profusely by the time we got through Customs. As we stood in the passport queue, I felt as though I was wrapped in cellular blankets; my hair stuck to the back of my neck, and the palms of my hands slipped along the straps of my handbag.

Robin noticed the smell first. He sniffed the air like a Bisto kid and a look of amazement came over his face.

'There's the most fantastic smell of pot in here,' he said, pinching in his nostrils, 'I've never smelt anything like it.' I sniffed too and, although I have only had the odd joint and pot smoking is an amusement that does not appeal to me, even a novice could tell what he meant; the air was thick with a sweet, rather sickly, smoke that drifted past us in thick clouds.

We seemed to be the only Europeans around; the majority of the crowd were Indonesians, mostly men, with darkish faces and straight dark hair. Nearly all of them were smoking peculiar thick, long cigarettes with red bands around them. It was a peculiar sensation; imagine being in a country where everyone smoked pot openly in the middle of the day, even at the airport!

Thoroughly bemused, with our heads swimming, we finally got through all the official paraphernalia of passports and immigration papers and were greeted by a Cornish friend, David Treffry, then working for the International Monetary Fund in Jakarta. Even in a short-sleeved Balinese shirt with a flamboyant pattern, he looked eminently distinguished and frightfully British. He also looked maddeningly cool. Thank

God for David (we were to say that many times over on our journey), with his large car and chauffeur. The airport was a totally confusing conglomeration of strange languages and strange people with men, women and children pushing this way and that. The noise was appalling, the heat oppressively sticky and rising in hot, shimmering streaks from a line of taxis battling for custom and blowing their horns. Efficiently, David got us sorted out and away in a matter of minutes. He also solved the pot question, laughing when we asked about it.

'You soon get used to that smell,' he told us. 'Indonesian cigarettes, Kreteks, have cloves in the tobacco. Apparently they are supposed to have some kind of an effect but they certainly aren't pot; everyone smokes them.'

My first impressions of the city were hazy ones. Fast traffic darted in between brightly painted tricycle passenger carts, peddled by long-legged, hungry-looking youths in tattered shirts and shorts. The pavements were a jostling kaleidoscope of colourful saris and men in large straw hats who were half running, half walking, with a twisting, jogging movement and carrying enormous weights in baskets suspended from either end of a pole balanced across their shoulders.

A short area of slum shacks, tumbling around either side of a railway line, gave way to a wider thoroughfare as we drove past elegant, colonnaded Dutch eighteenth-century buildings gleaming with new paint. Around them, skyscraper buildings were rising upwards in various stages of completion.

I had the impression of a boom town, of money being poured out on a staggering level and of foreign investment very much in the fore as I read the signs along the road: Japanese, American, United Nations, Australian and Chinese. I was confused by the contrasts of straight wide canals – empty but for a black sleazy slime at the bottom – massive skyscrapers rising inside impossibly flimsy bamboo scaffolding, and of sleek, imported cars weaving past beaten-up vans and lorries which looked as though they might, at any minute, crumble into a heap of rusty iron.

We circled mammoth statues, towering over the roundabouts, of rather tortured-looking men with bulging muscles, and a high central obelisk toppled by a rising flame covered with pure beaten gold, raised by the last President, Sukarno.

We had originally planned to spend a week in Jakarta on that first visit, trying to clarify our itinerary and, above all, to get our visa permits increased from one month to three. In London, they had refused to give us more than a month's tourist visas at the Indonesian Embassy and we were praying we would not have to fly back to Singapore to renew them.

Robin got in touch with some of the people he had written to from England, avoiding the official government departments which dealt with visitors who wished to carry out any kind of anthropological research. He contacted the head of the Protestant Missionary Organization about the chances of chartering small missionary aircraft in the more remote areas. While Robin and the tall, rangy American pored over maps and talked of tribes, I bit my nails and refrained from smoking or from ordering anything stronger than orange juice – we knew we might desperately need missionary help at some time or another and I did not want to make a bad impression.

We visited the British Embassy and had a disappointingly cold and unhelpful reception, despite a sheaf of the most favourable and high-ranking introductions. The staff looked slightly as though we might smell of trouble and made it plain they wanted nothing to do with us. That was a blow. Your Embassy, after all, is something that should be rather like a parent in a foreign country; always there and ready to give advice. The Ambassador made no comment on Robin's book about our journey to Brazil, *A Question of Survival*, which he had left as a present, and we walked out, feeling very alone.

After four days, Robin began to become edgy. Nobody that we met in Jakarta seemed to have any interest in Indonesia outside the capital; the British did not want to know and the Indonesians, although they smiled continuously and were polite and hospitable, talked vaguely about official permissions and government departments and then changed the subject. Also, we were spending a small fortune each day in the hotel.

'Let's get on,' said Robin, 'or we'll end up spending our three months in Jakarta. We'll leave for Sumatra tomorrow and hope for the best.'

Chapter 2

We flew to Medan in central Sumatra feeling more cheerful after having lunched with Mr Pringle, the First Secretary of the American Embassy.

Bob Pringle was the first person to be constructively helpful. He had travelled widely in Indonesia, and gave Robin some useful information and guidance. He had also been to our first destination, Lake Toba, in northern Sumatra, and confirmed that it was a fascinating place well worth a visit.

We arrived at Medan after dark. Like Jakarta, although on a smaller scale, the airport was hot, crowded and very bewildering and we were quickly and efficiently conned by one of the great horde of rough-looking youths who swarmed around us touting taxis. Robin picked one at random out of the bunch who pulled at our elbows and screamed 'Hullo, sir. I take you where you go to. This way, sir.'

We had left the bulk of our luggage in Jakarta. What remained went into the boot of a battered car and in less than five minutes we were dropped outside a dreary, modern building which seemed to be in the middle of nowhere. The youth grabbed his money and left and, too late, we discovered we were only at the airport hotel with the town some distance away and no other transport available.

Robin tried out his Indonesian on the attractive girl behind the reception desk. He has done a crash course in London and had found Bahasa Indonesia, a new modified form of the Malay language introduced by Sukarno to unite all the thousands of dialects in the republic, almost too confusingly simple to learn. After an hour of stilted conversation, she came out with some ideas.

We could take a bus from Medan to Lake Toba but that would probably take two or three days. We might hire a taxi but that would be very expensive. Best of all, we could get a 'collective' taxi if there were other people wanting to go in the same direction. We settled for the collective and the girl said she would tell one to arrive at eight the next morning.

The collective arrived at nine and turned out to be an even more scrap-heap car then the taxi we had hired the night before. Our driver was a middle-aged Indonesian with large ears sticking out at right angles from the side of his head. He looked morose and had to wedge his door shut with the help of an ageing rubber shoe. After hard bargaining, he agreed to take us for five pounds each to a town called Siantar, about two-thirds of the way to Lake Toba, and then arrange for another collective to take us to Prapat on the shores of the lake.

Medan was already sweltering. The streets were busy and full of traffic. Bechaks, the tricycle carriages we had seen in Jakarta, with bright primitive paintings on the back, each with a name (some extraordinarily out of place, such as *mon amour*), raced each other along crowded streets, all ringing their bells. Bicycle garages on the street corners mended blown tyres and greased chains. Cars, lorries and military jeeps drove wildly across crossings regardless of oncoming traffic. Under the shade of large trees lining the roads, buffaloes, goats, chickens and ducks wandered around untended.

We began to wonder just how 'collective' this particular taxi was going to be. Already a man from a military barracks, a rather tarty lady in Western dress, a small, smelly youth and another man wearing a beard of three long whiskers had joined us. The old Chevrolet was sagging visibly on all its few remaining springs when we stopped outside the cinema, blowing our horn in a strident tattoo.

'What now?' I asked Robin, expecting the worst. It turned out to be four crates of film, *The Scourge of the Monster*, to be taken to Siantar. They wouldn't fit in the boot so they were jammed onto the back seat beside us; the boy sat on top and the other four passengers somehow squeezed into the front seat.

We drove north past huge rubber plantations with straight rows of thin, tall trees, each neatly nicked with a series of Vs on the trunk where a small metal cup hung to catch the dripping trickle of raw rubber. The road was quite good and we made progress. After the rubber country, we drove through terraced fields of young rice, astonishingly bright yellow-green, the colour of acid boiled sweets; neat and tidy with the blue sky reflected in the water deep around the plants. Women with straw hats and sarongs hitched around their waists worked in the fields, small children led or rode large buffaloes along the grass verges. The country became hilly with wide, hazy views and we passed through small crowded villages of painted houses which would have been attractive if they had not all had rusty, corrugated-iron roofs.

This would not be the most exciting part of our trip, Robin warned me. 'The Bataks are a large and now highly civilized race. Once cannibals, they had been pacified by Catholic and Protestant missionaries in the late nineteenth century, and ate their last missionary in 1923.' Apparently, they were still very proud and tough people but this wouldn't exactly be 'jungle bashing'.

Robin was interested in the Bataks because they were said to retain many of their old customs and culture, and in Lake Toba because he had been told it was one of the most untouched areas in Sumatra. We were aiming for the island in the middle of the lake where Robin's Indonesian teacher had a cousin who was a keeper of the graves of the Bataks. Samosir Island had been the original home of all the Bataks and was a sacred place.

'People go there from the mainland,' Robin told me, 'but they aren't allowed to stay. With luck we might be an exception.'

On the road north, we were stopped three times by a block of policemen who wore guns and looked menacing but waved us on when the driver thrust a fistful of money through the window. Robin asked the military man in the front what it was about.

'It is bribery,' he replied in remarkably good English. 'They stop you and you have to pay something.'

'What happens if you don't?'

The man shrugged his shoulders. 'Then they find some excuse to give a fine. Bad lights or bad wheels or something. That would be worse, so it is easier to pay.'

By early afternoon, after having to push our taxi for a few miles, we wound down a steep road and got our first breathtaking view of Lake Toba, so large it looked more like a sea than a lake. It was beautiful. The mainland slopes were heavily wooded and across a stretch of shimmering water the island of Samosir rose up to a high central plateau, which was a bright, fresh green with occasional streaks of dark, tropical growth.

The small town of Prapat is built round an inlet facing the island. We passed an attractive modern hotel built out onto a point and went on along the main street bordered by small, tin-roofed houses, and had the driver drop us outside a *rumah makan*, an open-sided restaurant, furnished with dirty wooden tables and the meeting place of a thousand flies. A deafening blare of some kind of an Eastern pop song came from a decrepit juke box.

After we had finished a most unsatisfactory meal, a sourfaced youth agreed to take us to the island in a small motor boat. He jerked a disdainful thumb towards the island.

'You will find plenty of friends over there,' he said.

'What do you mean?' Robin asked. 'I thought no-one stayed on the island.'

'Oh, yes, there are plenty of you hippies living over there. Hippies stay on the island; tourists stay in the hotel here at Prapat.'

It took us about three-quarters of an hour to cross the water to the small cluster of little houses round the jetty on Samosir. One of them was a whitewashed coffee shop, wooden shutters in the place of windows and a group of men lounging at grease-stained tables. Outside, some old women squatted over baskets of fruit, shading under umbrellas. We asked for Mangoloi, our contact, and were directed up the hill towards a group of traditional Batak houses. They were the first we had seen and, at a glance, they were very spectacular; built twelve feet off the ground on thick, round, wooden pillars; rectangular buildings, end on in a neat row of three each side, with high, deeply pitched roofs and some dramatic carvings on the supporting beams. Then we noticed that, instead of weathered grey-brown thatching, three had rusting iron roofs and on the carved balcony of one, a group of hippies were staring down at us with suspicious hostility.

We climbed narrow wooden steps, balancing our luggage, and no-one spoke until we went in through the low door and a blond freak with steel-rimmed glasses said, in a slow drawl, to Robin, 'Take your shoes off, man.'

There were twelve of them sitting in sagging basket chairs on the balcony, bare feet propped up on the wooden balustrade. Five were girls in creased mother-hubbards, jeans or sarongs; five were men with long hair, matted beards and grubby sarongs or torn-off jeans; the remaining two were completely sexless – shaven boys or hairy girls. They looked dirty, although their feet were fairly clean, and there was a strong smell which was not from Kretek cigarettes.

They went on ignoring us, reading well-handled paperbacks, grunting to each other or just staring into space, occasionally lifting a tired hand and shouting out 'hot lemon' or 'get me a coconut milk, man'. The 'man' turned out to be a small, ragged Indonesian girl of about eight who rushed up and down from a lean-to kitchen at the back, carrying hot drinks precariously balanced on a small tray.

If you forgot the clothes and the voices, they could have been a group of crusty Indian colonels on their clubhouse balcony, each with his own chair, demanding their stengahs.

Robin discovered Mangoloi was coming back later from the mainland, and soon found out some of the party knew of

Survival International. The atmosphere of hostility changed and, before long, he had an admiring crowd hanging on his words. I felt very square and totally out of place, even with my shoes off.

Mangoloi arrived at about seven. He was a young man of thirty, very good-looking, with short hair, a well-built body and steady, honest eyes that were full of enthusiasm. He clasped our hands, talking in good, but halting, English.

'I am glad to see you. How long do you stay? You must forgive the many people but my friends recommend me and more and more come.' He led us up some steep wooden steps to the top floor under the eaves, where sleeping bags were laid out in tidy rows with only a foot in between each bag. Rucksacks were neatly stacked, books and personal things in heaps against the walls. He showed us to a small empty space about six feet wide in the back corner opposite a blanket covered by a mosquito net.

Robin blew up our lilos and as he had a migraine that was causing havoc, lay down and tried to sleep. I wandered downstairs and tried to talk to some of Mangoloi's visitors.

In the large room, furnished only with clean straw matting and some hard, square cushions, two men were stretched out on the floor; they could have been twenty or forty and both were Belsen thin. One was dressed in a tatty sarong, wrapped round his body from his shoulders. He wasn't wearing any underpants and he gave low groans every now and then. The other, blond and parchment white despite the sun, opened an eye and said, accusingly: 'You got any chocolate? Milk chocolate?' When I told him I was afraid I hadn't, he screwed his eyes at me.

'You sure you aren't hiding any? I crave for chocolate, man. I'd die for chocolate bars. I've got this terrible gnawing in my stomach.' He rolled over and sighed. 'Actually, it's cheese I really crave. Cheese with pickles.'

Outside, a Venezuelan boy with dark curly hair tied back in a pigtail with a red ribbon was playing chess with an Austrian and a plump Australian girl was trying to learn

Indonesian and told me that most of the group had come to Lake Toba from Bali.

On a pillar the list of prices for bed and board had been pinned and I was amazed at the low prices Mangoloi was charging: 50 rupiahs for the night, 150 for dinner, 100 for lunch and 80 for breakfast – less than 50p all in. While I was reading the list I heard Mangoloi gently chiding a girl for coming up from the lake in her bikini.

'Please to dress more correctly for walking around. On the mainland I am getting a bad name; they accuse me of allowing free love and nude bathing here and they try to make trouble.'

After a communal supper, eaten sitting crosslegged on the floor, a thin, golden brown, Australian girl in a bronze kaftan with tawny eyes and long blonde hair, took Robin's arm and led him outside into the darkness, saying she wanted to 'talk and talk' about his 'fantastic scene with tribes and exploring'. Another girl beside me nudged my arm and said she had a 'thing going' for my boyfriend; she giggled and disappeared upstairs with one of the shaggy, bearded, darkglassed freaks.

Mangoloi was a born conservationist. Next day he took us round the coast to show us Batak houses over three hundred years old, beautifully carved and still being lived-in in the traditional fashion with three open fires glowing in the first-floor room and each family living in their appointed corners. Musical instruments were stacked in the beams and, at one end, a gallery could be used for dancing. From under the house, he brought out an enormous canoe that must have been carved from a mammoth tree and told us how the Bataks used to sail across the lake in such a boat with twelve people rowing.

'All these things are going,' he said. 'New iron roofs and square stone houses are not good. I want to try to preserve the old things, to build new Batak houses and new boats in the traditional style.'

After the first few hippies had found their way to the island,

Mangoloi decided to run his house and the others he bought as a kind of hotel. He was endearingly naive.

'I am not popular with the government. They want tourists to stay at Prapat at the hotel, but it's expensive, so most of them come to me. Sometimes,' he said, sadly, 'they forget to pay me. I leave it to them to work out how much they owe.'

That night, we were to cross the hills to a village on the south coast in order to catch a boat leaving for a weekly market at five the next morning. We left after supper, in pitch darkness, with Mangoloi coming with us and another man wheeling a bicycle piled high with our luggage. Almost immediately it began to rain in a steady, heavy torrent. Within minutes, the narrow mud track we were following became an ankle-deep mire, uneven and extremely slippery.

Robin and Mangoloi were talking nineteen-to-the-dozen. (Mangoloi knew the track blindfolded, he said, as he'd come this way every night for a year when he was courting and then traipsed home in the morning.) I concentrated on keeping upright. After an hour, I began to see and move better and forget my soaking clothes. The air was warm, bats the size of pigeons flitted across our faces, and competitive choruses of frogs sang out of tune from all sides.

We reached the other village in just under four hours and Mangoloi (he seemed to be related to everyone) woke up a cousin who lived in the coffee shop. The doors were heavily barred but, although it was well after midnight, the whole family were up and busily working. The cousin, a dour-faced man who reminded me that we had been told the Bataks were very similar in character to the Scots, produced glasses of some fiery spirit, which was very welcome, while vague shapes in the room crowded with tables and benches, lit by one low lamp, brewed the bitter coffee which the Indonesians drink with tinned milk and the grounds floating on the top. Women in the background were tearing banana leaves into neat squares and wrapping them around small parcels of cold rice.

Before we dozed off to the lullaby of near-dead flies and hornets buzzing on the dusty floor beside strong-smelling heaps of onions, we talked about Mangoloi, hoping his plans would succeed, that the island would be preserved and that, if tourism was inevitable, it should somehow steer a course between his romanticism and the government's apparent dreams of skyscraper hotels and overcrowded lidos on the peaceful, beautiful shores of Samosir Island.

Chapter 3

Robin's usually reliable wristwatch alarm failed to wake us next morning and we had to leave the island in a hurry, thrusting a pound to our host, who looked horrified and tried to return it, running down to the jetty where the boat had been supposed to leave an hour before and scrambling on board in a confusion of lilos and carelessly packed baggage. We need not have bothered; loading for the market was still going on and time seemed to be standing still.

I had not yet become used to the overcrowding we saw throughout Indonesia; an overcrowding that was in marked contrast to the many areas of empty jungle, mountains or scrub we were to experience as well. That boat was a perfect example. It was about sixty feet long, covered with a flat tin roof and sitting frighteningly low in the water. Both the inside and the roof were jam-packed with produce and people; old women with weatherbeaten faces, their mouths red and distorted through chewing betel nut, their heads wrapped in bright coloured turbans or crowned by carefully wound coils of black hair, and young, good-looking girls with shy glances and natural grace. There were very few men.

We settled ourselves and our luggage on the bows and watched whilst sacks of rice were heaved up by these tough ladies, straw mats were bundled into spare corners and huge baskets of red onions or small potatoes were balanced one on another. In between loading, the women chatted and bought small, hard cakes or packets of banana-wrapped rice (from a vendor in the back) which they threw at their menfolk who stood watching, not helping much, on the shore.

At last, the boatman decided we should go and everyone settled themselves on their particular pile of goods as we churned away. It seemed a miracle that such a small boat could hold so much and so many. It was still quite cold at this time in the morning, the sky was grey, and there was a sharp wind that made the boat rock. The mainland looked some way off.

To our amazement, we hugged the coast of the island and stopped at two other villages to pick up more produce and more people, the boat grounding at one point and having to be manhandled into deeper water by about twenty men using long poles. By now, we were sitting shoulder to shoulder with other passengers and my hair was being tugged by a girl who wanted to see if it was really yellow. Everyone stared and gossiped in a local dialect about us; some shyly offered us pieces of toffee with sesame seeds in it. Many crowded closer as I wrote in my notebook and Robin recorded in his pocket tape recorder.

It was impossible to see how these people could make a living out of the things they were taking to sell; a basket of onions, a string of fishes no more than five inches long or a roll of matting which must have taken months of intensive work to make. Yet they were amazingly clean and tidy, gay and laughing and, once they got over their shyness, openly friendly towards us.

We finally reached saturation point and the boatman veered away from yet a third potential pick-up place. I felt upset for the people standing on the bank until I saw that we were not the only boat on the water; four more, identical in shape to ours but all painted in different bright colours, were also streaming towards a dot of a town on the opposite coast. We raced and began to beat them to the forest-topped hills of the mainland and a long silver ribbon of water that fell from the side of a bare smooth precipice to the water below.

Encouraged by the passengers, shouting like coxes, the boatman picked up speed and we drew level with a dark and pale blue boat called the *King Kong*, obviously a great rival. We reached the small market port bow to bow, grounding in shallow water beside a dozen other boats which had got there first. Robin and I were almost pushed into the water by the hasty exodus which took place almost before we stopped moving as everyone scrambled to get their stuff off the boat and into the market, which was already a teeming, seething mass of people and colours. Grabbing bags, baskets and sacks, they hurried past us and ran down a five-inch-wide pole onto the sand, stopping to lift their baskets onto their heads or to tie up a loose mat. We left last and it took me twice as long to clamber down that pole as it had any of the Bataks.

Our next destination was a town called Kabanjahe, about 200 miles north, where Robin had heard an Australian anthropologist was working. I sat on the beach with our luggage while Robin went to try and arrange for a taxi. It was embarrassing. Obviously, the hippies never reached here because everyone stared at me as though I had come from Mars and I soon had a ring of curious spectators, men and women, all in saris, watching my every movement. I found it a bit disconcerting and hid behind my camera, fitting in a colour film and training it on the women washing their fish, a pig wriggling in a wicker basket, the sun glinting on a row of colourful boats and the circle of steep hills rising behind the rather pretty little wooden and tin market town.

The market was marvellously gay. A few thousand people spilled into the main street and onto the beach, selling everything from coarsely printed cotton sarongs to cheap plastic toys and tiny lemons the size of marbles. Food stalls had been set up with charcoal fires blazing, and omelettes, noodles and spiced rice dishes were being served at little wooden tables with upturned boxes as chairs. The colours were blinding: the scarlet of chillies, the shocking pinks and citron yellows of cheaply dyed cloth, the dazzling array of patterned sarongs,

35

and a background of the natural blue of the sea and the varying greens of the hills.

At the edge of the town, as we drove through an almost stationary queue of horn-blasting buses packed with people and baskets, we were stopped again by the police. This time, our driver argued with them as they returned a 100-rupiah note and demanded more. In the end, he sullenly handed up 500 rupiahs and we wound our way up the steep hill away from the town and the squat wooden church which dominated it.

For the next few hours, we churned slowly up hills and saved petrol by free-wheeling alarmingly fast down slopes and winding roads, through pleasant rural country, intensively farmed, with the most staggering variety of verge-side flowers I have ever seen – yellow daisies the size of dinner plates, elephant-high cow parsley, things that looked remarkably like wild dahlias and others that must have been the common or hedgerow zinnia, all untouched by chemical poisons or insecticides.

In Kabanjahe, we dropped off the other passengers from our 'collective' and drove to the police station to try and trace our anthropologist, Bob. Robin had been told about him at second hand and had no idea what he looked like. However, he was an Australian, and since there did not seem to be any sign of other non-Indonesians in sight, we hoped to track him down.

We were lucky. Robin answered 'yes' on spec to the police questions of: Did we mean the white man with the dark hair? The man with the wife? The man who rode on the small motorbike and had cashed a cheque for 30 000 rupiahs that morning at the bank? We were directed to a small wooden house on the outskirts of the town and greeted in amazement by the young Australian couple. Janice, the wife, petite, attractive and a long way from home, was especially overjoyed to have our company and at once asked us to stay for the night.

Robin and Bob went winging off on the motorbicycle to see

one of the Batak villages Bob was working with, while Janice and I wandered back into the town to yet another market – this time for some serious shopping.

We passed a newly built market, whitewashed and attractive, with traditional Batak roofing crowning the central gateway. When I said how pretty it looked, Janice shook her head.

'It may look pretty but it doesn't do much good. The government put it up and now they are charging so much to rent the stalls that the people can't afford them. We go through here into the old one.'

Behind the gleaming façade was a crowded squalor of makeshift stalls built around mud paths oozing slime and debris.

From Janice, I learnt more about the Bataks in the region and, from what she said, they seemed in a mess. Having been pacified, the men had no-one to fight and nothing to protect; all the work was left to the women. Driving into the town, we had seen them – lean, tired women coming back from the rice fields in a long stream, bowed down under the large clumsy hoes and heavy spades they balanced on their heads. The older men sat around the coffee shops all day gossiping and the younger men roamed the streets or tore about on motorbicycles looking for trouble.

For those who had jobs in the government, wages were rock bottom; three pounds a month for a clerk. Yet the equivalent of the mayor of the town, who only earned thirty pounds a month, could somehow afford cars for all his family and a large house. A co-operative rice venture with a large storage building had been built by the Bataks; permission from the government to run it had never come through because the Chinese owners of another large rice concern were prepared to pay massive bribes to prevent competition. The women, it seemed, had the hardest time; they did all the work and managed the money but remained servile to the men and were virtually slaves in their homes as well as in the fields.

In the evening, the four of us, with an Indonesian couple, walked into the town to have supper before going to the cinema, the only form of local entertainment. On the way, we passed the coffee shops, all packed with men, loafing about, sipping glasses of coffee, talking and playing chess.

'Chess,' Bob said, 'is the great game here. In fact, an Indonesian champion comes from this town. He's brilliant and should have gone to a world tournament this year. The trouble was, he is totally illiterate and very peasant. They decided it would be a bad advertisement for Indonesia. Now, they've given him a job in a government office to try and educate him a bit before the next championships.'

As we crossed the main road to the cinema, we passed a wild, bearded figure standing in the gutter; chains were wrapped round his hands and his tattered trousers were dropped below his hips, exposing everything. Hundreds of people were pushing past, making for the cinema, and not one of them payed him the slightest attention.

'Once he was a professor at the university,' Bob told me. 'Then he suddenly went like that. People are very tolerant towards insanity in Indonesia and he seems quite happy with his life.'

The large cinema decorated in pale blue and apple green was packed out with people squatting or standing in the aisles. Small children climbed over the seats, babies were being breast fed and the air was full of the smell of the food being eaten all around us. The film was scratchy, the screen slightly lopsided and the projectionist had not quite got the focusing right. It was an Indonesian epic with everything from Balinese temples and dancing to erotic kissing in brothel bedrooms and the volume was turned so high that the sound blended into an ear-splitting, blaring roar. The crowd went mad; they lived and loved every minute, shrieking themselves hoarse and whooping every time another Indonesian lovely appeared fuzzily on the screen. We came out exhausted and rather deaf.

There was a wildness about these people that one could almost breathe in the air and it was not hard to believe the story about a cannibalistic killing which had happened in the town only a couple of months before.

The Bataks are fanatical Christians; the majority of Indonesians are Muslim with groups of those also being extremely fanatical. On this occasion, a Batak boy had fallen in love with a Muslim girl and wanted to marry her. His father was incensed and had insisted that, not only did the boy marry a Batak girl of the father's choice but that he also killed and ate the Muslim girl. With five friends, the boy had done just that and apparently they had enjoyed the taste of the girl's flesh far more than the local highly prized delicacy of dog. The Bataks, as I have said, seem to be pretty tough people. At the height of their cannibal days they lit fires round their live victims, barbecue style, slicing off sizzling flesh from the still living carcass. The cheeks and buttocks, apparently, were the most favoured portions.

Our time was at a premium. We would have liked to spend longer with the Australians, but there was not time. Instead we picked up another collective to Medan next day to catch the daily flight to the south-western port of Padang. The flight went across a vast panorama of uninhabited virgin land; mile after mile of green, jungle-covered hills broken only by winding rivers ending at the coast, where the sea, an aquamarine blue, stretched along a gently curving seashore of pale sand with curling white waves licking at the edges. Out in the ocean, small, circular paradise islands were bullseyed with emerald vegetation, and ringed with white and the palest, palest blue.

Padang, from the air, is the sort of place one dreams of, sparkling white in the blazing sun, with a large silver-topped onion globe mosque in the centre and a semi-circle of green hills fanning out around it from the sea.

During the short time it took for us to circle round and drop to the airport, the sun disappeared, the sky blackened over and we slewed along the runway in heavy sheets of horizontal rain.

In England, Robin had corresponded with a German called Helmut Buchholz who had worked on a little-known island called Siberut, in the Mentawai archipelago west of

Sumatra. Rather tentatively, he had sent a telegram to Buchholz from Jakarta, giving the time of our arrival in Padang and saying we hoped to visit Siberut. To our delight, the large, obviously very shy, blond-haired man was at the airport to meet us and we began a friendship that was to be one of the highlights of our expedition.

The Buchholzes were living north of Padang in the hillside town of Bukittinggi, formerly a popular resort of the Dutch, in the Minankabao area. We drove there in a Volkswagen bus with Robin dredging up his rusty German in the front and me sitting in the back with a pretty little girl, one of the Buchholzes' five children. She did not speak English, nor I German, so I had plenty of time to look at the view.

During our stay with the family, we drove that three-hour journey to and from the hills five times, and each time it was a new experience and one that I do not think anyone could ever tire of; it was also extremely frightening.

Once he got behind a wheel, Helmut turned from a gentle giant into a crazy rally driver, obsessed with speed, swinging wildly round corners, shaving past buffalo carts and playing 'dares' with the many brightly painted buses, each with its own name splashed in fairground characters along the side.

The changing scenery, as we left the plains and climbed higher and higher into the volcanic hills, was better than anything I had seen so far. We crossed a series of wide rivers, busy with water traffic, women washing, small naked boys swimming like fishes against the current. The road was bordered by fountains of sago palms with pineapple stems and dark green, feathery branches, or groves of coconuts, grey-trunked and tall. Little wooden houses were set back in gardens of maize and fruit trees and small villages were clustered round newly painted mosques reflected in the fish ponds which surrounded them. In some of the villages, streams ran in channels beside the road and each house had a little arched stone bridge in front of it. Occasionally, there was a large traditional Minankabao house, similar to the Batak houses but much more ornate, the carving painted and the roof an incredible great curving structure in the shape of two pairs of buffalo horns, one on top of the other.

Most of the time, the road ran alongside a single railway track, built by the Dutch in the late nineteenth century, along which the original train with a Puffing Billy engine and gay coaches still chuffed once a day. Up in the hills, this followed a tortuous route across suspension bridges criss-crossing a high, rocky gorge where jungle growth clung and tumbled over sheer grey cliffs to a fast-flowing river cascading in white foam over huge stones. At one place, a high waterfall plummeted down into a large, deep pool just beside the road, the spray dancing with rainbows. Children were bathing in the pool and women with brightly patterned sarongs wrapped tightly over lean hips washed clothes in the clear, cold water.

At the top of the pass, we stopped for a moment to look out across a plain to further hills and Bukittinggi, perched on the top and sides of a small plateau and ringed by blue, hazy mountains, with sheer, craggy sides. Terrace after terrace of rice paddies rippled across the valley and, to our right, a faintly smoking volcano rose steeply beyond a lake where buffalo wallowed amongst pink and white waterlilies.

On the whole, the road was reasonably good, tarmacked and quite wide but, whereas the railway bridges looked brand new, the road bridges were nearly all being repaired, so that one often crossed wide gullies on a couple of worn-out-looking planks. One structure of concrete piers and metal framework had been being rebuilt for the past four years.

The Buchholzes had an attractive, rambling bungalow with a large garden which included the ruins of a one-time hotel. A black-and-white cow stood with its calf on what had once been the steps, nibbling at overgrown weeds. A large dog came bounding out to greet Helmut and, beside Helga and the other four children, rolling like an old sea captain, came a two-foot high, jet-black, ridiculously long-armed dwarf black gibbon who threw herself into my arms, squeaking and chattering, hiding her woolly face in my chest and clinging to me with little rubbery fingers; she was introduced as 'Bilou' who hated men.

There was a lot to arrange, but fortunately Helmut had two weeks' leave from his job with the World Bank, and was free to come with us to Siberut and perhaps, later, to take us to central Sumatra to a nomadic tribe called the Kubu.

The Buchholzes' story is a strange one. After marrying, they had been sent to Siberut as missionaries from an extreme fundamentalist Protestant sect in Germany. They arrived speaking virtually no Indonesian, having no house, little funds, no idea what the Mentawai would be like and no experience of missionary life in the wilds. During those first two years, they lived at starvation level, their first child nearly died when Helga was unable to feed it, and they had no milk. Gradually, Helmut built them a house and, moving amongst the Mentawai, learnt their language and came to love them. Helga learnt how to grow fruit and vegetables and they began to recover their strength. She also learnt, the hard way, the elements of nursing, having four of her five children on the island and helping with over a hundred Mentawaian births (there was, of course, no doctor on Siberut).

As he worked with the people, Helmut gradually came to the conclusion that the policy laid down by the fundamentalists in Germany was not one that could be of any positive help to the Mentawai islanders. He wrote telling his mentors this and followed what he felt was the best course to teach them about God but, above all, to help and protect them. After seven years of battling, he was excommunicated by the German sect and his salary was cut off, leaving them totally penniless.

They stayed on as long as they could in Siberut but were eventually forced to go back to the mainland so that Helmut could earn some money. Their longing, however, was to be able to return to the island and carry on their work there.

Although their beliefs had been radically shaken, their faith had miraculously remained. Both Helmut and his attractive wife were totally good Christians and managed to combine being devout with humour and tolerance. Their children, though shy through the strange, isolated life they had lived for so long, were beautiful and well-mannered, and seeing them singing hymns that evening, grouped around their blond parents, was a moving experience.

Helmut had chartered a boat to take us to Siberut and then to remain there until we returned as there was no regular transport to the island. All the family, except the baby, were to come too and all of us sang as we raced down the hills back to Padang but I suddenly lost my enthusiasm for the trip when we reached the docks. I saw the tramp ship and shook hands with the fat, elderly Chinese captain who owned it. The palms of his hands were sweaty, the skin pudgy and the colour of old dough. He looked like a night-club bouncer from the sleaziest of establishments, but I knew Helmut had faith in him and that he adored Helmut for the very good reason that, during the time of the Night of the Long Knives, in 1965, when a Communist coup had been exposed in Indonesia and many thousands of Chinese were murdered, Helmut had saved his life and the lives of his family.

The boat, the *Anggrek III*, was moored to the docks on the outskirts of the town. It was filthy, covered with black grease, encrusted with rust and rode low in the muddy water of the river. Clinging to the rails were a collection of incredibly dirty and ragged boys dangling fishing lines into the scummy water and occasionally pulling out silver small fry no larger than their grubby fingers.

It was a long, miserable and stormy overnight crossing and all eight of us were exhausted by the morning.

Chapter 4

The sky was still grey and overcast as we put down the anchor quite a distance from the Siberut shore and gathered up the wet pillows, soaked baskets, and the damp sarongs the children had slept under. Helmut, the only one of us who looked in the least fresh, pumped up the dinghy, attached the outboard and took the first load to the island. Already, people in canoes were coming out to greet us and we could see women, wading with high triangular nets in shallow water along the palm-fringed shore, calling excitedly to each other.

We passed the collection of grubby shacks that make up the main township of Muara Siberut and went upriver to the small missionary settlement where a neat Protestant church stands at one end of a line of wooden houses on stilts and a Roman Catholic mission stands at the other. We were to stay in the latter, but first we had to check into the police and military posts on the island, to let them know who we were, why we were there and what we intended to do on the island.

The head of the police force and the head of the military, both neatly dressed in uniforms and each with a small entourage of lower ranks behind them, withdrew into a small hut with our passports while we were given gritty coffee and Helmut chatted politely to the remaining Indonesians. After half an hour they returned, saying, slightly reluctantly, that our papers seemed in order but we must be sure to check again before we left. Later, we got used to this permanent checking and re-checking with the authorities, but it was not always to be quite that easy.

The three Italian priests and two nuns at the mission were wonderfully hospitable and produced an amazing lunch of minestrone, spaghetti and frito del mar, washed down with ice-cold beer and accompanied by Rachmaninoff from a stereo record player. After it, Helmut, Helga and Robin persuaded me to have a rest and they set off to walk to the nearest Mentawai village.

It was so hot that each breath seemed a fight to draw in air through the heavy warmth. The little room we had been allocated buzzed with insects despite mosquito netting on the windows and outside the mission school were playing a football match with over a hundred Mentawai boys of all ages, shouting and cannoning over a pitch knee-deep in black mud after the night's rain. I sank into a deep, dreamless sleep and remained there until Helmut knocked on my door four hours later.

'Robin says, come,' he said, in his very halting English. 'Follow me.'

I wanted to sleep on but he seemed determined; so I followed him, past the Protestant church and into the shade of the jungle beyond.

Helmut, barefooted, moved with enviable ease as I slipped on a narrow path, breathless in the all-enveloping humidity. I was very relieved when we reached the village of four or five houses in a clearing, surrounded by thick trees, with the river not far away. One of the verandahs was crowded with people, Helga sat with a group of bare-breasted women on one side and Robin was using his new camera with obvious enjoyment. He leaped down the pole steps and came up to me, talking in shorthand whispers.

'The most fantastic thing I have ever seen. Such luck, such unbelievable luck. The witch doctor is performing magic to try and cure a sick woman and they are having a feast. In a moment, they are going to start sacrificing the pig and chickens.' He cocked his camera again and added, 'If you open a packet of cigarettes, lay them on the ground for everyone to help themselves.'

I took off my sandals and climbed on to the verandah, edging past the seated women to a corner where Helga sat looking cool in a sleeveless cotton dress. A young girl with full, perky breasts made room for me and, as I squatted down, an old woman took up a piece of coconut husk and scraped off the fudgy mud clinging to my feet. Aches, pains, and swollen legs were forgotten as I looked round to absorb the staggering scene of a Mentawai feast, the fifty or so men and women sitting around us, the bright colours and a strange, heady scent mixed with the acrid smell of strong tobacco.

The sick woman, young but skeleton thin, her hair lifeless and matted, sat in the shadows near the door at the back; men sat on one side and women on the other. In the centre, the medicine man and his apprentice weaved their spells and chanted their magic, both in a deep trance. Despite the seriousness underlying the occasion, the Mentawai looked happy and smiled often, as they talked softly together, both men and women dipping into the pile of tobacco Helmut placed on the floor or passing little twists to those at the back, wrapping them in tightly curled leaves and lighting one from another. Some helped themselves to my cigarettes, examining the tips and sniffing them. The older children sat quietly watching while the young ones lay on their parents' laps or fed from their mothers' milk-laden breasts. Even large children were still breast feeding; one, leaning against his mother's side and dragging at her distended nipple, looked about five and his rows of white milk teeth must have been extraordinarily painful.

There was a beauty and perfection about these people that I find hard to describe. They seemed a golden and almost godlike race, with Polynesian features, skin the colour of liquid honey, black hair, heavy, straight and shining, twisted at the back of their necks or hanging in a curtain around their faces. Colour came from the pale, faded sarongs of the women, from the off-white bark loincloths of the men, from the beads they all wore, row upon row, around their necks and, above all, from the flowers the men, women and children wore in their hair, behind their ears and around their waists; red hibiscus, brilliantly scarlet, delicate white day lilies with that heady scent and bunches of lacy grass and velvety dark green leaves. All the grown-ups were tattooed on faces and bodies with finely traced, intricate patterns – apparently a slow and painful process and requiring great courage. Small children ran naked except for flowers and necklaces of coloured china beads. They accepted us without question as friends of Helmut, smiling at us shyly.

The medicine man, with a coronet of flowers coming from a headband embroidered with small beads, and a long tail of grasses sprouting from his loincloth, held in his hands a short stick like a magician's wand. Two girls moved behind him, bearing wooden platters of fruit and flowers mixed with articles of the sick woman. His eyes were glazed, his voice high as he intoned the ancient ritual and weaved amongst the people, drawing out their strength to help him fight the evil spirit embedded in the invalid.

A group of boys brought a pig and eight white cockerels for sacrificing. At first, the crows and squeals were ear-splitting, then, as they were handed, one by one, to the witch doctor, he touched them gently and they became silent. Holding the first of the cocks, he moved again amongst the Mentawai, stroking the head of the live bird along the arms of men and women and apologizing to the bird for having to kill it. He did the same with the small supine pig, holding it in his arms like a baby, his wrinkled face full of compassion.

The pig and the birds were killed on the steps of the verandah, by cutting their throats with one quick stroke. Dripping, dark red blood was caught in a bowl and the sacrifices were taken off to be singed over a fire smoking on the ground near the house. Then two men neatly dissected the still raw animals, pulling out the entrails and adding them to the blood in the bowl. While the portions of meat were laid out along a carpet of banana leaves, the medicine man, sitting cross-legged on the floor, lifted up the entrails from the bowl, examined them closely, and intoned, still in a heavy trance, as he gazed through the stretched skin of a bladder which shed ruby droplets of blood over his legs.

'It is good,' Helga whispered to me. 'The oracles are favourable and the woman will get better. Our presence has helped.'

The deep concentration of the medicine man was catching and I found I had been sitting tensed and still, almost not daring to breathe for two hours. I looked at the gory hunks of flesh and the bowl of entrails and wondered, feeling sick, if we would be expected to eat any of the raw meat, and I must admit to being relieved when Helga said we must go because now the Mentawai would begin feasting and we had not been invited.

The atmosphere relaxed and the sick woman, who had moved out from her place at the back, did indeed look remarkably better. Perhaps it was imagination but her hair seemed less dull and lifeless and suddenly there appeared to be more flesh on her frail bones.

Helmut and Robin went running through the darkness. Helga followed slowly with me, explaining more about the Mentawai.

'They believe that all things have spirits, and they never kill except for the necessity of getting food or sacrifices. Before they kill they spend a long time explaining to the victim why it is necessary to do this thing and apologizing to its spirit so that it will not be angry.'

The Mentawai, she told me, were proto-Malay and might perhaps be the most pure-bred Malays left in Indonesia; only she, Helmut and the children spoke their language fluently.

Like all isolated, so-called primitive peoples, the Mentawai were coming under pressure. An attempt was being made for laws existing on the mainland to be imposed on them, laws concerning the following: men not having long hair, the people not being allowed to build their large communal houses, not keeping pigs (Muslim influence), not tattooing their bodies and wearing clothes.

Around the coast, where these rules were being enforced, a large party of Mentawai men had been tricked into attending a police feast and had their hair forcibly cut off. Traditionally dressed Mentawais were now an unusual sight in Muara Siberut, but in the interior of the island, life still went on in the old way. Police and military patrolled the larger rivers and the two missions had set up small schools at the settlements along their banks, but few ventured off the main streams where we were to go the next day.

Perhaps the biggest threat of all to these people was a Filipino lumber camp to the south of Muara Siberut. There the forest was being massacred and game killed over a large area. With the lumbermen came the inevitable drunkenness and prostitution that accompanies such settlements, and stories that Mentawai women were being sold to the workers as slave wives.

Helga was to stay at the mission with the children and I set out alone the next morning with Helmut and Robin on the start of our journey to the interior. I stepped rather nervously into a long, wooden canoe driven by a twenty-five horsepower Johnson. We carried presents of rice, tea, sugar and tobacco for the people we were to visit and four jerry cans of petrol to see us through the journey.

Somewhere on the way, Helmut acquired a large, evil-smelling golden fruit the size of a large pineapple, covered with spines like a horse chestnut. Even now, just saying the name 'durian' evokes that revolting smell of rotting flesh and bad drains. 'It's delicious,' he assured us, 'the best fruit to grow in the Far East.' The smell got worse as he cut the flesh in half and offered us the row of bright golden, flesh-covered seeds from the centre, putting them into his mouth, sucking them well and then spitting out the smooth brown stones. I managed to eat three but, to me, it tasted the same as it smelled, and I felt nauseated as we chugged slowly up the twisting river between banks of jungle fringed with sago palms.

Robin teased me for thinking of my stomach before everything and said it was the first time he had seen me turn up my nose at anything eatable. We were gently bickering when we rounded a bend of the river and came across a family of Mentawai pulling their canoes up the mud banks. They looked like something from an eighteenth-century print of 'discovering savages in the jungle'. The man, two women and a child were dressed totally in banana leaves, all with long skirts of green and the women with layered tops of the same material hiding their breasts. On their heads were hats of plaited green. When they saw Helmut, they rushed into the water, chattering excitedly, and he drew into the bank. He took their hands and they all laughed and laughed until our canoes rocked and we were nearly pitched into the water.

'They thought we were the missionaries,' Helmut gasped with tears of laughter coursing down his cheeks. 'They heard the engine about half an hour ago and, because the missionaries forbid them to go naked, they rushed off to make clothes from banana leaves. Oh, they look so funny.' We shared their laughter and were given gifts of bananas and another repulsive-smelling durian.

It was becoming dark by the time we reached our destination of the village of Sakaliou, which was hidden deep in the jungle fortification of nature. As we walked through it to the clan house at the end – past fat, odorous pigs and the sago press that smelt sweet and sickly from the trunks rotting in turgid water below – people called out greetings: 'Maronsita?', 'Aileweta', 'Where are you going?', 'Stay with us'.

The house was larger than those we had seen before with a wide, open verandah of bamboo and a long room behind with two fireplaces in the centre covered by pole shelves which housed cooking utensils, long drums covered with snakeskin and weapons for hunting. Spoons made from a piece of wood threaded through half a calabash hung from the sides beside long bows and arrows. Men cooked over the fires while women played with their children. There was no evidence at all of the modern world.

The chief of the clan and the medicine man, with his embroidered head band and a tracing of stars following the curves of his buttocks, clasped Helmut to their breasts in that curious silent and unmoving embrace that the Mentawai use to indicate a friend, long lost. We were greeted cautiously, accepted because we were with Helmut, but carefully scrutinized through slightly narrowed eyes; our baggage closely examined, unpacked and re-packed again with interest.

While sitting cross-legged on the floor we ate, with our hands, tough, dry sago baked in young bamboo and a stew of pig, boiled with freshwater crayfish, and drank the greasy liquid they were cooked in from tin cups. Watched by about thirty people and a black spider the size of my fist, we arranged our lilos side by side, stringing our large mosquito net over them, as insects were already clouding thickly around the one wick in an old tobacco tin which gave the only light apart from the fires from inside. The smell of pig, sago and tobacco was drowned by the scent of lilies worn by the people around us.

'What have you brought us?' the Mentawai had asked of Robin when we arrived and we felt ashamed at coming empty-handed until we realized, as Helmut said, that we had nothing to give them. They needed only things that could work for them, such as knives or mosquito netting, or things we could never provide, such as protection from the outside world, the proof that the medicine of their witch doctor should be effective, and the knowledge that their religion and family ties would remain strong. The only thing they coveted to any degree was a round cigarette tin I carried in my handbag. Eventually, I gave it to the witch doctor who was overjoyed and, in return, gave me a Mentawai tobacco container of a small coconut shell, polished to a dark brown and carved with gibbons.

Girls giggled as I discreetly wiggled into my long white cotton nightdress and Robin put on the nightshirt he always wears. We had bought sarongs in Bukittinggi but had not yet mastered the art of tying them so that they did not fall down every other minute. Under the blur of the mosquito net, I could still see people moving around and hear their voices as I eased myself into a position on the lilo where my hips did not dig quite so painfully into the bamboos and, closing my mind to the still motionless spider, fell asleep. Near us Helmut lay stretched on a thin mat with no mosquito net and no lilo.

Our original plan had been to stay there one night and then go further up the river, finally walking across the central range of mountains to the far coast. I was relieved Robin and Helmut agreed to stay where we were, getting to know the village and making small expeditions to other settlements in the area. I was not finding the jungle easy to cope with and the walk from the river to the village that evening had almost finished me; over an hour of pushing our way through muddy, brackish swamps or balancing on logs wallowing on the surface.

In the morning, we woke to find a circle of Mentawaians still sitting around us. Helmut was chuckling as he shaved in a piece of cracked mirror – his only luggage beside a sleeping mat, a change of shorts and shaving things.

'There is a taboo against men and women sleeping together in the clan house,' he said through a mouthful of lather. 'They had to watch all night to see what you were doing under that netting. Luckily, I gather it was just sleeping, no more.'

Surrounded by a droning haze of mosquitoes, we made our way back through the jungle to the river and went upstream in a narrow, rounded canoe, paddled by two Mentawai. It was extremely unstable although surprisingly fast and we squatted on the bottom with a hand on each side. Helmut told us more of the taboos as we slid through narrowing waterways under overhanging branches and long tentacles of twisted leanders. He explained how the Mentawai castrate the young pigs soon after they are born and how human sexual intercourse is allowed until the young sows are old enough to be bred. When the sows are in pig, intercourse is taboo. Sex is also forbidden during the feasts, some of which go on for weeks and at times when the moon is in a certain phase. Few women have more than two children; if they do become pregnant with a third it is usually aborted by massaging the foetus out of the body.

Of course, the Mentawai are not all so physically perfect as they had appeared at first. During the next few days, as we canoed up the rivers and walked through the jungle to more hidden villages, we saw plenty of malaria and men and women shrivelled to bare bones and parchment flesh from tuberculosis, spitting blood and coughing wretchedly. We saw cases of cancer of the throat and face with huge, bulbous growths distorting the features and a woman with a skin disease which had turned her legs black, the rotting flesh giving out a smell of bad fish.

That morning, with the two Sakaliou men, we walked through the jungle, cutting our way in some places through thick undergrowth, fleshy plants and bamboos, to a fast-flowing river which led to a waterfall which, until then, Helmut had been the only non-Mentawai to see. The men now called me 'moile, moile' (slowly, slowly) with friendly familiarity, urging me on up the slippery river bed and across sharp, jagged stones.

At last we reached the waterfall, coming suddenly round a bend in the river and seeing a breathtakingly beautiful expanse of scenery ahead. The water fell in a white curtain from a staggering height, was shot with rainbows and looked like a shaft of light against the dark greens of the jungle. The two Mentawai, as always with flowers threaded through their long hair, shared our cigarettes and looked more godlike than ever as they stood against a background of the foaming water in the strange pale green light. They leaped across the spray and stood like statues at the edge of the black pool, as Helmut told us the story they had about this place. How two sisters had climbed to the top of the waterfall and been lured by evil spirits into jumping down the cascade, how their souls still called from the pool and their hands could sometimes be seen rising from the bottomless pool.

Trudging back to the main river I stepped on a small green plant which looked harmless enough but which sent a pain like fire up my legs. A red, angry rash appeared at once, with the symptoms of nettle sting but a hundred times as strong.

Luckily it prevented me from using the plant as loo paper which I had thought of doing. The pain was still raging when the others came back but I got no sympathy from the tough Helmut.

'You were lucky,' he said, examining my leg. 'That is just the mild form of poisoning and only lasts for three or four days. There is another variety which goes on stinging for weeks.' He was far more fascinated by a long snake skin recently shed on the banks of the river.

I was a mess. The pain was atrocious for three days and got unbearable every time my legs got wet, which with my balance was frequent as we crossed one after another tortuous network of slippery branches. At times, to my shame, it had me in tears and at night I had to take massive doses of sleeping pills before I could even close my eyes. My legs were raw and bleeding from running my fingernails across the rash in an effort to subdue the itching.

In the evenings, the Mentawai shared their one meal with us and made tea in a black pot. We drank the tea from tin cups while they sipped from the calabash spoons. One night, they held a feast in Helmut's honour and we saw again the ritual of sacrifice with the medicine man craving the pardon of a fat, black-and-white pig about to have its throat cut.

Dogs were swept from the room by an old woman who held a bunch of leaves on the end of which a nest of ants with formic acid stings ran in mazed frenzy, jumping under the dogs' tails when the branch made contact and sending them howling out of the hut.

We ate with the medicine man who, because of his status, claimed a larger share for his wife and family. The cooked meat, entrails and some green, bitter leaves were placed on a large wooden platter beside young, baked and charred sago shoots. Before eating, he blessed the food, passing his hands over it, falling into a glazed trance and rocking on his haunches as he intoned a musical, warbling grace.

The medicine man had become my special friend after helping me to the waterfall. He offered me the fattest bits of meat, saying 'moile, moile' (eat, eat), watching with concern as I had trouble chewing the undercooked, glutinous pieces. He smiled at me with eyes creasing up at the sides and a rather suggestive jerk of the head which I had at first thought meant 'come outside' but which I learnt meant merely that he was content. We could not talk to each other but we were able to communicate by glances.

After the feast, we all moved onto the verandah; the men and women of the clan sat round us and children slept on the bare floor or on their mothers' laps. Through Helmut, the Mentawaians asked questions of Robin: Where had we come from? Why had we come and would we come back again? Most of the questions were put by the younger men, while the elders watched and weighed up the answers from an outer circle.

Robin told them about a plan of the World Wildlife Fund to make Siberut into a game reserve. 'Would you accept it if you were told not to kill the apes and gibbons?' he asked. There was a stunned silence when Helmut translated and then a burst of angry voices. It was astonishing how quickly an atmosphere of frightening hostility arose and one could feel the Mentawai mentally withdrawing from us. Helmut calmed them. It was not Robin's idea, but the plan of other men; Robin was there to help them, he explained.

'Who are these men?' they asked. 'Are they apes themselves? Certainly, if they think to take away our land, they must be stupid and should live in the trees themselves.' Gradually, they relaxed and admitted that they disliked killing and only did so for food to supplement their diet; they would go on killing as long as they needed meat.

The medicine man leaned forward. 'Would you rather live here than in your home?' he asked us.

'Yes,' Robin replied. 'Your culture is strong and your life here is good compared to many aspects of ours.'

'Then stay,' he said, simply, 'and if you must go, then come back. Come back to us, to no-one else.'

We had to leave the next morning to get back to the mission, struggling through the swamp to the river bank for the last time. No-one said goodbye as we left; the Mentawai only have words for greetings, but many of them stood by the river and watched as we loaded up the canoe. At the last minute, the medicine man picked up a fat cockerel from the ground and presented it to Helmut, blessing and soothing it while he attached a rope of liana to a scaly yellow leg. In silence, Helmut started the engine and we began the long journey back to the coast and the mission.

We had learnt many things on that journey, from Helmut about the jungle and from the Mentawai about their way of living. On our journey back from the waterfall, Helmut had pointed out to us a young bamboo-like stem which we had cut on our way through. In just three hours, it had grown a new shoot 15 inches long, pale yellow-green and tender, a miracle of nature and one that made me realize what an astonishing place the jungle is. He had shown us orchids growing high on the branches of trees thick with parasites and made us open our eyes to see the gibbons which sometimes swung through the thick forest, swift and almost invisible.

From the Mentawai, we had caught a glimpse of natural happiness. Those people laugh and smile more than any people I know, and they respect each other and their fore-fathers. They mourn the dead but look towards the future, taking each day as it comes, live strictly by their clan rules, following, without argument and with total discipline, the taboos of their tribe; they show happiness and sadness without restraint, have loyalty to the clan and suffer none of the diseases of civilization – of boredom, nervous or mental problems. For our modern world with its paper money and gaudy trappings they showed no envy or desire.

But it was the children who impressed me most. They never cried, never whined and never nagged. They had no toys yet they played their own games, laughing together; they were loved by everyone. I will always remember the pictures of happiness as a mother held a small boy in the curve of her arm and suckled him from her full golden breast, fanning away flies from his forehead with a scarlet hibiscus flower. And a young father, dressed only in the traditional bark loincloth with a streamer of green leaves hanging down his buttocks, who washed his small daughter as she stood in a wooden dish, pouring water over her head again and again, rubbing her with his hands and laughing with her all the time.

Chapter 5

After the peace of Siberut, returning to civilization was an almost shattering experience and the next few days passed in a hectic, mind-bending whirl as the *Anggrek* ploughed back to the mainland, through another miserable, storm-filled night. We flew to Palembang and then a small town called Jambi in central Sumatra, before returning to Java and Jakarta to begin the second stage of our journey, this time to the jungles of Kalimantan (formerly called Borneo) where we hoped to visit some of the Dayak tribes.

The capital was hot and exhausting once more. Trying to find information about the outer islands was unrewardingly frustrating and it was a relief to leave and get the expedition on the road again and at least we had succeeded in having our visas extended and we now had permits for travelling around Kalimantan.

Once airborne and flying east, we cheered up. Robin was never happy in big cities, and though we were very vague about our plans for Kalimantan, he was full of confidence about the journey.

Originally, Robin had hoped we would be able to fly into the centre of Kalimantan, up near the Sarawak border to spend two weeks or so with the Dayak tribes at the head-waters of the Kapuas river. The only possible way to get there would be by chartering a lift with the Protestant missionary plane which we had been told flew regularly from the west to the east coast. When we talked to the head of the mission on our first visit to Jakarta, this had seemed a possibility, but when we contacted him on our return, he told us the idea was quite out of the question; they were not making any flights for two months.

It had been a blow. Our only other tenuous contact in Kalimantan was an anthropologist from Hull University (the only one working in the country) called Terry King. He was said to be somewhere way up in the interior – no-one quite knew where – and all we had was a vague address through the Catholic mission in Pontianak. Since it was almost impossible to find out anything constructive about Kalimantan or the tribes in Jakarta, we decided to get to Pontianak, the capital, and play it by ear, hope to make contact with Terry King and somehow find our way to the Dayaks, one of the largest ethnic groups in Indonesia.

The airport at Pontianak was a small, open-sided, wooden hut. There was the usual crowd of people, but nothing which looked like a taxi. After hours of standing around, we managed to find a jeep to take us into the town and a driver who recommended we stay at the Friendship Inn.

Our room had a double bed and an Indonesian bathroom, the usual seatless lavatory with no flush and a tiled tank of water in one corner which looked astonishingly clear considering the colour of the only-inches-deep water in the canals running by the sides of the streets outside. As it was the first double bed we had slept in so far during the journey, we were delighted; it was not, however, made for any violent love-making, for across the headrest ran a glass-covered cupboard where a nightmarish collection of china 'objets' had been carefully but hazardously displayed on two sagging shelves. As in our Palembang hotel, there were no windows and the walls ended three-quarters of the way up and were topped by wire meshing, separating us from the rooms next door.

Robin went to the mission and was then directed to a small house. It was still deserted but a small boy playing outside recognized the name 'King' and took him to the house of the Protestant missionary some streets away. He found Judy King staying with the family.

Judy astonished me. She had lived all her life in Great Yarmouth (Terry came from there too) and as soon as they married she was whisked from her job as a secretary and brought to Kalimantan. For eight months they had been living in a Dayak community up the Kapuas river, totally out of contact with the rest of the world. For an anthropologist, the living and the travelling would have been quite tough, but for a girl from Great Yarmouth it must have been unbelievable. Yet there was Judy, tall and willowy, with blonde hair neatly tied with a yellow ribbon, a terribly English cotton frock and fingernails the length of a pampered socialite, looking as though the nearest thing to a jungle she had ever got was Great Yarmouth beach on a Bank Holiday Monday.

We had unfortunately missed Terry by minutes. He had caught the plane to Jakarta that we had flown in on and must have passed us somewhere on the road. Judy had no idea for how long he would be gone, but at least, with almost unbelievable luck, our arrival had coincided with one of the Kings being in the town and able to give us advice on what to do next.

'We came down to do some shopping,' she explained, 'then the police got hold of Terry and said his papers weren't in order and he must go and get them renewed in Jakarta. We had them checked and checked before we arrived here and hadn't any idea what they were talking about, but they said he must either go immediately or we must both leave the country.'

Bob, the anthropologist we had stayed with in Sumatra, had told us that strict checks were being made because of the Wyn Sargent affair and, although Judy had not heard anything about this, it seemed obvious Terry was under scrutiny in case he too might cause an international incident in some way.

Through Judy we met the local Protestant missionaries who organize a network of small missions around the country. It was Wednesday and, by that evening, Robin had fixed up that we could fly on Friday with one of their planes to one of their more remote outposts, a small town called Nangapinoh on the Melawi river.

'It will be quite expensive,' Robin reported, 'but I think worth a gamble. From Nangapinoh we should be able to charter a boat and go up river from there, visiting Dayak tribes in the area and, with luck, seeing some of the long-houses the Dayaks are famous for.'

The missionaries had been dubious about the hiring of boats; they only went downriver from Nangapinoh and felt it un-likely we would find anyone prepared to take us north – that, Robin thought, was a chance worth taking.

'You know what it's like on these trips,' he told me. 'If one doesn't take every chance which crops up, you end up achiev-ing nothing at all.'

The Dayaks, Judy had told us, were marvellous people; incredibly hospitable and very brave. They did not allow her to cook or do any kind of work (that explained her immaculate nails). Sadly, the group they were living with were giving up many of their old traditions and beginning to move out of their longhouses. She envied us our proposed trip because, on the Melawi river, there was a chance the ancient 'adat' of the people might still be reasonably strong. She had not heard anything about the region but that did not mean much as no-one seemed to know anything about the interior and even the missionaries kept very much to their own small areas.

It was raining again when we came out of the restaurant so we took two bechaks, were enclosed in polythene sheeting and pedalled slowly, in convoy, through the dimly-lit, now desert-ed streets of the town, past the smart, floodlit bungalow of the head of the police force, bristling with armed guards, and along the small back roads, bordered with now half-full canals, to the house where Judy was staying.

The family she was staying with were typical of the American Protestants we had seen both in Brazil and in Indonesia, living in a house packed with 'mod-cons' in an antiseptic atmosphere. Clean, severe people with pale com-plexions that looked as though they had never seen the sun, let alone lived in a hot country for any length of time; people protected from their environment by their faith, the comforts

61

twentieth-century America provided them with and the self-satisfaction of knowing that they were living an unselfish life. And indeed in many ways they were.

I found them difficult to talk to and, in their company, I inevitably longed to chain smoke and thought of alcohol with a consuming desire. I do not swear much normally but, paradoxically, amongst these Protestant missionaries, I was liable to punctuate every sentence with 'bloody' or something worse.

The pilots who fly for the missionaries have a much wider outlook on life, and we spent a fascinating few hours in Pontianak listening to the stories of one of the team's experience in Irian.

Flying over a remote and hilly part of the island, he had caught sight of the glitter of metal on the side of a mountain. Later, he went back to the area, located the spot and flew low enough to identify a crashed plane. He plotted the point and, after a few days an army helicopter dropped him as near to the crash as was possible. He walked alone across the mountains to the spot and, because of bad weather, had the sinister experience of discovering the skeletons of a plane-load of Australian prisoners, released at the end of the war and on their way home, who had hit the mountainside over twenty-eight years ago. They had been declared lost without trace.

The missionaries, he told us, had a really efficient network over the island with first-class radio contact from post to post.

'With the radio network they have here,' he said, 'the American Protestants could do the most efficient take-over coup ever attempted. What with the system and the air fleet they could overrun Kalimantan in a matter of hours.'

We found this to be a fascinating idea and speculated wildly about it as another of those slowly-pedalling bechak boys trundled us back to the hotel.

We had a day to fill in before we could fly to the interior. In the morning, we took a round trip ticket to the other side of the town on the far bank of the Pontianak river on an ancient, re-painted, war-time, Japanese leftover that did duty as a ferry. Coming back, we saw a scene which brought home to us how much the Chinese were hated throughout the country, and although we had felt the tensions already, this was the first time we saw open hostility between Indonesians and Chinese.

A bunch of students crowded onto the ferry, carrying bundles of school books, their clothes meticulously clean, although many of them looked as though they were about to fall to pieces through endless washing.

An old Chinese lady stood in the centre; her small feet were planted widely apart to bear the weight of a heavy body which sagged onto swollen ankles above minute embroidered slippers. She wore the baggy pants and high-necked shirt, crisscrossed by frogging, of her country. Her hair was so tightly scraped back into a dull grey bun that it accentuated the naked look of lashless, narrow eyes in a wrinkled, jaundice-coloured skin.

I did not see what started it off; we were just aware of a sudden scuffling and some of the older Indonesian students began to bait the old lady, shouting insults at her in the now familiar, high-pitched tone of the Indonesian language. The others quickly joined in, screaming and yelling, surrounding her in a circle, like the savages they despised in their jungles. The other passengers watched impassively and we did not dare to intervene, although we were both itching to, as the Chinese lady stood her ground, ignoring their obvious taunts, staring in silent stoicism at her miniature feet.

When the ferry landed, the boys had worked themselves up into a state of mob mania and, as she crossed the planks onto the shore, were brave enough to start touching her clothes, and jostle her along the heat-steaming tarmac. Her temper snapped and she began screeching back at them in Chinese, flourishing her umbrella like a female Errol Flynn and beating around her in a really fearsome way. By the time she reached the end of the street, the crowd had dispersed and I had the feeling that the prices in Chin's, Chee's or whatever shop it was that her family monopolized, would be rising within the next twenty-four hours and credit would be cut to a minimum.

In the lobby of our hotel – a noisy place because the room behind it was used, night and day, for a series of shift classes in English – we had frequently passed a middle-aged, comfortable-looking, European woman. A couple of times, I had said 'good morning' as we glanced at each other with curiosity – the only white woman under the same roof. This time when we returned there I stopped to talk to her.

Mrs Davidson was a Canadian, married to a road engineer working in Kalimantan. Until prefabricated houses would be erected for the crew in a few months' time, she and her husband were living in the hotel. For her it was a lonely life, with her husband working long hours and often being away for days on end.

'Still, the Indonesians are very friendly and they like to practise their English on me, but have you noticed,' she said, 'how inquisitive they are, how personal?'

'Oh, yes,' I answered. 'They seem to want to know all one's most intimate details in five minutes.' I was constantly amazed by the people we met who, on very short acquaintance, asked me the most minute details about us and our children and always, when they heard our children were so widely spaced, enquired: 'So you take the pill then?'

Mrs Davidson nodded her head. 'I got so fed up with them asking why I had no children, I invented a couple to make life easier. Do you know, I've almost come to believe in them now myself. A girl and a boy, fourteen and sixteen years old, and in school back in Canada. We never had any because we were always travelling from one part of the world to another and there never seemed to be time. Now, it's too late and, to be honest, I rather regret it.'

'Now, I make do with the letters I write to myself pretending to be from them,' she said, after a pause. 'I show them to the Indonesians and they all seem so interested.'

She was such a friendly, kindly sort of person, it saddened me to think of her sitting alone in that hotel day after day. I longed to give her a big hug and plant a huge kiss on that faded, plump face with a frame of carefully curled, greying hair. Instead, I gave her a couple of paperbacks we had finished and left our excess luggage in her charge.

When we returned to Pontianak after our adventure up the Melawi river, she looked even more sad and faded than before. Her husband had contacted a bad fever in the interior, probably malaria. She had been unable to get a doctor to come to the hotel and had, very bravely, I thought, woken up the head of the military in the middle of the night, demanding he produce some kind of medical attention. He got over the crisis but was still a very sick man and the two of them were spending most of the time in their depressing swelteringly hot bedroom, painted a sharp apple green to head height and a rich cream above that.

'When things were at their worst,' she told me, 'I clung to the thought of the children. Only yesterday, I had a letter from Janet and she sounded so happy at school.'

Next morning we flew to Nangapinoh in the interior with George Boggs, one of the mission pilots and a good-natured, bluff, 'no-nonsense' character. After a flight across deserted jungle and scrub-covered hills we landed on a small, grassy strip, some distance from the small town and seemingly in the middle of nowhere, beside a wooden shed and a couple of dark, round-faced Indonesians carrying a post bag and a sack of sugar. George Boggs hurried us out of the plane, loaded the sugar and within minutes was strapped in for take-off again.

'I'm late,' he said. Like the white rabbit, he always appeared to be in a hurry. 'Two more trips to do before dark.' As he taxied past us, he remembered, at the last minute, to shout out that a tractor should be coming up to collect us before too long.

Together with the two men, we stood in the shade of the wooden shed by the runway and soon heard a tractor in the distance. From the men, we gathered it was driven by the Protestant missionary from Nangapinoh, a man called Van Patten who had been in the area for a 'long time'. That was about all we did gather as they spoke some sort of dialect and, because of the jumble of languages he had been speaking since we arrived in Indonesia, Robin's Bahasa Indonesian still was not all that fluent. The four of us smoked in silence until a small garden tractor pulling a trailer came into sight, then the two Indonesians self-consciously stubbed out their butts like naughty school boys and we hastily followed suit.

Van Patten is an exceptionally tall good-looking man with a thin, chiselled face and a well-groomed head of iron grey hair. He dwarfed the reception committee of Indonesians who sat rigidly upright in the canopied trailer behind him. They all got out and Van Patten introduced us with ceremony to the prefect of the town, an elderly man with a worried monkey face, the chief of police and the chief of the military. All of them looked nervous and rather embarrassed and, although they gave us a great welcome, it was impossible to know whether they were really pleased to see us or not.

'Sorry about all this,' Van Patten said as we all squeezed into the trailer, 'but it's the first time tourists have ever come to Nangapinoh and they were determined to give you full honours. I suppose you do know there are no hotels or modern facilities here; this isn't exactly the centre of civilization,' he added, obviously wondering what the hell we were doing anyway.

It was a bumpy half-hour's drive to the outskirts of the town where we stopped at a small military and police post to produce our papers. Van Patten was worried that we had no official permission to visit the interior but the officials themselves appeared not to be concerned. In fact, they seemed rather confused about what they were expected to do with our passports and visas when Robin brought them out. In the end, we lent them a biro and they copied every number in sight onto a piece of rough paper torn from my notebook and we all shook hands once more.

From there, we continued our ride to a large, one-storey wooden building overlooking the river. This, we were told, was the prefect's house and office and was where we would spend the night.

The building had obviously been the town hall or the white

man's club in the Dutch days and had been running downhill since the colonizers left the country. What had once been the garden was now an unmown football pitch with a deer, tethered by a wide, leather collar, quietly grazing in the middle. Paint was peeling from the roof of the long verandah, cobwebs hung from the eaves and, in a dusty room inside, a row of seedy plastic-seated chairs were lined up alongside half a dozen knee-high wooden tables. The only decorations in the room were some tin ashtrays overflowing with cigarette butts and a faded print of President Suharto. The prefect showed us into a second room where four mattresses were laid out on the floor. Woven mats surrounded these beds and, in the corner, a clothes line had been strung and a pair of trousers was hanging beside a pair of towels.

The prefect spoke no English and was plainly rather ill at ease with his 'tourist charges'. It was a relief to all three of us when two other men appeared and our host was able to escape to his home at the back of the rambling bungalow.

Our room mates were two charming and helpful lumber prospectors from a Singapore firm with a branch in Jakarta, a Malay and a Chinese. Mr Chee, the Chinese, spoke excellent English and, with his help, we were able to plan an expedition up the Melawi river. When the prefect returned, he managed to convince our host that we had no objections to sleeping in native houses, were used to discomfort and actually wanted to get to the wilder, upper reaches of the river.

While the men were talking, I left and wandered through the town, an attractive place, built by the Dutch and seemingly untouched for at least a hundred years. The short main street was bordered by shops, raised on stilts and reached by wooden steps. The buildings were of clapboard, weathered silver grey, with balconies along the first storeys, some supported on elegant pillars, giving the effect of a stage set for a Western epic. Below the town, moored by the banks of the wide river, was a second township with rows of flat, barge-type houseboats topped by wooden sheds.

Before long I was joined by fifty or more children, following about ten yards behind me, staring in amazement and whispering amongst themselves. At first I found their presence rather amusing, then they began to crowd round me, shouting something that sounded like 'Hip, hip, hurrah', in louder and louder voices until the noise became almost deafening. There must have been over a hundred of them and I felt the beginnings of panic as I tried to walk at a reasonable pace back to the prefect's house. Once I reached it, the noise died down although they stayed as close as they could, crammed round the windows and doors, occasionally shoved away gently by the prefect but returning almost immediately to stare unwaveringly at us. They were attractive children, surprisingly clean despite their ragged clothing, with intelligent monkey faces and straight, heavy black hair, and they might have seemed enchanting if someone had only told them it was rude to stare.

In the committee room, things were moving fast. Mr Chee produced a fellow countryman with skin the colour of old parchment and a riveting pair of crossed incisors in an otherwise toothless mouth. He said he could provide us with a sampan and motor and our new friend agreed to bargain for the price of hire and petrol on our behalf. He did this with such polite firmness that they soon came to a sum which Robin considered reasonable for the journey.

In semi-darkness, we walked down to the river to inspect the boat. It turned out to be a shallow sampan without an engine and half-full of water. Mr Chee was furious. He shot a stream of angry Indonesian at the boatman and then told us not to worry; a new boat, with an engine, would be waiting for us next morning at seven o'clock.

With this small, kind and exceptionally neat man who had the most beautiful manners, we wandered along the main street to do some final shopping. By now it was dark, the houses were dimly lit by a few oil lamps and a delicious smell of cooking drifted towards us from a wooden barrow where an old woman was frying golden banana fritters over a charcoal fire.

In the little boxlike shops, we were served by elderly Chinese gentlemen, dressed in pyjamas, who burrowed through a strange assortment of goods – from Sloane's liniment to green ginger – to find the soap and towels we wanted. Children crowded into the already stuffy rooms behind us, growing even more cheeky now, touching us to see if we were real, making a noise like the monkey house at the zoo, giggling continuously and knocking over boxes of stinking salt fish and tripping over rusty tin kettles. Mr Chee was highly embarrassed.

'I am so sorry for the bad behaviour of these children,' he said, looking as though it were all his fault. Being the perfect oriental, he apologized for everything.

He took us to the kitchen of one of the houses and we sat round a stained table top supported by wooden crates while a large Chinese lady performed miracles with the strange ingredients she mixed into a concave saucepan over a wood fire. Mr Chee looked miserable.

'I am so sorry this is such humble food. Unfortunately, they are not used to visitors in this town and there is no other place to eat.' He went on looking unhappy and continued apologizing for everything despite our telling him again and again that the food was delicious and we were very content.

Outside the stars were bright and a large silver moon swung in a dark midnight blue sky. Kerosene lamps shone dully, the colour of old copper, from the houseboats on the river, people crouched over charcoal fires burning on the decks and the wooden town looked more like a stage set than ever.

Mr Chee's partner did not join us. He was a Muslim and we, of course, had eaten pork in our Chinese establishment.

Sleeping with three men may be some women's idea of Heaven, but it is not mine. Despite the travelling I had done with Robin and however tired I was, I still found it hard to sleep in close proximity to strangers. As I quickly undressed while the other three discreetly kept their distance, I knew this was going to be a bad night. I settled myself on the thin mattress and hoped for the best, trusting that a chapter or two of Dickens, read by the light of a candle stump stuck on the floorboards, would help send me to sleep. Bats played 'dare' with the candle flame and above my head a family of swifts twittered hysterically as they tried to squeeze themselves into a small nest built under the eaves of the room; someone had shut and barred the shutters which served as windows.

It was a bad night – for everyone.

The Indonesian had lit a smoke coil to keep away the mosquitoes. The sweet incense-like smell in the stuffy, airless room, puffing out in a steady stream of smoke, did its job well. There were no mosquitoes, but for some reason the smoke gave me a chronic dose of hayfever. My eyes watered, I sneezed a thousand times in succession and my throat felt like a nutmeg grater.

After what seemed like hours, Robin, who had been sleeping like a baby till then, woke up and also began coughing with a rasping noise.

'I've got to have something to drink,' he gasped. 'My throat's like straw.' He lit a candle and at once Mr Chee, neatly wrapped up in a sarong, was by our side, full of apologies again.

'Perhaps there was too much seasoning in the food. I have some beer, you must drink it, the water is not good here.' From a suitcase, he brought out the beer and an opener. Seeing my eyes and my face, which by then had puffed up like a football, he immediately snuffed out the smoke coil, fussing over us like a nanny, almost in tears because, horror of horrors, he could produce no glasses. The beer, being as hot as the room, exploded into a cascade of foam when it was opened and Mr Chee watched in admiration as Robin put the bottle to his lips and neatly sucked up the white froth.

'Oh, that's better,' Robin said with relief, passing the bottle to me and wiping his mouth with the back of his hand.

'Good, good,' said Mr Chee delightedly as I gurgled down the warm liquid. 'This just like public school midnight feast in your country. Yes? Perhaps you would like a pillow fight?'

Chapter 6

The sampan Mr Chee led us to early the next morning looked identical to the one we had seen the evening before and still had, in the bottom, a good six inches of water which, in the daylight, we could see came from gaps along the side. The small craft was low in the water under the weight of a large petrol drum resting on planks in the centre. In place of seats was an old piece of straw matting and the engine at the back had no top to it. There was no cover and although it was still quite cool, the morning mist had already cleared, and when the sun came up in earnest I knew we were going to fry out there on the water.

Two strange men, middle-aged and shabby, loaded our baggage into the front of the shaky-looking boat, piling in a small cardboard box of food, Robin's briefcase, our knapsack, my expensive handbag-satchel I had bought at vast cost because it was hand-made in real leather and I hoped it would last me through the journey, a bottle of beer and one of cold tea. There was not much room left for us and it was a slight shock to find we were to have yet another companion for the journey.

The prefect appeared to say goodbye (along with a couple of hundred children and an interested crowd of adults) and introduced us to a young man dressed in a sand-coloured uniform and sporting a black velvet peaked cap with 'God is with you' embroidered in gold lettering across the front. He was a policeman, the prefect explained, and would be going with us to see we would be kept safe. Yet again the prefect warned that we would not find much comfortable accommodation where we were heading and Mr Chee had one last apology as we thanked him for his help.

'It is necessary for you to have this policeman as a guard. You see, they are not used to tourists here and it would be most embarrassing if anything happened to you. Also, you have to check in with the police up the river.'

I had rather unhappy memories of the guide we had had forced upon us in Brazil, but this man looked pleasant enough despite his strange head gear which, I am afraid, reeked of Protestant missionary influence. As it turned out, Amri Bachtiar (we soon nicknamed him our 'courier') was a marvellous help and asset on the journey, and being half Dayak and half Chinese he was equally as friendly with the Chinese traders we met on the way as he was with the local people living on the banks of the Melawi.

The boatmen (one already bailing hard with half a coconut shell) and Amri Bachtiar settled themselves in the back of the boat while Robin and I half crouched, half lay, in the front, and we set off past the scores of shabby houseboats, all roped together with their owners standing on the narrow decks, throwing buckets of water over themselves as they performed their morning ablutions. Never have I seen people so conscious of cleanliness as those we met on that river journey; they seemed to be always washing.

We had only a hazy idea where we were heading. There were no detailed maps of the area and all we had was a rough drawing of the river which Mr Chee had done from the air during his lumber prospecting. Like all Indonesians, Amri Bachtiar seemed astonished we should want to venture into the interior – instead of going to Bali – and he looked dubious when Robin explained that we were particularly interested in visiting the more remote Dayak villages and in staying in longhouses. We discovered that morning that he spoke quite a bit of English.

The river was about a quarter of a mile wide at this point and small settlements on the banks were still quite frequent, many of them clustered around romantic-looking mosques with tiny spires and onion domes. Below each house, a small jetty was built out into the water, supporting a small three-sided wooden wash house and lavatory. Banana and manioc plantations encircled the villages.

In the afternoon the engine packed up and immediately we were swept downstream at a dizzy pace – through the fast-flowing, swollen river – spinning like a top, only just managing to steer towards the bank to tie up beside a small trading post. A grinning boatman borrowed a large hammer and some long nails from the trader and began bashing at the engine with a lot of enthusiasm, which Robin and I found most alarming. Apparently, we had not only broken the solenoid, which they luckily had a replacement for, but the engine had only been attached to the boat by one screw and was in danger of falling off the end.

The damage took well over an hour to repair and, without any movement to create a breeze, we sweltered under a palm canopy Amri had erected, sweat trickling down our necks and faces in the breathlessly hot and humid air. Despite the heat, we stayed put as the jetty was covered with a layer of rubber which stuck to everything. The smell of salt fish was claustrophobic.

The engine finally firmly in position, we were off again. All seemed well for about an hour, although our courier told us we would not, as had been hoped, reach the last village of any size up the river that evening. There was a Roman Catholic mission there, with a priest Robin hoped to meet, and it had been planned to spend the night in the mission.

'If you really want to stay in longhouses,' Amri said tentatively, 'I know of one we should reach by nightfall.' Of course, we said we were delighted.

The further we got upstream, the faster the swirling water seemed to be racing past us and the next time the engine stopped we were again swept crazily back the way we had come; whirled about a mile downriver before we could get to the bank, careering past huge trees with coarse leaves the size of dinner plates and occasional hidden paths with crude steps, cut from narrow tree trunks, leading to houses in the jungle. The boat rocked as the boatmen tried to steer for the shore and it seemed inevitable that we would be pitched into that muddy debris-strewn water.

This time we seemed to be in serious difficulties. Smoke poured from the engine and there was a strong smell of burning oil. Robin, who knew a bit about outboard engines, was horrified when they began pouring a mixture of petrol and oil straight into the engine. As usual, the Indonesians seemed unperturbed; they ignored Robin's mutterings and worked slowly, at their own pace, miraculously managing to get the motor going again after another hour.

A few hours later, we pulled into another small settlement, a collection of only about half a dozen wooden houses. 'We will eat here,' Amri informed us, leading the way from a landing raft across a wide tree trunk which rolled as we crossed it, onto the bank and up an incredibly steep wooden ladder to a surprisingly well-stocked shop at the top. He introduced us to the Chinese proprietor, an enormous man, stripped to the waist, wearing striped pyjama bottoms and exposing a flabby paunch belly rolling over the top of the corded tie of the trousers.

'Mr Samosee does good business,' Amri said, and it certainly seemed as though he did. We sat on the wooden counter in the shop while Mrs Samosee, also dressed in pyjamas, rushed off to prepare some food for us. A steady stream of half-naked Dayaks – tough, wiry men with tan complexions and intelligent faces – poured into the shop, bent almost double under sacks of raw rubber or palm-oil nuts. The large Chinaman was full of nervous energy, moving around the shop with surprising speed for one of his size, checking in the sacks, totting up the amount owed on an abacus with fingers flicking across the beads, and then converting the money he owed them into goods from the shop: cheap, bright-coloured materials, candles, tobacco and sticky sweets. He seldom produced any cash and the system seemed to consist mainly of an exchange of goods. When he did bring out the 'ready', it was handed over in small bags of shining 10-rupiah pieces.

Many of the Dayaks looked painfully thin, with large, sticking-out ears flanking hollow cheeks, and it was not difficult to see that the effect of a bad rice harvest the preceding summer was taking its toll. One couple, particularly, looked pathetic – a youngish man whose bones stuck out as he heaved three heavy sacks up the wooden steps and a woman who sat waiting for him and carried a small child crying with a thin, reedy wailing as she sucked at the exposed, withered and sagging breasts.

Rather to our surprise, after supper we went back the way we had come, downriver, and turned off the main stream after a few miles into a narrow waterway cluttered with the dark bulk of huge trees which lay where they had fallen, almost spanning the stream in places. Our courier sat on the front bow of the sampan, shining the pale beam of a weak torch to direct the boatmen between innumerable snags. We lay flat on the bottom so as not to obscure their view, looking up at the interlaced silhouettes of towering tropical vegetation, at huge bats flitting across the sky, and at the myriads of tiny fireflies dancing on the high banks.

Night can be scary and we had no idea where we were going. Suppose, I thought, they were taking us here to kill us; a quick, easy murder, three against one and a half; a couple of dead bodies sent to the bottom of the river and the murderers would gain some reasonably valuable equipment and considerable money. We had enough cash, travellers cheques and papers of all kinds to make killing us well worth while to these people, and any others who knew we were around could surely have been easily bribed to keep their mouths shut.

I shivered. It was getting chilly, a storm was brewing and a giant black cloud, like a misshapen hand, crept across the sky, bringing with it streaks of forked lightning and loud rolls of ever-nearing thunder.

The motor stopped again and, as the boatmen worked to

fix it, a canoe drifted silently out of the blackness. A Dayak, naked to the waist, a sarong hitched high on his hips, drew up beside us, a panga glittering as a flash of lightning lit the sky. The men up in front whispered together as they worked over the motor and finally got it re-started.

The stream narrowed until branches met over our head, tunnel-fashion. We passed a small houseboat tied to the bank, the glow from a kerosene lamp inside making it look safe and cosy as it rocked gently in our wash.

At about eight, the engine cut again and we sat up to see we had arrived at a largish floating jetty, topped by the usual bath house. Two men stood on the high bank, scrutinizing us with severe and almost undisguised reserve. It was not the most welcoming reception committee, and it was a committee which I, after hours of cramped deprivation in the sampan, would have preferred to be more genial.

We waited while Amri climbed like a monkey up one of these vertiginous tree-trunk ladders. He came back looking depressed.

'I have not been here for some time. The people are Protestants now and the chief no longer lives in a longhouse, but it is too late to go on now. We can sleep here.' He held out his hand to help me cross the plank from the jetty to the bank and then went ahead to shine his torch down the slippery ladder and across a yard, thick with pig shit, to a small, square, wooden house perched on high piles. The light inside, coming from an oil pressure lamp, hissing loudly, was blinding for a minute, then my eyes got adjusted and I saw we were in a windowless room with a small partition in one corner. We shook hands with two women wearing sarongs tied above their breasts, with an old man wearing a loincloth and a grey turban wound around his head, and with the chief, a young man dressed in Western clothes.

Dogs and chickens were shooed from the room, rattan mats were unrolled and we sat cross-legged on the floor; Robin, myself and Amri were on one side of the room and about a dozen Dayaks on the other. They were good-looking people, the men about five foot five, the women slightly smaller, all well built, with straight, black hair, dark complexions and clean-cut features with straight noses and widely spaced eyes.

Glasses of hot coffee were produced, hot and sickly sweet with sugar, and Amri talked fast in a dialect we did not understand. Suddenly, he seemed to come to a decision, turned to Robin and asked in English: 'What absolutely are you doing here? Are you missionaries?'

Robin said emphatically that we were not and tried to explain how he was interested in the more remote peoples of the world and in seeing how people lived in Kalimantan, their culture and their traditions.

'The chief wishes to know if you are Protestant or Catholic,' Amri plunged on, shifting his cross-legged position from one buttock to another in an agony of embarrassment.

'Neither,' I said firmly, because the American Protestant missionary movement is far removed from the Anglican church as we know it. I drew a sketch on a piece of paper. 'Here is the American Protestant church on this side and the Catholic church on the other.' I drew two lines from the names and joined them halfway down the page. 'Our religion, Anglican, is halfway between the two.' Robin said he thought that was totally confusing but I was rather pleased with my simplified explanation.

We offered round cigarettes and, to our surprise, all the men shook their heads, although the old man in the turban put out his hand and then hastily withdrew it, looking miserable. Everywhere we went in Indonesia, men and boys from about the age of fifteen smoked cigarette after cigarette and it was strange to be in a community where we were the only ones puffing.

The old man in his dirty loincloth looked so unhappily at our cartons of cigarettes that I managed to slip him a packet later on in the evening. He took my hand in his wrinkled brown fingers and his way of thanking me was so full of gratitude that I gave him two more.

'It is the Protestant missionaries,' Amri explained. 'They forbid smoking and dancing. This makes the people most unhappy.' Amri, we discovered, had managed to escape 'missionarization', despite the cap he wore. Traditionally, the Dayaks are animist – if you destroy their religion you also destroy a large part of their culture. Amri, once he decided to trust our motives and got over the misapprehension that we might be some new kind of missionary, turned out to have many of the same views as Robin.

Inside the room, the heat of the kerosene lamp, the close proximity of people and the glowing fire brought the temperature to a level at which we were all sweating, the faces of the Dayaks, and ours, shining in the light. Outside a bell rang and the children crowding round the door ran off into the darkness.

'That is for school,' Amri said. 'The children work in the day and during the night they have an hour of lessons from a Protestant teacher.' In the distance, we could hear them singing the doleful tune of a joyless hymn.

We were taken back to the jetty to wash, Amri stripping to his underpants, sloshing the cold water over himself with great vigour and changing into a clean set of clothes which he produced from a minute suitcase. We were soaked through a score of times during that journey, yet Amri always changed in the evenings and always managed to look immaculate despite his bag being not much larger than my handbag. I envied him as, having washed each evening, I invariably slipped into squelching mud, off the rotating slippery poles leading onto the jetties.

Earlier Amri had said the longhouse in the village had been pulled down but now, school being over and our courier having decided to trust us, we were led through the darkness, accompanied by the sounds of ringing, deep-toned gongs, to a long, wooden building, supported about twelve feet from the ground on high wooden poles.

It was exciting, at last, to be inside one of these strange buildings typical of the Dayak tribes throughout Kalimantan.

The reason for raising it above the ground was for protection from hostile neighbours; the narrow ladders leading to openings spaced along the building could easily be raised in case of trouble. Inside, the whole tribe or clan lived in one large construction that seemed to stretch forever. On one side, a verandah made from bamboo poles was raised about six inches and covered with finely woven rattan matting. This was the community area. Down the centre ran an unmatted path and, to the right, a series of doors led to individual quarters where each family had a small room with a fire for cooking and a screened-off area for sleeping.

On the community area, about two hundred Dayaks sat cross-legged on the floor, men on one side, women on the other and children in between, their faces dark, features finely chiselled. At one end, a bank of brass gongs of different sizes were laid out. Amri pointed to me to sit with the women, so I sat in the front row between an elderly smiling lady and a younger woman, both with rather flat, heart-shaped faces, their hair pulled tightly back and twisted into a knot at the back of their necks. Both wore colourful sarongs and tight-fitting lace jackets and the younger woman carried a child in a dark green sash tied like a sling. Everyone stared at us, silent, waiting.

An old man, thin and unsmiling, rose from the floor, picked up a drum and squatted with the instrument between his knees. He drummed with his fingers, very loud, rhythmically and fast, accompanied by another old man who struck three gongs of varying sizes, held steady by small boys.

The music was strange with a steady beat, a fast yet firm sound which echoed slightly down the long building, disappearing into the blackness beyond the area dimly lit with small oil lamps. Soon, the old man's veins showed up on his hands and arms in a network of dark blue, throbbing knots and, after twenty minutes, he was exhausted. The music drew suddenly to an end, leaving a silence that was only broken by the high squeaking of bats flying in the rafters. There was no clapping; merely a general shifting to get more comfortable as most of the male audience pulled aside corners of the mats to spit between the bamboo poles and the women loosened the knots of their heavy, black hair, threw their heads back, pulled back the tresses and neatly wound it up again in a complicated twist without the help of combs or grips.

A group of younger boys took over beating the drum and the gongs in the same style but with a faster rhythm. From behind came laughter and giggling as three teenage boys scrambled into the empty area in front of the band.

The Protestant influence was obviously having its effect, because they soon began faltering in the steps, camping up the dance and giggling to each other self-consciously, infuriating the older men in the audience. One old man, wearing only a baggy loincloth and a grey turban, even limped across and caught one of the youths roughly by the arm, arguing with him. The dance ended in confusion and the boys were replaced by four women.

The women also seemed embarrassed by having to perform and from our point of view it was a disappointing display. They looked beautiful and were richly dressed in sarongs threaded with gold, with elaborate gold belts around their waists and tight-fitting, ruby-red jackets showing off lithe figures, but their movements were slow and clumsy with little grace.

Even on the long, open verandah, it was hot and stuffy, and my eyes were beginning to droop when the women ran off giggling, but I woke up quickly as a slim, fantastic-looking boy – dressed in tight-fitting jeans and a white tee-shirt decorated with a large blue butterfly – sprang onto the stage. He began to dance and, this time, the performance was breathtaking.

He could not have been much more than fifteen. His body was compact, his movements amazingly controlled and his face beautiful. Dark hair was brushed sideways across his high forehead, cut short at the back, showing off the pure Grecian shape of his head. His wide-set eyes were large, tilted up at the corners and fringed with long black lashes, the eyebrows above them perfectly arched. His ears were slightly pointed

Robin in a Batak country market, on the shores of Lake Toba

Mentawai tribesmen perform sacrificial rites, watched by a witch doctor, on Siberut Island

Marika plays Pied Piper in Nangapinoh

A young Mentawai husband by a jungle waterfall

A young girl picks nits out of her mother's hair

at the top, giving his face a gamin, elfin look, and although his face was a study of concentration, a slight smile played at the corners of his mouth as he danced, producing a puckish effect.

After a couple of dances (the rhythmic music of the gongs and drums was so strange it was difficult to see where one ended and another began) the butterfly boy was joined by another youth and together they went through the movements of a cock fight, leaping in the air with arms flailing, legs in a high scissors action; circling around each other, faces glistening in the pale candlelight, the crowd motionless as they watched and the air cloudy with dust and heat.

The gongs rang faster, the drum beat louder, both boys leapt again and again, parodying the fight until the second boy won and the butterfly boy sank gracefully to the ground in one fluid movement, a dead bird with feathers limp and lifeless.

After that, the evening dragged and I was grateful when, as a dozen children began to dance in a circle, Amri said it was time to finish, and we were led back to the chief's house where we slept on the floor alongside a dozen men in the suffocatingly hot small room.

Next morning we left early again, chugged monotonously upriver, stopped at another remote police post for a check and another meal with a Chinese trader and then continued our journey.

Our engine ran smoothly and it took us three hours that afternoon to reach the final village of any size up the river. The sun came out, beating vertically on the water, and dried our wet clothes into stiff, muddied boards, bringing sweat beading on our foreheads and almost blinding my eyes. Large herons occasionally flapped along the bank against a wall of jungle, but, apart from them, there was little movement. Sometimes we saw a small canoe with a couple of Dayaks fishing amongst the reeds, men and women stripped to the waist, their heads shaded by large straw hats with brims two feet wide.

We dozed and read under our palm canopy and I tested

Robin on his Indonesian from one of those infuriating phrase books containing only such useless sentences as: 'What time do the blue buses leave from the railway terminus?' – the sort of information that seemed way out of place as we moved past the thick, jungle-covered banks of the Melawi, still racing against us with more and more debris floating down after recent rains.

Each time we rounded a corner, criss-crossing to avoid the worst of the current, a new panorama stretched ahead; the wide river curled around heavily vegetated islands, fed by streams on both sides, and ran between high, muddy banks. Far in the distance, a range of mountains could be seen, slightly hazy and pale purple against the still clear sky.

It was a long day with almost twelve hours spent on the water and, although we had not taken much physical exercise, we were both tired by the time we reached the village where we were to spend the night. It was still just light enough to see and, as we crossed another of those tortuous tree-trunk bridges onto dry land, stiffness and tiredness were forgotten. Above us was a longhouse such as we had dreamed of, built high off the ground, stretching on and on, the wood silver-grey with age. In front of it, carved from coconut palms still rooted to the ground, were a series of strange tall poles, a dozen or more varying in height from ten to twenty feet, each fashioned into the shape of a god or ancestor.

Chapter 7

This time, I managed to negotiate, without disaster, the bridge – a long, narrow trunk with notches as footholds – and a slippery stile across a wall of sharp bamboos and the final high ladder to the centre of the house. An old man came to meet us; Amri explained who we were, and we were led down the central passage dimly lit by small kerosene lamps to the very end of the longhouse. Our footsteps echoed on the floor of bamboo poles, faces peered at us from doorways along the sides, and the shapes of large wooden storage chests and heavy troughs for pounding rice were shadowy in the half-light.

The old man indicated we should sit in the corner on finely woven mats of thin rattan, shiny with use. Too late, we realized we should have removed our shoes, as Amri and the boatmen had done, before entering the house. Now a crowd of a score of more silent men, wearing sarongs, their faces expressionless, watched as we struggled to undo laces clogged with mud.

A brighter lamp was brought out from one of the rooms and the silence continued as we sat cross-legged, the circle of men around us, and offered round packets of tobacco and Kretek cigarettes. They regarded the tobacco with suspicion, sniffing it and placing it untouched on the floor, but the cigarettes seemed to be more successful and soon everyone was smoking hard, thickening the air with a grey haze as they continued to stare.

What were they thinking? The Dayaks had been headhunters; some still were. Were these people upset by our invasion: strangers, uninvited? Were they friendly or hostile? It was impossible to tell from their faces and the glint of steel blades from long, pointed knives began to unnerve me.

Then, at last, the old man began to talk to Amri and the atmosphere relaxed slightly. More cigarettes were offered and accepted, a few of the men began shredding the tobacco in their fingers and rolling it into the thin paper we also had with us.

'They have little food here,' Amri reported apologetically. 'Perhaps I could give one of your sardine tins to the women to cook.'

So far, we had not really seen any women. They remained hidden in their houses along the passage, peering out as we followed Amri down to the river to wash and stepped over some of the fallen idols lying on the ground. They shone silver-white in the moonlight and the squarely carved faces and bodies looked strangely real and human. Around us the nightly chorus of frogs and cicadas was in full swing, and above us flying foxes by the dozen were silhouetted against the clear, starlit sky.

We were in Indonesia to find out how the isolated tribes of that country were situated in the twentieth century, but it was not easy to get close enough to these people to understand them fully, and once more time was at a premium. Very few of the Dayaks spoke more than a few words of Indonesian and, although Robin's command of the language was improving daily, local accents complicated the Malay-based language. Their controlled features, though full of dignity and politeness, were almost impossible to penetrate.

The Bataks in Sumatra had been almost aggressively open; the Mentawai had been naively and enchantingly uninhibited; these people were extremely isolated and yet, because they had the communication of the river Melawi on their doorstep and had, for centuries, traded with the Chinese, they had a highly developed cultural tradition. They displayed the minimum of emotion through their features and, at first, talking through the interpretation of Amri, we felt how totally foreign and alien we were in their midst.

Although it was about nine o'clock, work for the day was only just finishing and a stream of men, their sarongs rolled high around their waists, the rest of their bodies bare, came into the house carrying sacks of rice and palm nuts. They unrolled the lengths of cotton cloth, pulled them out to the full width, crossed the slack over and neatly tied them tightly around their waists again as they came to sit with the other men. Women now appeared from their houses, dressed in their best, in colourful sarongs and tightly-fitting jackets, hair tightly scraped back from their high foreheads. Again, they sat by themselves, brought out brass trays bearing an assortment of small pots and busied themselves by preparing betel nut. This was accomplished by crushing the nut (a round, hard, brown knob the size of a walnut) and placing it on a leaf with a pinch of lime, then rolling up the leaf and popping the whole thing into their mouths, chewing methodically and occasionally spitting out the juices through the gaps in the bamboo floor. Their gums were red from the nut, their cheeks distorted as they kept the package in one side. Some of the women would have been beautiful but their otherwise fine features and smooth nut-brown skin were spoilt by teeth discoloured and rotting from lime.

One of the women brought out a tray of glasses filled with sweet acrid coffee, thick with grounds, and sank gracefully to her knees as she offered it first to Robin and then to me. When the coffee was finished, she disappeared again and this time returned with a brass tray on which there were a dozen glasses and a large earthenware jar. From it, she poured a pale milky liquid, offered it to us and then filled the remaining glasses, passing them round amongst the men.

'Palm wine,' said Amri, grinning, 'very strong, very good.' It had a sour, bitter taste but was cool and not unpleasant. When that jar was empty, someone fetched another and the pouring began again. The women did not drink, concentrating on their betel nut.

Men were still coming up into the house with sacks and baskets on their backs, many of them tired-looking and dirty. By now, there were about a hundred and fifty people sitting up our end of the long, long room which seemed to stretch into infinity in the darkness. The air was thick with smoke and heavy with the smell of wine, the pigs under the house and betel nut.

A set of gongs was carefully carried onto the mats and some children, a few of them now dressed in cheap, skimpy cotton dresses instead of their sarongs, brought out a large pole with three crossbars and hung with chains of coloured paper. Spiders and other insects, disturbed by the activity, rustled in the palm-thatched walls behind our backs and ran scuttling across the rattan mats.

The people were relaxed now, talking softly amongst themselves, often turning to smile shyly at us. Some of the men rubbed muscles which ached after working in their rice fields, most of which were up to three days' walk from the village. Many were pitifully thin; there were notably few old people and only one man with grey hair, but the young men looked strong and the women, although their faces were often drawn, had a grace that I envied.

One of the young men produced a strange instrument made from bamboos and small gourds, fashioned rather like an organ. At the bottom was a gourd with a curved stem like a maraschino pipe through which he began to suck, his cheeks drawn in, his body unmoving in total concentration. There was silence again and strange music filled the room and echoed down the long passage. The sounds were soft and haunting, a low reedy bagpipe, sighing with notes that lingered and undulated. After a time, he was joined by another man, this time with a crudely-carved, elongated banjo, playing softly in accompaniment. Then the gongs joined in, tinkling and light, and a group of young girls danced around the colourful pole, swaying in time with the music, their hands twisting and curving.

Now the stage was taken by a man wearing only a sarong,

richly coloured in greens and reds, tied between his legs to make a loincloth. On his head was a large and complicated turban. At his side was a long dagger sheathed in an ornately carved wooden case.

'This is a war dance for when the Dayaks are attacked by the Punan hill tribes,' Amri whispered, and we watched fascinated as, very slowly, the dancer began to perform the complicated steps of an ancient ritual, pivoting on the sides of his feet, arms twisting smoothly, crouching to the ground with a hand shielding his eyes as he looked for the Punans. Slowly the dance built up to a crescendo, faster and faster as he leapt into the air, legs outstretched, with a great cry of: 'The Punans are coming.' He drew his sword, which glittered as the light fell on a razor edge, swinging it round with more cries as he killed one after another of the enemy and then sprung once more into the air with a leap of staggering height as they were at last defeated.

Again there was no clapping and the crowd settled themselves more comfortably, accepting more cigarettes and sipping at the palm wine. Many of the men were now chewing betel nut too, taking time over the ritualistic preparations; some were getting glassy-eyed and the air was so thick with smoke it stung my eyes.

There was a sway of bodies as another dancer moved through the crowd to the centre.

A woman's sarong, a tight-fitting white lace jacket and a beautifully embroidered scarf tied gracefully around the head, hiding both hair and face, did not totally disguise the fact that this was a man, although his dancing was totally feminine. It was a woman's dance with a woman's motions and an over-riding aura of sex. Hands curved and fluttered with female elegance, hips gyrated in a sexual flowing movement in time with the singing wail of the pipes, gongs and the string instrument. He pivoted and swayed, sinking and rising to the ground with pelvis forward and his back arched, the scarf never once moving to expose his face and the jacket padded in some way so that even the breasts were those of a woman.

It was a transvestite dance performed as part of a culture and tradition, not for amusement. No-one laughed as the crowd sat motionless, watching.

After more children danced, their childish movements showing signs of the grace that was to come, a second man gave another beautiful performance. He was straight from the fields, hands calloused, face still streaked with dirt, and he wore ragged torn trousers that were caked with mud. I found it amazing that a man who had laboured all day could then transform himself into a thing of such exquisiteness. Again the dance was effeminate; many of the movements reminded me of Thai dancing I had seen in London as his feet remained on one spot and he pivoted slowly round, his body curving and arching and his arms waving slowly. The incredible movements of his hands and fingers must have taken years of practice to perfect.

The dancing ended, but the party seemed to be continuing and the palm wine was still being passed round, although it was now into the early hours of the morning. Both of us were yawning, I was aching from sitting on the floor in the same position for what seemed like hours and hours, and my head was spinning.

Amri, our faithful courier whom we were getting to like more and more, came to our rescue. 'You want to sleep?' he asked, and, looking round the crowded open area of the longhouse, decided we would be better in one of the houses. We left our luggage where it was. We were slightly nervous about it but Amri assured us it would not be touched.

In an eight-foot-square room at the back, thin mats were unrolled and straw pillows, covered with coarse, heavily embroidered linen cases, were laid on the ground. We had nothing to cover us as our knapsack and the thin blankets inside it were soaked through from the rains.

Although it was swept and clean, there was a smell of dust in the room, and we could hear the noise of the Dayaks, talking, spitting out their betel nuts and occasionally singing. A dim light filtered in through the plaited walls and I could hear the scurrying of small animals moving along the edges of the room and in the roof above.

As soon as I lay down, I felt sick. Desperately, violently sick, with gorge rising into my mouth and a sour taste as it filled my mouth. It might have been the palm wine, but I had not had much to drink. I was more certain it had been the few chews I had had of another revolting durian that I had to accept out of politeness earlier in the evening.

I began to panic. I could not go out into that crowd in my nightdress and risk being sick in front of them, and although I shone my torch along the boards there was no crack large enough to be sick through. I sat up, I walked around the tiny room, and I stuffed a handkerchief into my mouth, watched by Robin who was powerless to do anything except hold my hand.

Hour after hour, it went on. Wave after wave of nausea swept over me and each time I fought back one I was sure I would not be able to control the next. Outside, the noise of the Dayaks talking and singing continued.

Sleep finally conquered. At last I was able to lie down again and we huddled together on our mats like two puppies as, by then, I was cold and shivering.

The revelling of the night before had obviously had its effect, as we were up before anyone else seemed to be moving the next morning. We took a walk past two smaller long-houses, also built on high stilts – protection from attack from hostile tribes – across a fragile bridge of bamboo, across another bamboo stockade and into the forest surrounding the village, disturbing an occasional large, coarse-haired pig not far removed from its wild cousin, the boar, long-nosed, small-eyed and viciously tusked. From the jungle we could hear the sound of monkeys chattering to each other from tree to tree.

In the daylight, the carved idols looked less spooky. They were dotted in amongst coconut trees, some obviously very old indeed, primitive facsimiles of men wearing loincloths with their hair in a sort of top knot. More modern carvings depicted dead ancestors wearing crudely fashioned shorts and one sported what looked extraordinarily like a bowler hat and carried what could only have been a pair of binoculars in his hands. Some of the poles had offerings of earthenware pots and gongs tied to them, green with age. A few had been roughly painted in a now-faded royal blue and turquoise.

In one of the smaller houses we had a breakfast of rice and a little thin soup, drinking boiled water that was grey with mud, and then joined the chief who sat cross-legged on the floor with his wife and two older women around a betel-nut tray. We gave them some tea, coffee and soap which seemed little in return for their hospitality and the dancing we had seen the night before, and they accepted the poor presents with dignity. As they accompanied us down to the sampan, they asked us to return again, or to stay longer.

The river was even higher that morning and seemed to be moving at an incredible rate, swirling around debris brought down from the mountains – trees eighty feet long, pulled up by their roots. Soon the sun blazed down in full force and this time we had no shade as frequent, lashing rain had ruined our plaited canopy. I could feel myself burning up but at least our clothes and kit dried out.

Before long, the river narrowed and we battled through tumbling rapids past banks that were masked with thick jungle, bamboos and trees overhanging the water that had strange, fleshy plants growing on their branches and were festooned with vines. On the opposite bank, a strange, large bird, the size of a turkey, flopped clumsily amongst some bushes, half hopping and half flying, with a large, russet-brown wing span and a fan spread tail. Once we saw a whole tree, stripped of its leaves, covered with monkeys as many as twenty to a branch, swinging from their tails and scratching themselves. It was a fantastic sight and I scrambled carelessly to a crouching position with my camera poised, the sudden movement almost upsetting the shallow craft.

Around mid-day, we chugged round one of the twisting corners and arrived at a surprisingly modern-looking collection of brick-built houses, glaring white in the sunshine, each with a little garden in front of it. This, Amri told us, was the Camat's office of the area and once again we must report and show our passports and our passes.

The office was surprisingly large and one wondered what on earth the eight Indonesians sitting in it could possibly have to do. Their two large typewriters were dusty and none of the faded notices pinned to the wall were dated later than 1971. By now, we were getting far enough inland to be within reach of the Sarawak border where, since confrontation, there had been constant fighting, so perhaps this post of Ambalou was there in case of trouble. All the men wore pale khaki uniform but it was impossible to know whether they were police, soldiers, or merely members of the Camat's staff. They laboriously copied down every page of our passports and gave us coffee, strong, delicious and very welcome.

By late afternoon after frequent heavy rainstorms we finally reached the village of Sabun which, as it turned out, was the end of the trail. On the few vague maps Robin had seen, it had looked as though we might have been able to go another ten or fifteen miles up the river, but this was obviously going to be impossible by boat. Above a collection of six long houses on the banks, the river rose in a series of rapids so steep they were more like waterfalls with white water tumbling over a high mass of black rocks. Beyond us the river swerved sharply around a great fountain of giant bamboos and disappeared out of view.

The village had – to my delight – no raft or bath house here and no perilous log bridge. We tied up against the bank and followed two young women, their sarongs, soaking wet and clinging to their bodies, outlining shortish, strong figures. On their heads they carried large circular gourds heavy with water.

The houses were smaller than the one the night before but in much better repair, and Sabun had an air of prosperity about it, although here there were virtually no signs of Western or any missionary influences. The Dayaks too looked stronger and more healthy. They were much shorter and more stocky than the people we had met lower down the river and, in many ways, far more open and less reserved in their attitude towards us.

In the centre of the village was a strange shrine, a wooden platform on high stilts covered with a thatched roof that was obviously still very much in use. At each end a primitive carving of a man and a woman faced towards the village below them; in the centre was a grotesquely grinning devil face. On the ledge, offerings of plates with small mounds of rice were surrounded by dried pigs' trotters, bunches of herbs and the skulls of wild boar, and what I supposed were monkeys. A woman passing it – her head covered with an incredibly wide-brimmed hat patterned with strange oriental designs – carried charms in her hands, more tinkling pigs' trotters and a string of strangely carved objects designed to bring good luck, as she went off to fish.

In the largest house we met the chief, an elderly grey-haired man with a high forehead and deep widow's peak, who invited us to sit and offered us betel nut from a highly ornate brass tray with the ingredients in equally intricately decorated small brass pots. Both Robin and I refused; the idea of chewing raw lime and the red-lipped results were too much for either of us, although we both tried it later.

Children played around the feet of their parents, quiet and well-behaved. The man sat cross-legged, in that yoga style I had not yet managed to perfect, with legs entwined and bare feet flat side up, and the women squatted on firmly planted feet, their bottoms almost touching the floor, backs ramrod straight, breasts exposed above their sarongs. The house was simple, unfurnished except for exceptionally fine mats on the floor and some knives hanging on the walls beside wide cartwheel hats, decorated with tiny pearl buttons, painted red and with tassels of human hair hanging in a pigtail tightly tied with coloured ribbons coming from the coned crowns.

We were sitting in the communal area outside the door of someone's house, and each time a member of the family or one of the children wanted to enter through the half-closed door, they had to push their way through about fifty people sitting on the ground outside. They did this with the curious deferential politeness we saw throughout the interior of Indonesia, half-bending to the ground as they passed and holding an arm out straight in front of them as they moved. This we learnt was an ancient tradition which had grown up to show they were not moving in anger; the crouch was an apologetic gesture and the outstretched arm was to show they were not armed. Even the smallest children performed these motions every time they went to or from the door.

One of the older men went to sit by the main door to the longhouse and banged out a rhythmic pattern on an ancient brass gong.

'He calls the people to the chief,' Amri, who had changed from his uniform to the traditional sarong, explained, and within seconds the Dayaks began arriving, more and more; men, women and children squeezed into the small longhouse until there must have been nearly a hundred of them sitting almost shoulder to shoulder on the floor. Brass betel trays were passed between small groups and everyone was busy chewing, rolling and crushing the betel or spitting out saliva between the floor boards. A fascinated row of chickens and cockerels perched on the two window frames and blinked through red-rimmed eyes into the room. Our Chinese boatmen stayed very much in the background.

Though similar to the music we had heard with other Dayak tribes, the entertainment that evening had a purer, simpler quality to it and there was no dancing. Men played alone or in harmony on strange bamboo pipes and stringed instruments: soft, haunting notes that floated through the air, echoing slightly, with a gentle, sighing sound.

It was a pleasant, soothing way to spend an evening but, much as I had enjoyed the music, I was glad when the party seemed to break up at about ten-thirty. The instruments were put away and, although no-one moved, that was obviously the end of the entertainment.

'I think they are waiting for us to do something,' I whispered to Robin.

'You may be right. Let's go and wash.'

We walked through the crowd, pushing out our right arms politely and moving with a half crouch, clutching our washing things in the other hand. It felt a bit silly, but 'when in Rome...'

When we returned, the room was empty except for Amri and his boys already stretched out in a row at one end of the room. Beside them was a paraffin lamp, turned down low and surrounded by thousands of small insects and a few enormous moths. At the other end of the room, our luggage was neatly stacked against a wall and two of the most beautiful mats we had yet seen were laid out on the floor. The rattan was so fine it was almost impossible to see the weave; both mats were shiny with use and patterned with intricate black lines.

From the chief of this tribe Robin had learnt earlier in the evening that, even if we carried the sampan above the rapids, the river was virtually impassable even in this high water and, in any case, the villages beyond were few and far between and difficult to locate. He also told us of a sensational waterfall, about three or four days' walk away. Amri, who was helping to translate, said he had also heard rumours about this fall but, as far as he knew, no-one outside the Dayaks living in the area had ever seen it.

'I believe it is higher than Niagara,' he had said, and I could see Robin's eyes gleam. To be the first outsiders to reach such a waterfall would be an achievement indeed. The instincts of an explorer did battle with his instincts of trying to keep to our tight schedule. Was the fall really only four days' walk away at the outside? Could it be done in less? How tough would the walking be and could I keep up? Could we get a guide? All these were questions which had to be taken account of. If we went we would never be back in Nangapinoh in time to get our lift back to Pontianak and it might be days, or even weeks, before we could get the plane to come in again for us. Reluctantly, he decided we ought to return. We had already taken an extra day to get this far and, if we had trouble with the boat going back, we might not return in time

It gets light early in the tropics and it seemed no time at all between falling asleep and being woken by the cocks crowing outside. After we had had some coffee, Amri asked me to go and look at a sick girl lying in one of the little houses built off the main longhouse. I took our medicine chest and followed him into a small room where the personal things of the family were neatly stacked around the walls beside large porcelain jars, used for storing wine, oil or the spirits of the gods; jars which had been brought up the river by the first Chinese explorers centuries ago and which, at Sotheby's or Christie's, would have fetched a small fortune.

The girl was obviously very ill. She lay in the centre of the room, her smooth, walnut-brown skin tinged with a greenish-yellow hue, her forehead damp with beads of fever sweat and her hands chill and clammy. She shivered constantly and I managed to find out that she had been very sick. She obviously had a high temperature.

Amri had not followed me into the room so I went out to confer with him.

'She should go to hospital,' I said.

'Yes, they will take her to hospital but it will take them three days. Can you give her something to make her better for the journey?'

What should I give her? We had all sorts of anti-biotics and pain-killers but I did not know if the girl had malaria or polio. The people standing round her shook their heads when I said malaria, so I supposed they knew better than I would. Just in case, I gave her mother a supply of malaria pills, some codis and some stomach pills to stop her being sick. I told her carefully what to do with them; none of the medications could do her any harm and I just hoped they would help to make the journey more comfortable.

We went down to the river with her family to see them off. Careful preparations had been made for the journey. The shallow canoe was covered with an arch of freshly plaited green palms; gourds of water and wine were packed carefully in the back with a sack of rice and two live chickens. Two men laid the sick girl carefully on a straw mat, laid over more palm leaves and wrapped some freshly picked banana leaves around her head. Her father and mother picked up their paddles and joined her. A small child sat motionless in the centre of the small craft beside the girl's legs as the rest of the village stood on the bank to watch them go.

We re-packed and left soon after, sad to leave so soon this village in its idyllic setting and the people who lived there.

'Some day,' Robin said as the boat drew away from the bank and we waved to all the people who lined it to see us off, 'some day, we will come back here and find that water-fall.' It was a nice thought but both of us knew if we left it too long the village of Sabun and its surroundings would be sadly changed. The prospects of wealth from lumber and minerals were beginning to boom in Kalimantan. Already, much of the forest and jungle further to the west had been raped and the ground left barren; there had been a French team of mineralogists in Nangapinoh before we arrived and, if deposits were found, it would be people like these Dayaks up the Melawi who would suffer. With their land destroyed, the cloak of poverty would quickly encompass them and almost certainly little, if any, of the profits of this pillage would go into their pockets. Perhaps institutions like Survival International and others like it around the world could help to protect the rights and the lives from such pillage.

We had not got far before we met trouble. The rapids which had nearly swamped us the day before were even rougher now that the level of the water had fallen. We drew into the bank above them while Amri considered the situation.

'We will leave the baggage in,' he told the men. 'Mr Tenison and the lady will walk on the bank and we will pull the sampan through.' Robin was not terribly keen on behaving like a white Rajah – he liked to be 'where the action was' – but Amri was in charge and we obediently climbed out of the boat onto the bank.

Although the bank was heavily covered with undergrowth and our way often blocked by thick vines so that we had to wade through the water around the edge, we made better progress than the four men dragging the boat over the rocks. Three times it tipped sideways and I thought it would over-turn, but somehow they kept it steady against the current and the rushing river and an hour later they were out the other side and into smooth water again. We slid across sandy boul- . ders to join them, surrounded by a cloud of white and yellow butterflies, many at least six inches across from the tip of one wing to the edge of the other. They danced round our heads and settled on our shoulders as we walked and then flitted off as we stepped back into the boat.

We shot the next two rapids, careering madly through the water with waves breaking over the side of the sampan, swinging and bobbing with what seemed to me virtually no control at all. It seemed almost miraculous that nothing disastrous happened to either the boat or its occupants.

At Ambalou, we stopped to reload the petrol drum which seemed suspiciously lighter than when we had left it there. Robin swore a bit but there was nothing we could do about it, and Amri's usually fluent understanding of his Indonesian suddenly went to pieces. While we were standing on the raft jetty arguing the point in a friendly fashion, the boatmen disappeared into the jungle and came back with armfuls of small fruit with smooth, yellowish-brown skins. They heaped them into our laps with broad grins and Robin's sense of humour triumphed over anger at being gypped over the petrol.

'Oh well,' he said, grinning too, 'they always say that fair exchange is no robbery. These had better be good, these fruit.' Luckily, they were.

Once again, we had to check in at the Camat's office at the little whitewashed settlement below the village of Ambalou and this time we got VIP treatment. The Camat was wearing his best uniform, looking rather hot in a suit that had obviously been made some years before, and breathing heavily under the weight of a dozen rusty medals. His second-in-command was wearing his best false teeth, of shining white porcelain, which made his jaw jut and his ears stick out. They did not quite meet in the front but the back clashed with a terrible clatter.

We were invited into the Camat's house, tatty and cheap-looking compared to the longhouse at Sabun, with old pages from a prudish girlie calendar pinned to the wall beside a faded print of the President and an eight-inch-long, heavily armoured beetle, which one of his children had tied by a long piece of cotton to a shelf on the wall, buzzing sadly in the background, occasionally beating its wings with a whirring sound.

Lunch, by Dayak standards, was a splendiferous affair: huge bowls of rice, a dish of stewed chicken, hard-boiled duck's eggs and some peppery sauce. At the end of it, the Camat leaned back contentedly, making every medal pinned to his chest bounce up and down with the vibrations of a mammoth belch. The finale of the meal was glasses of a white liquid which I thought must be palm wine. No such luck. The Camat and his minions were Indonesians (probably from Java or Sumatra), belonging to the Muslim religion and therefore teetotallers. The liquid turned out to be our first taste of a speciality we were to be offered many times again on our journeys – lukewarm, diluted, tinned milk, heavily sweetened and thickly sickening. I found it unbearably cloying and almost impossible to swallow. Robin, on the other hand, who has always retained a nursery palate, loved it. Often, he had to drink mine as well as his and we got very nimble about switching glasses so as not to cause offence to people to whom tinned milk was as precious as gold dust.

After lying motionless in the blazing sun for an hour, the boat was burning to the touch when we set off again. The petrol drum was so hot, it was positively dangerous, and it was difficult to get comfortable under the palm canopy without touching something red-hot. Sweat trickled along our bodies and a foot that Robin left carelessly dangling outside the shade soon turned an ugly red, but at least the motor kept going and we made good progress now that we were no longer fighting the current.

Nangapinoh – reached the next afternoon after a night in another village, where conditions were bad and the people near starvation, and then a long, hot day on the water – seemed like a return to another world. The feeling was intensified when, after checking in with the Camat, we hurriedly changed and walked to the outskirts of the town to take 'tea' with the American Missionary, Mr Van Patten, and his wife – an invitation accepted before we had left the town.

Their house was, staggeringly, straight out of *American Homes and Gardens* with a 'country flavour'. I felt as out of place in it as a prostitute at a deb dance, sitting on my hands to stop myself smoking, on the edge of a chair upholstered in pale linen. The room was coloured with pastel hues and contained cotton tablecloths with frilly skirts, 'snaps' of smiling children and little things from 'way back home'. I shivered slightly in air that was stirred by a fan and carefully screened from mosquitoes. Mrs Van Patten looked cool and ladylike in a knee-length cotton 'frock'. I felt hot and sticky and longed for a long, cold beer. My feet, sticking through open sandals, had a decaying, greyish tinge to them although I'd spent ages scrubbing them in the primitive bathroom of the Camat's office, using a piece of coconut husk as a nail brush. I hid broken, mud-engrained nails under the table as Van Patten said grace, calling on the Lord to bless 'our visitors, the Tenisons, who eat with us today' and asking Him to watch over our journey. 'Amen to that,' I said under my breath.

The Van Pattens had been in Indonesia for twenty-eight years and were able to fill us in on a lot of background history of Kalimantan. During the conflict between the government and Communism in 1965, they had seen many graves being dug for anti-Communists, had seen two prepared for their own bodies, and then witnessed the massacre of scores of Chinese as the revolution was crushed.

'Many Chinese are still being hunted down as suspected Communists,' Van Patten said, as we supped off a good American meal of eggs scrambled with tinned meat, toast with cranberry jam and a salad of grated raw carrots and raisins. 'They hide in the jungle with remote groups and there have been many unfortunate cases of Dayaks being murdered to prevent them disclosing their whereabouts. Recently, the Dayaks rose up against the Chinese because of this and there was a lot of bloodshed. But of course it's often almost impossible to tell who is Red and who isn't in this kind of situation – everyone suspects everyone else.'

He told us about a young Chinese photographer who had been arrested for Communist activities the week before. He was the official Nangapinoh photographer and had gone on a trip with the MAF plane to take pictures of the town from the air. Soon after, some officials took him away on the charge that he had been at a party with some identified Communists some years before.

At that moment, the man in question walked in. He looked as though he had been a prisoner in a concentration camp, thin to the point of emaciation and exceptionally pale. Although he was obviously nervous about saying too much in front of us, he did talk a little about his experiences in prison.

'They didn't beat me up but they did interrogate me for over ten hours and they removed my film – all my films. I was lucky. It wasn't too uncomfortable and I could pay to be released.'

'How much?' we asked, but he shook his head and smiled thinly. That was something he was not prepared to divulge. I thought about the photographs we had taken of Nangapinoh and I sincerely hoped no-one was going to think we were potential Communists.

That evening, we had one of the nicest experiences we were

to have on the whole expedition, one of those moments when one is touched to the point of tears.

Our courier, Amri, who had disappeared immediately we reached the town, appeared again at the Camat's house and sat down with us on one of the dusty plastic-ribbed chairs still standing in a straight row down the central room.

'How was everything at your home?' I asked him. Amri smiled broadly.

'Everything was very well,' he said. 'My wife had a son. A big boy, very strong and our first man child.'

We were astonished. Amri had never said anything about his wife expecting a baby while we were away, although, now we thought about it, we realized he had been in a bit of a hurry to get home. He cleared his throat a few times, rose to his feet, clasped his hands in front of him and began speaking very fast, in English, as though repeating a well-learned lesson:

'I should like, with your permission, to call my son Tenison Amri Bachtiar, and for you, Mr Tenison, to be his godfather.' He hesitated and, obviously feeling I might be hurt at being left out, added, 'The Lady Tenison too, of course, would be very honourable.'

I did not know about being 'honourable', but both Robin and I were terribly touched. We gave Amri a copy of Robin's book about the Indians of Brazil, *A Question of Survival*, and promised to keep in touch with him and little Tenison. I would love to have seen the baby but Amri, regretfully, said his wife was not yet 'arranged' for visitors.

Just then we were joined by the Camat, looking neat and official in a sand-coloured uniform. He too obviously had something important to say because once more there was again a considerable amount of throat-clearing and some hastily whispered words in Indonesian to Amri, who went pink about the ears. Amri was chosen as the one to speak.

The people in Kalimantan, Amri said, were having too many babies. We had produced only two children in fifteen years of marriage. Did we take the tablets they had heard of which prevented babies? Did we know where they could get these tablets? Was it true that abortion was allowed by our religion? Both men kept their eyes fixed on the overflowing ashtrays on the shabby tables in front of us as the questions were asked and we tried to answer them.

These people were living far into the interior of an island which was itself far from the governing capital of Jakarta, yet they were highly aware, and desperately keen to do something about, a problem which the Western world has really only recently opened its eyes to. Their attitude was refreshing.

The conversation lasted for about an hour and then Amri left to get back to his family. We were sad at parting company. At the speed we were moving, friendships tended to be fleeting things and in Amri we have found someone we considered very special. Apart from anything else, we had him to thank for the tremendous success of our trip and the ease with which we had been able to visit the Dayaks and their longhouses.

Van Patten took us out to the airstrip next morning and waited with us to collect the post from Pontianak.

Two Indonesians cleared the runway of cows and picked up their droppings to spread on the missionary garden, and after an hour's hot wait, with flies and mosquitoes buzzing annoyingly around our faces, the MAF pilot, George Boggs, arrived out of the sky. Within five minutes we were airborne with the wooden town of Nangapinoh, the houseboats (bandungs) and the small dagans (motor canoes) only a colourful blur in the distance.

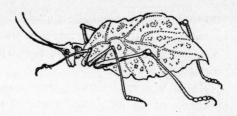

Chapter 8

In Pontianak, we found the anthropologist, Terry King, had returned from Jakarta with a new set of papers. He told us he had been ordered to send back weekly reports of his activities to the authorities in the capital.

'How they think I can do that from eight weeks up the Kapuas river, God only knows,' he said a little wryly. 'In Jakarta they seem to think every bend of the river has a post box on it.' The confusion over his papers had, as we had thought, been caused by the incident over Wyn Sargent, the American anthropologist who had been thrown out of Irian by the Indonesian government. There was still the bad feeling and anthropologists in Indonesia (what few had been allowed in) were 'marked men' at the moment.

The four of us dined at the 'best restaurant in town'. We laughed over the menu which, surprisingly, had a page of English translation and included such delicacies as 'crap soup' and 'fried shrig'; we swopped stories about our travels and from Terry we learnt more about the Dayaks and their problems.

The government, he told us, were against the building of longhouses both for hygienic and political reasons. Community living, they said, led to the spread of diseases and it was this community living which also led to war and bloodshed when chiefs and elders got together. Recently, Terry had heard of a group of Dayaks who had begun building a new longhouse, starting with the row of kitchens which would make up the back of the house. Local officials had forbidden them to continue with the passage and the long, open verandah and families of up to twelve were now living in claustrophobically cramped quarters that would normally have been used only for eating.

Robin was saddened by this news. He had found in the principle of the longhouse a way of living that he felt could well be adopted in the Western world. We had talked about it a lot on the journey and compared the busy community life of the Dayaks with the lonely existence of people, especially the elderly, living in tower blocks in our own cities. The four of us drank welcome bottle after bottle of beer as he talked.

'Longhouses are exactly what is needed in the crazy world of skyscrapers and limited space. They could be built in London, New York, Singapore – everywhere new buildings are being erected by governments. Instead of putting up a series of identical little self-contained box flats, one on top of another like a tower of minibricks, where no-one has any contact with anyone else and loneliness is inevitable for young and old, governments should copy the longhouse system, building modern facsimiles, one on top of another, to make a skyscraper that can be a community on every level. Each one would have the long recreation and communal area running along the length of each storey, with picture windows and even perhaps small strips of garden. A place where people could meet and talk; spend the evening talking, instead of watching the television in solitary isolation and get together with their neighbours. Their private living areas could be scaled down in proportion but they would still each have their own front door and it would lead onto a sort of Coronation Street instead of the limbo of a blank passage.'

We made plans to revolutionize the world and built castles in the sky and, in Terry, Robin found one of a new breed of anthropologists, a man who was not just interested in recording the past history of the tribes he was studying but who was also deeply and genuinely concerned about their future.

Apart from the obvious problems of lack of food and protein, the Dayaks were suffering from a rapid population increase which they wanted to control. With the infiltration of the outside world into their lives, old methods of contraception and abortion were quickly dying out, yet no government programme of birth control had been introduced to replace the old and successful, if sometimes somewhat violent, habits. It was a well-known cycle. More mouths to feed inevitably meant more food must be found to put into them, while, at the same time, game in the forests – deer, pigs and monkeys – was growing more and more scarce, especially since the price for live animals for sale to zoos made hunting an attractive proposition to outside trappers equipped with modern techniques. A summer without rain had drastically cut the last season's crop of hill rice, and the Dayaks had no knowledge of how to grow the wet rice which would increase their harvest. In addition there was, as we had seen only too plainly, a desperate need for medical help amongst the people of the interior.

The Dayaks were a people between two worlds, the old and the new. As civilization encroached on their jungles, they were losing the customs, habits and adat of their old life together with much of the knowledge which had strengthened them in the past and, until now anyway, they had found nothing to replace these vital elements of life.

The work of the missionaries in the interior of Kalimantan appeared to be of little value and, in fact, merely seemed to cause unnecessary and often unhappy confusion to the tribes. Their gods, they were told, their cultural traditions and their adat were evil and their half-nakedness an insult to the real God. But who was the real God? The missionaries themselves seemed to have different points of view on this subject.

Terry summed it up, having to shout above the clamour of voices and clattering of crockery in the restaurant which, that evening, was crowded with soldiers and prosperous-looking Chinese families whose fat babies rolled on the floor between the tables.

'What can those poor Dayaks be expected to believe? A Roman Catholic arrives out of the blue, tells the women to wear bras, tells the elders to worship a new God and frightens the people into believing that if their babies die unbaptized (by a priest who only appears about once a year) they will go to hell. Then along comes a Protestant who says the other white man got it wrong and they will all burn in the fires of hell anyway unless they stop smoking, dancing and drinking palm wine at feasts. Finally, an Islam missionary appears on the scene, puts up a mosque beside the Roman Catholic and Protestant churches, preaches a totally different religion and leads them to believe that all white men are dogs and infidels. I ask you,' Terry said over the 'crap soup', 'what could anyone, let alone a so-called "savage" from the jungle, be expected to make out of that lot?'

The Garuda flight to Jakarta next morning was scheduled for eleven and once more we had the frustration of trying to get some form of transport to the airport.

Robin came back to the hotel from taxi-hunting hot and unsuccessful. Time was getting on and we were panicking about what to do next, when we heard a hoot outside and found that Terry had at the eleventh hour persuaded one of the missionaries to pick us up. Within hours we were back in the teeming, noisy heat of Jakarta, and again Robin was not looking forward to the experience. Staying in big cities put a big strain on our finances; he had already made most of the contacts he had in the capital and every day spent in the concrete jungle meant one less to be spent in the green jungle of the interior. We expected to have to stay about a week in order to get papers for Sulawesi and the Moluccas and the vital permit which would allow us to visit Irian Jaya.

I, on the other hand (although I did not like to mention it), was only too delighted by the thought of such luxuries as hot baths, regular meals, soft beds and a respite from being mosquito-ridden and continually dripping with mud.

Reasonably clean again, for the first time for weeks, we lay on our respective twin beds, me reading a lurid paperback, avidly bought at a ridiculous price from the hotel bookshop, and Robin going through his list of telephone numbers.

I wallowed in secondhand lust while he, looking like a Roman senator with a towel wrapped around his waist, made a series of ineffectual calls. The British Embassy had closed at mid-day; the travel agent would not have any news on our Irian visas until Monday; the well-known Indonesian writer, Mochtar Lubis, was away for the weekend; so was our friend David Treffry at the International Monetary Fund; so-and-so would be unavailable until next week, and so would so-and-so and so-and-so somebody else. In the end, he slammed down the receiver in disgust.

Neither of us, I think, quite realized how tiring the journey up the Melawi had been, or how little sleep we had really had during the past weeks. After a quick supper, we fell on our beds and slept for an uninterrupted stretch of twelve hours.

At ten the next morning, an Italian, called Sergio dello Strologo, rang. We had met him in Jakarta with Francis Lang, and in the limbo we were in at that moment his voice was the manna from heaven. He was working for the United Nations and was involved in a project to restore the old buildings which made up the Dutch colonial square of Jakarta in the original centre of the city down by the docks. Like Robin, he is an ardent conservationist, apart from being a tremendously attractive man with all the charm of a Latin successfully combined with American dynamic qualities.

'I have arranged a small lunch for you at my home,' he said, 'and then tonight we will dine with Muni Gastel, whom you will meet at luncheon. After that, who knows?'

Hair, fingers, face – everything was a mess. I scrubbed, massaged and dug in suitcases for unused make-up, frantically trying to become a picture of glossy sophistication, until a chauffeured car, large, sleek and air-conditioned, appeared to waft us away to another world, the weekend began and we stepped into a long colourful dream.

Sergio's house, like Sergio himself, was exotic. Looking like a character out of a James Bond film in a spotless white safari suit, with most of his face hidden behind enormous dark glasses, he led us into the verandah of a white one-storey building. The verandah, richly oriental and flamboyantly exotic, made me feel pampered, important and luxurious as I reclined as elegantly as I could on the soft cushions of an enormous wooden Chinese bed with ornate carvings of dragon-like creatures on three sides and four posts supporting a plush canopy. Tropical plants luxuriated in the corners of the room, two emperor-sized white cane chairs with fan-shaped backs flanked the bed, brilliantly coloured cockatoos and parakeets flashed in the garden outside and a silent man-servant in white served us with astonishingly large vodkas and tonic, clinking with ice, from a silver tray.

I forgot the itching flea bites on my buttocks and the agony of a nasty attack of foot-rot in my right toes.

Inside the house a large cool living room and opulent dining room reverberated gently with classical music and a hundred rich and rare antiques were arranged with the utmost perfection of taste.

I sipped my drink while we looked at exquisite drawings of old Jakarta with the pillared Dutch colonial buildings and cobbled squares as they would be once more and listened dreamily as Robin and Sergio discussed subjects of preservation and conservation. Twice Sergio, full of nervous energy, leapt to the telephone and talked rapid Italian accompanied by dramatic Latin gesticulation from the hand not holding the receiver.

'Muni is always late,' he explained. 'I'm telling him to hurry or the lunch will be ruined and my cook demented.'

At last Muni Gastel arrived; tall, dark, with an exaggeratedly aristocratic face and a dynamism that matched Sergio's. He was dressed identically to Sergio and accompanied by a most beautiful girl, an Indonesian and a grand-daughter of the famous Sultan of Jogjakarta. Nanouk looked delicious in this setting, her slight plumpness giving her body a feline appeal; her large, dark, almost jet-black eyes were luminous against a golden brown skin that had the sheen of satin on a velvet complexion; heavy black hair was knotted loosely at the nape of her neck. She tied the knot without the aid of pins or combs and every now and then the sheer weight of the tresses caused it to become loose and cascade down her back. When this happened she would throw her head back in a loose, liquid movement, gather up the gleaming curtain of black and quickly twist it back into a new shape.

Muni is a natural entertainer. He took my hand to his lips as though I was the one person he most wanted to meet and gave us a most graphic description with Italian interspersing his English of the dramas of his morning.

'Everythinga was terrible. I woke with a hangover, my coffee it was cold and Nanouk wasa so unsympatice. The telephone it rang constantly with people I had never heard of who kept talking, talking, talking. We went for the shopping and Nanouk had to find some strange foods for dinner this evening which were not in this market or that market.' He grinned broadly, sank in a chair, ran a hand through crinkly hair and said comically, 'Mama mia! It is a miracle I live to be here.'

The food and wine were gloriously Italian and a delicious contrast to the rice we seemed to have been eating for so long. The conversation sparkled, Sergio scintillated, Muni made us laugh and I felt I was sitting in a glorious pink bubble. And the deliciousness went on until in a haze of happiness it was almost impossible to believe that only two days ago we were sleeping on bare boards and stinking of mud.

Late in the afternoon we drove down to the harbour to look at speedboats with Muni and Nanouk; Nanouk who was as beautiful as only Indonesian girls can be with her large, dark eyes, heavy curling eyelashes and her gleaming aureole of velvet black hair; Nanouk, who was a princess, who moved like one and was surrounded by an air of sumptuous confidence.

We had dinner with Muni at his house. House? It was a palace, spaciously cool yet comfortable at the same time with a garden of tall trees that stretched into the darkness. We had been asked for eight-thirty, but arrived late. It was difficult to find the large wooden gates in the unlit street and it must have been nine by the time we arrived. We need not have hurried for the other twelve guests went on arriving over the space of the next hour: Indonesians, Americans, a Frenchman and another delightful Italian (Gerardo, smoothly self-assured and every inch the diplomat he indeed was) with a sweet Chinese girlfriend.

Nanouk took me into her bedroom where silks cascaded from a cupboard like rainbow-coloured jewels. She had cut a plant like a thick green sword from the garden and she showed me how the sticky sap inside could be rubbed through the hair to make it thick and rich in texture. Muni, she said, had been going bald until he began to rub the sap on his head.

'And look how much hair he has now,' she said laughing. And it was true.

In the drawing room, amongst woven hangings from Bali and breathtaking antiques, a huge bowl of gigantic fruit carved from wood glowed as the centrepiece of a mantelpiece. I felt my stomach churn, for the crowning glory was a durien, that stinking, rotten tasting fruit which had already made me violently ill on two occasions. I had to ask them to remove it while I was there. I knew it was stupid, but even the shape, oval and covered with plump spines, was enough to set me off again and I did not want to ruin the dinner which was to be pure Indonesian and which Nanouk had cooked herself.

That evening was still part of this beautiful, beautiful dream.

A cockatoo, white with a salmon-pink crest, sat on Muni's shoulder nibbling his ear and screaming furiously when anyone went too near him or when the two dogs, a spaniel and a large bumbling mongrel, tried to get his attention.

'I'll send you away, Coco,' Muni teased, and Coco went into a frenzy of agony at the thought, displaying his crest to show how beautiful he was, rubbed his beak through Muni's hair, and cooed with tenderness. Before we went in for dinner he did have to be taken away, on a perch, by one of the servants who glided silently around, and his outraged shrieks could be heard in the distance as we ate.

'Coco's better than a guard dog,' Muni said. 'Burglaries are common in Jakarta but I think he'd kill anyone who tried to get in here.'

I sat next to a Franco-Indonesian who told me some of the mysteries involved in the printing of the complicated patterns that are the secret of Batik materials, from which all good sarongs are made; how the patterns change from region to region and how it was possible to tell a good cloth from a second-rate one.

Coco was brought back at the end of dinner, and Muni was forgiven and covered with kisses in between sidelong glances of triumph the intelligent great bird shot at Nanouk. Then Muni made a speech, his accent heavily Italian, his English perfect and his hands gesticulating elegantly.

'Tonight we are taking you to the mountains. It is wonderfully cool up there and the sunrise is unbelievable. After a drink and a little more talk we go back to your hotel, you get some jeans and things and then we take off. Tomorrow we will go to the botanical gardens at Bogor. There,' he said, smiling triumphantly, 'you see, it is all arranged. We will stay with Gerardo at the Italian residence which is just a cottage but quite comfortable.' Gerardo looked a little surprised but not too much put out and left the room to telephone to the residence.

It was amazing. They wafted us up and we drove in the early hours of the morning to the mountains with Muni treating his car like Fangio, narrowly missing unlit lorries, the crowds of people who seemed to be on the streets in every small village we went through, and the occasional bullock dozing in the middle of the road. We raced up a curving mountain road, wheels screaming, and arrived at the residence, high up on the side of a hillside, at about three in the morning.

The dream went on. Upstairs in the house, which looked like a Swiss chalet, Robin and I curled up in each other's arms and took advantage of being in a comfortable double bed once more. I find I really miss this double-bed thing as we travel. Impersonal hotel twin beds or mats on bare floorboards just are not the same as a nice, large double bed in a room where there are just the two of you and not an audience of gentlemen numbering maybe up to fifteen or more. In that particular bed, it was actually cool enough to have two blankets on top of us – unbelievable bliss after sweating almost every night in Kalimantan. We even had to cuddle up closer than ever under those blankets because of a definite nip in the air.

Despite the comfort, we woke after only a few hours' sleep. A pack of what sounded like bloodhounds appeared to be running in full cry through the valley below, with their barks and howls echoing against the mountains and, for us anyway, sleep was impossible. We imagined them hunting tiger or wild boar. Later we learnt they were just a neighbour's pack of guard dogs. Anyway, they woke us up completely, so we took Muni's advice and went onto a wide balcony to watch the sun rise. As he had promised, 'spectacular' was an understatement.

We were high on a range of hills at a town which had been popular as a holiday resort in the Dutch colonial heyday. Below us stretched a heavily cultivated winding valley banked by slopes neatly planted with tidily pruned tea bushes – even from a distance they looked trim and faintly smug, like domesticated, spoutless teapots. Waves of early mist drifted over the winding river, half-concealing one of those romantic mosques we saw all over Indonesia, all spires and minarets connected by a silver-topped onion-shaped dome. (I am sorry to say they were actually made from beaten corrugated iron that would soon rust.) Jagged volcanic mountains to the south were touched with pale geranium tints.

Later, an elderly manservant, wearing a white dinner jacket, a muted sarong and a black Muslim hat, served us all breakfast. While we drank coffee and covered toast with honey, a throng of traders filed up the drive, past the window, to gather on the lawn where, despite it being Sunday, two boys were clipping the coarse, thickly-bladed grass, inch by inch, with pairs of shears, squatting on their haunches and edging forward like flat-footed birds.

The caravan continued up the hill in a seemingly endless stream of men with sarongs wrapped neatly round their waists. Some were young, some elderly and, moving slowly, every one carried a bundle wrapped in cloth.

'What are they doing?' I asked Sergio.

'They come to sell antiques. Some of the stuff is trash or cheap reproductions, but some is good and one can still get a bargain.'

'But how did they know we were here?'

'Word gets around quickly. Probably some of them are relations of the servants who get a cut out of the spoils. Once one comes, the others quickly follow.'

By now, there must have been about thirty of them, sitting cross-legged on the ground, carefully unwrapping their precious bundles and spreading out objects on the ground around them, and we wandered amongst them, examining Ming plates and silver-sheathed kris.

Later that morning we drove down to the local market which was the usual riot of colour with banks of fresh fruit and vegetables; carrots, clean and brilliant orange; oranges, lemons and even apples; purple, shining aubergines; pineapples, mangoes and strange things I had never seen before. Nanouk went mad, filling the boot of the car with great armfuls of fruit and vegetables.

Everyone caught the spending fever. Robin nearly landed himself with a small, green-and-orange parakeet which flew onto his shoulder and ran up and down his arm, twisting its head sideways, cackling gently. Muni fell head over heels in love with a large, young, fish-eating owl, brown-feathered with huge, blinking, amber eyes and tufts like horns on the top of its head. It stood in the middle of the market, uncaged and seemingly oblivious to the noise around, the feathery edges of its plumage making it obvious that it must be very young indeed. Seduced, Muni bought it and put it on the back window ledge of the car where it continued blinking and turned its head almost completely back to front to see what was going on, balancing on huge, clawed feet with talons that were sharply barbed and at least an inch long.

'We will keep it in the garden where it can fly between the trees,' he said to Nanouk. She was realistically dubious about the owl's effect on the cockatoo, Coco, and she was right. Coco threw tantrum after hysterical tantrum when they returned home with the owl and, after a few days, Muni had to give up and present it to the Jakarta zoo, apparently one of the best in the world, run by a dedicated zoologist.

After lunch, we drove back towards Jakarta, stopping on the way to visit the botanical gardens at Bogor, but not arriving there until just after five when the gardens were officially shut.

My admiration for Sergio grew minute by minute as he summoned the gatekeeper from a small lodge, announced imperiously that we were official guests given permission to visit the gardens by the Governor himself and demanded the gates be opened. They were – at once.

We wandered until darkness through the magnificent gardens which had been started by Raffles in his heyday, past the elegant white palace resplendent with Palladian pillars which he built for his home. Sukarno too had lived there and filled the rooms with flashy twentieth-century oil paintings, and now Sergio had hopes of turning the building into a museum. A large lake – covered in Victoria Regina lilies wide as tabletops, where frogs croaked with strange warbling noises and small crocodiles flopped in and out of the water – spread out towards the gardens behind the house below a lawn slightly scarred by heavy bronze statues, which were more relics of Sukarno's reign.

We strolled under bamboos, high as skyscrapers, arching across the path and past giant ferns and strange trees with thick tentacle-roots spreading for yards around them. Orchids clung to high branches and made splashes of fantastic colour against the dark green background of leaves.

Raffles fascinated me as a swashbuckling, romantic person who gained and lost vast fortunes and power. Someone whom one had not heard a word about at school and yet who must have been one of the great characters of the nineteenth century and a major force in the building of the English colonies.

In the early nineteenth century, he had governed Indonesia in the brief colonization before the Dutch took over, had begun Bogor, and collected the amazing quantity of botanical species which began the foundation of the garden. He had ruled over Singapore, been exiled to Sumatra and made another amazing collection of butterflies and specimens, been shipwrecked on his way home and gone back to repeat the whole collection. He had written, built and created much that still remains, yet I had never even heard of him until I went to the East.

We crossed a swinging wooden bridge over a natural gorge, over water tumbling in a foaming stream, and went to look at the grave of Raffles' wife, Elizabeth, a white monument with Grecian canopy and pillars. Then, all too quickly, the dream was over. Tomorrow was Monday, we had our papers and visas to see to and we had an expedition to get on the road once more.

Miraculously, it all took a much shorter time than we had thought or dared to hope it would. Our Jakarta travel agent had come up trumps. They had our Sulawesi and Moluccas papers in order, our Irian visas could be obtained from the government building dealing with that department and our flights were all booked. From the Australian Embassy, we obtained visas to enter Papua New Guinea.

At the government department, we were passed from official to official and filled in form after form, and were asked question after question about our background and our reasons for going to Irian Jaya. We wrote 'tourist' and 'tourism' again and again, handed over passports and a stack of photographs of us both (luckily we had come equipped with fifteen each, but they were disappearing fast now) and then were told to go away and come back the next day.

We waited nervously and the time passed slowly, although we had a fascinating lunch with Mochtar Lubis. He is one of the great intellectuals and editors of Indonesia. In the evening we drove with Sergio, Muni and Nanouk to see the old Dutch square, the centre of old Batavia, which Sergio was restoring to its original grandeur. Work had only just started, but one could well understand his enthusiasm for the perfect symmetry of the graceful colonial buildings and the central plaza now to be recobbled, a copy of the original fountain to be resurrected and palms planted once more at the four corners.

We dined in a walled fortress where many of the Chinese had holed up during the 1965 wave of feeling against them which had swept through the country. Since then, a small city had been built behind the huge iron gates guarding it, and inside it was all Chinese with shops, restaurants and food stalls jammed tightly together. Nervously, we looked at the stalls and sampled small dishes of monkey, snake, iguana and dog, supposedly the greatest of delicacies. I tried all but the dog, which I balked at, although we had already eaten that in Sumatra unknowingly. However, Robin chewed a portion and said it was far the best. That was just for starters. We had dinner in a bare restaurant with neon lighting and a soulless atmosphere, but food that surpassed anything I had ever experienced – crab, lobster, prawns, chicken, and smooth, silkily textured abalone and crisp vegetables in a steaming soup. There were intermissions for the steaming, cologne-scented face cloths which a Chinese lady offered every now and then with a humble bow.

Knowing my interest in cookery, Sergio led me to the kitchens where chefs with wide girths performed miracles in a temperature that must have been well over one hundred, tossing rounded frying pans over raging fires and chopping and slicing with an art that never ceases to amaze me. I was relieved they weren't dissecting a dog while I was in there, but I did watch with fascination as one, using a cleaver fit for an ox, neatly boned a chicken, cutting the flesh into wafer-thin slices and leaving the bones clean as a whistle in under a minute flat. It made the Cordon Bleu look ridiculous.

Next day, we returned to the Irian department, sat in a waiting room, sweating in the sticky heat, for what seemed like hours. We ran the gauntlet of officialdom once more and finally emerged with those small bits of paper which were so vitally important. Robin was jubilant and we raced back to the travel agent to try and put our flight to Makassar forward by two days so we could leave the next morning.

We repacked for the last time in Jakarta. The bulk of our luggage was to be left in the care of David Treffry at his house and this time we decided to jettison our lilos and a lot of the stuff we had been carrying before. From now on, we had to travel with the barest of essentials for, although we knew basically where we wanted to go, we had no idea what travelling conditions would be like when we got there.

Chapter 9

The flight from Jakarta to Makassar was an experience.

We both had filthy hangovers, not improved by having to be at the airport at 5 a.m. and, even at that hour, the terminal was unbelievably noisy and crowded. Having checked in, we joined what must have been a few hundred other passengers in the small waiting area and slumped down onto the only small space of wooden bench left empty.

One of the things that continually fascinated me about Indonesia was the mixture of races one saw everywhere. That morning there were Indonesian colonels in smartly pressed uniforms, carrying short leather sticks and looking extra military; a couple of Chinese girls, carrying armfuls of purple orchids, paraded around self-consciously on six-inch-high platform shoes that elevated their bodies forward in an extraordinary way; dark-complexioned, elderly men in sarongs, wearing Muslim hats and black jackets, ate hard-boiled eggs in a small café, and white Australian businessmen sat around in crumpled cotton suits fingering through yesterday's papers.

The loudspeaker system had broken down and was replaced by a young boy in a leather jacket, sporting large dark glasses, who tried to shout something through a loudhailer but was overcome by giggles and gave up.

We sat in the sagging, rather grubby seats of the first-class compartment (the ancient DC4 was ominously empty) and were given a free packet of stale cigarettes and offered a glass of beer immediately after a shaky take-off. These were followed by a curious breakfast of some cold rice wrapped in a banana leaf and our pick from a large bowl of fresh fruit. Since there was only one other passenger on the plane, we helped ourselves generously. I have always had a theory that fresh fruit helps to cure hangovers and it worked. By the time the sun had risen, we were feeling much better and able to enjoy the magnificent view as we flew shakily onwards.

We were cruising alongside volcanic mountains and in the early dawn light they were gently coloured in dove-grey and pink, wreathed in mist and looking romantically ethereal. Steeply jagged slopes flattened out to a platform at the pinnacle of each and one or two still gently belched out puffs of smoke.

Near Surabaya in the east of Java the scenery changed to a patchwork pattern of greens with little strips of rice paddies. Every inch of land was carefully cultivated and not a square foot wasted.

'They must be fantastic farmers,' I said as we circled over the city where faded red-tiled roofs fanned one on top of another as closely integrated as the fields.

'They need to be,' Robin answered. 'The population of Indonesia is 120 million. Java with the neighbouring island of Madura is about the size of England and two-thirds of the population live there. Everyone else lives on the remaining 93 per cent of land. Most of that is jungle, swamp or mountain.'

Makassar airport (the airports were getting smaller all the time) was swelteringly hot and it took forever for our luggage to be unloaded. While we waited, Robin asked two Australians if they could recommend a hotel in the town. They looked bored.

'Well,' one of them finally said, 'there's the Grand. It's pretty lousy but I don't know of anywhere else.'

'The Grand it is,' Robin decided. 'We might as well stay in the best.'

We had one contact in Sulawesi – Carl Bundt, orchid grower, who was reputed to be an expert on the island and its people. As we entered Makassar, Robin handed the driver a slip of paper with his name and address on it. Four boys squeezed into the front seat, passed it back and forth amongst themselves, fingering it curiously until we realized none of them could read. Robin tried saying the name and address in Indonesian and they all nodded knowledgeably, as we shot through three sets of red lights (I was convinced by now that the taxi driver had never actually driven before, certainly not in a town).

Makassar is not a very large town and, after we had driven flat out down what was obviously the main street for the third time, weaving wildly through droves of yellow and blue bechaks, it became clear the driver had not the slightest idea of what to do next.

'I don't think they've ever been here before,' I told Robin and he managed to persuade them to slow down so that he could ask directions. Half an hour and about five hundred yards later, we pulled up outside a sizable house near the harbour.

Three long green canoes with spidery outriggers were stacked outside a formidable pair of locked gates; outside, a sign proclaimed 'Carl Bundt, Orchids'.

The gate was opened by three smiling Indonesian girls, and a pack of yapping, smooth-haired dachshunds charged towards us sniffing and nipping around our feet, giving tongue to wild, high-pitched barking every time we moved.

'Dr Bundt,' one of the girls said, shouting above the noise, 'is with his orchids.'

We followed her past rows and rows of orchid seedlings, wombed in bottles of all shapes and sizes; gin bottles, coca-cola bottles, whisky bottles and jam jars packed closely together, each with a piece of cotton wool, a haze of moisture and a tiny green seedling; through more green gates into a yard, heavy with humidity, where rank upon rank of slatted wooden trestles supported pots of all sizes and orchids of a thousand varieties were growing. Canopies of plastic gave this world a strange, greyish-yellow twilight.

Carl Bundt came out from behind a forest of fully grown

flowers, swearing at an enemy snail which had somehow found its way into his garden. At first sight he was terrifying. A giant of a man who made Robin look like a midget. The shape of a Victorian spinning top, with an enormous head, an enormous torso, narrow hips and thin legs encased in black socks which stuck rather grotesquely from long baggy white shorts. He carried his huge head slightly at an angle, his hair was snow-white, and deep-socketed eyes were only half-hidden by dark-tinted, metal-rimmed spectacles. A wall, or blind, eye looked in one direction while the other glared sharply at us. He spoke English with a very guttural German accent and barked out words, sounding rather like his dachshunds.

This has not exactly been a flattering picture of this renowned orchid grower, and let me say at once that he turned out to be both fascinating to talk to and an enormous help, generously giving us his time and the benefit of his life-long experience in Indonesia. But that first impression was a little frightening – especially when one happened to feel shiny, red-faced, uncomfortably hot, and smaller than usual.

'What are you here for,' he barked, 'my orchids or my daughter's shells?' Robin explained that he had written to Dr Bundt from England about Survival International and our intended journey to Indonesia and that he had received a constructive reply. He gave him a copy of his book, *A Question of Survival*, producing it like a magician from his briefcase.

The doctor nodded vaguely and led us to see his daughter's collection of shells arranged in cases and displayed around the walls of three large rooms. They were staggering. Thousands upon thousands of shells of all varieties, shapes, sizes and colours gleamed under dim neon strip lighting; giant clams with satin pink insides, a multitude of cowries, brown bubble shells, purple transparent fans, and the shells of evil-looking crabs and spiny lobsters that must have weighed over twelve pounds when they had crawled across the bottom of the sea.

'She collected all these in only two years,' he told us proudly, waving an arm of an astonishing length. 'It is the finest collection in Indonesia and now she sells them all over the world.'

Abruptly he changed the subject. 'You have allowed too little time here in Sulawesi,' he barked. 'First,' he said, 'you must go and see my friend, Doctor Meyer . . . if he will see you. He is a very busy man. Busy with his hospital and the poor people. You must go now, immediately, to his house, and if you are very lucky you might find him there. Sometimes he is home for a short time in the middle of the day. If he is not, you leave a copy of your book and a note asking for an appointment. He will be impressed with your book.' Luckily, Robin still had a few copies with him.

Doctor Meyer sounded even more frightening than Doctor Bundt.

'Probably he will shout at you. He always shouts but, with luck, he will calm down and no-one knows more than he does about the strange people in Sulawesi. You must see him now, now, now,' he shouted, flapping his huge hands at us and pushing us towards the door.

He roared instructions on how to get to Doctor Meyer's house to the boys dozing outside in the car. The doctor's dynamism galvanized them into action, they put their shoulders to the back of the scrap heap, leapt into the car as it was moving and we roared up the road leaving the orchid grower still waving his hands and booming: 'Hurry, hurry.'

Doctor Meyer was in and had not yet started lunch. He looked surprised and gratified at being presented with Robin's book and never shouted once. In fact, he appeared to be the most gentle of men, thin almost to the point of emaciation with kind, grey eyes, a narrow, intelligent face, faded, rather dry-looking hair, thin, sensitive hands (the hands of a surgeon) and a soft voice.

He smiled when we said we had been sent by Doctor Bundt.

'Ah, the good Carl' (he also talked with a strong German accent). 'Did he shout and wave his hands at you and tell you frightening stories about me? He always does that.' He looked kindly at me.

'First, before anything else, we must have a long, cold drink.'

He disappeared and we looked round his room, which had the air of a bachelor about it. He was obviously a collector. Shelves were cluttered with rather dusty, primitive clay figures, ancient black pots with strange designs and ornate krises in silver and brass scabbards. Books overflowed everywhere, on tables, chairs and stacked in piles on the floor.

A woman in a sarong followed him back into the room and set a large jug, full of golden liquid, clinking with ice, on the table in front of us.

'This is Markessa,' Doctor Meyer told us, 'our local drink. I hope you enjoy it.'

It was made from passion-fruit juice, sweet and yet infinitely refreshing, and never has any drink tasted so good. From the way my head suddenly swam, I got the feeling that it might also possibly have been laced with gin. It was true nectar.

'Of course,' Dr Meyer said, rolling up the sleeves of a rather stained and crumpled white cotton suit, 'you must see the Toraja. Now tourists have started to go there and I'm afraid the beauty of the people and the place will soon change, especially as the government are talking of putting up tourist hotels in the heart of Toraja country. Still, there is much to see, and as yet the tourists only go to the one place and not at all off the beaten track.' Sulawesi is shaped rather like a long wrist hanging down with three fingers sticking out, one due south, one due east and the other in between. He pointed to an area roughly in the centre of the island as he went on talking.

'The Toraja are very colourful people with an interesting religion based on the worship of their ancestors. They have amazing funeral rites. I went to one of a famous Toraja king. The body had been kept for a year in the house of his family, mourned over continually, and the funeral feast

lasted for days with so many people and such a sacrifice of
buffaloes and pigs that it almost crippled his family.'

Dr Meyer planned our lives out for us. We would go to
Toraja, then north to Palopo where there were tribes of isolated peoples. After that, we would return to Makassar and,
if he could manage it, he would come down to the south
with us to visit the Bugi people on the coast and also a strange
religious sect he had long hoped to find. They were said to
dress in indigo blue and live in a sacred forest. He gave us a
bottle of whisky to give to a friend of his who was a Bupati
in Makali in the Toraja country, a good man who was very
knowledgeable about the people there.

'Have you money?' he asked bluntly.

'Yes,' said Robin. 'More than enough.'

'Good. That is very good because these things can be
expensive. You must find a jeep, or better still a Landrover,
and you must set off tomorrow, as early as possible, in order
to get everything in. Go back to Dr Bundt at around four
o'clock, after the siesta, and get him to arrange for the jeep.
He has the contacts for those things and will fix a deal for
you.'

He suddenly seemed tired and looked at his watch.

'I must go back to the hospital. I will see you in eight days'
time.'

The Grand Hotel was as grand as its name suggested from
the outside, a relic from another era with an elegant colonial
façade and wide Ionic columns. Inside, the bloom had faded.
On the verandah, ugly plastic chairs were grouped around
ugly plastic tables. The white marble floor was grey and
once-shining marble pillars had become dull.

'Shades of Somerset Maugham,' I whispered. 'I bet he stayed
here when things were swinging and the wallahs were swig-
ging stengahs on the verandah.' I was right; he had both
stayed and written here.

The porter showed us to room 1. Three beds were ranged
against a damp wall, the only windows were narrow slits
touching a sixteen-foot-high ceiling and it had a dank, dismal

air. With an antiquated DDT gun he attacked the haze of hungry mosquitoes lying in wait for us.

At our next meeting with Carl Bundt, he showed us, with almost religious fervour, how he cross-pollinated his orchids. He then summoned a male secretary who stood beside him, orchids brushing his shoulders on both sides, taking notes as Dr Bundt shot out a volley of orders.

'Find a jeep or a Landrover for twelve days. Make certain it is reliable.'

'Make an appointment to see the Governor's secretary, this evening if possible. You must [this to us] have papers otherwise there will be trouble. You must get a letter from the Governor.' The major-domo hurried away and returned within minutes.

The Governor's secretary would see us at eight the next morning. The jeep would be at the hotel by seven-thirty. We must check the tyres to make sure they were good and we *must* be patient and charming with everyone.

Over tea we learnt more about the orchid grower and his family.

The Bundt parents were Prussian, an aunt and nephew who were unable to marry by Prussian law. They were in love and had fled to Ceram in the Moluccas (an island we wanted to visit), married and farmed happily there. Somehow, they lost everything and came penniless to Makassar. Carl's father had contracted a wasting disease of open sores in Ceram and was unable to walk. While he lay in bed, his wife began a bakery business in the house where we now sat. Because the Dutch so loved sweet things, she soon had a thriving business. Then they started the orchid farm. Dr Meyer had performed a miracle on the elder Bundt and, after something like twenty years of being bedridden, made him walk again and completely cured his disease in only a few months.

We left after profusely thanking the giant man for his help and this time he stood in the street with his arm round his attractive daughter as we left, shouting, 'It is nothing, nothing. Be charming and have luck.'

Along the harbour wall of Makassar, palm trees were silhouetted against a staggering sunset of livid reds and orange. Tall ships with high billowing sails were setting out to sea and, in the distance, spidery erections looked like tarantulas waiting to pounce. At first we thought these were oil rigs, but they turned out to be fish traps.

Looking back, I think Makassar was the most attractive city we saw in Indonesia. It was surprisingly clean and seemed to have escaped the horror of unused Dutch canals. The colonial buildings there remained and were attractively proportioned; late nineteenth-century, solid family houses or colonnaded official buildings with a graceful air about them, and the original old Dutch town of grey stone and high slanting roofs, which lay almost hidden behind a high fortressed wall beside the sea, and plenty of trees in the streets, gave an impression of coolness. In fact, I think it was hotter there than any city we had been in.

After we had changed, we walked towards the sea front to find a restaurant for dinner, accompanied by half a dozen or more bechak drivers who seemed unable to accept that we actually wanted to go on foot. They were tough boys, with long legs bulging with muscles from eternal pedalling.

Strangely, the wooden chariots here were much more simple and crude to look at than the metal ones we had seen in Kalimantan or Java. Here in Makassar a monopoly, owned by a few rich Chinese merchants, rented the bechaks to the boys and took a major percentage of their earnings.

The life of the Bechak boys is a hard one. Often, they pedal more than sixteen hours a day and when they sleep they sleep in their carts, lying like rag dolls across the passenger seat. Like the bootblacks of America, their dream is to grow rich; few ever do and many end up having to retire to the gutters at an early age because they can no longer pedal as fast as their competitors.

On the sea front, a neon-lit building called the Sea View offered the attractions of a bar, restaurant and striptease club. We had a beer on the terrace at the top, served by plump little Indonesian girls who giggled a lot and wore very tight, short-skirted orange uniforms with large buttons on the point of each breast. Orange caps like those worn by many air hostesses were pinned at cheeky angles on the top of dark hair and we had a distinct feeling that their mothers would not have liked what they were doing.

The terrace was dimly lit, the night comfortably cool and it was pleasant up there, overlooking the sea, watching the bright lamps of fishing boats bobbing on the water in the distance, like dancing fireflies.

Despite the fact that we had eaten a veritable banquet of a meal, the bill was astonishingly small and the elderly Chinese waiter seemed like an old friend as we shook his hand and he bowed us gracefully to the door.

It was late when we got back to 'The Grand' but, too excited to go to bed, we went to the bar for a drink. Fairy-lights twinkled on and off behind the counter, giving the only light, and two girls sat on bar stools on either side of a considerably drunk Australian. It did not need much imagination to work out that these were the striptease artists as they both wore long dresses of shiny satin, one blood red and one black, both slit to the navel in the front and below waist level at the back, and there was something blatantly lascivious about them both. The Australian was not too drunk to be arguing with the red dress about the price for a night's 'fun'. She wanted 20 000 rupiahs, he was offering 10 000, which I thought rather mean as he looked fat and disgustingly rich. While they argued, both girls drank one double whisky after another, topping them up with Seven-Up while they chain-smoked cigarettes from the Australian's crocodile case lying open on the counter.

I was riveted and would have been willing to bet that red dress got her price in the end. When we left, the Australian had become considerably more drunk and was offering 20 000 rupiahs for both girls to accompany him.

'We'll have a ball, dolls,' he kept saying, 'ball for three or a three ball. Ha, ha, ha.'

The jeep had not arrived by eight o'clock the next day when we left for our appointment with the Governor's secretary.

In endless offices we met generals and police chiefs and smiled and smiled until I thought my face would crack. Finally we emerged triumphant with three lots of papers in quintuplicate, written in longhand by the Head of Information and infinitely slowly typed by a uniformed girl.

But we were not finished yet. We still had to go to the military offices where a lot of soldiers peered at our papers, asked more never-ending questions and at last stamped two rather tatty pieces of paper, looking like ancient bus tickets, which were carefully tacked into our passports. They reminded us to check with the Bupati (regional governor) in every town we went to.

'We will send ahead to tell them you are coming and to expect you,' the Head of Information had said rather ominously.

Our vehicle was waiting when we returned to the hotel. It was a dusty jeep that did not look too bad although the tyres looked a bit thin and, as Carl Bundt had warned us about this, Robin insisted the driver went and changed them before we left. He returned about half an hour later and, stupidly, we forgot to check on the replacements.

Robin and I sat in the front beside the driver, a youngish man with good features and a long, narrow nose. His mate, a dozy character of about sixteen who had the greatest capacity for sleep of anyone I have seen, curled himself up on our luggage in the back beside three spare cans of petrol.

I realized, as we drove northwards out of the city back towards the airport, that it was Friday the 13th, and, being wildly superstitious, kept my fingers crossed for almost the whole drive to Makali, a town on the edge of Toraja country, where we hoped to spend the night and where we had been told there was a sort of rest house

Chapter 10

Most of Indonesia is beautiful but some islands are breath-taking in their landscape, and Sulawesi is one of these. The route we drove that day lay through the most superb country we had yet seen, with scenery unfolding mile by mile in an ever-changing panorama of graceful lines, fantastic colours, and a gentle influence by man that enhanced rather than polluted the environment.

One thing soured the view. We had heard of the recent introduction in the island of dieldrin, introduced in theory to help increase the output of essential harvests. This chemical, which seemed by so many to be magic, had come under much misuse and when we saw men walking through their rice paddies with large yellow tanks on their backs, we were reminded of horrors we had heard that this ingredient (banned in England and America) had already caused in this area.

A man, we had been told, spilt a can of dieldrin over his harvested rice. He could not afford to lose the crop so he washed the grain, laid it out in the sun to dry, had winnowed it in the normal way and then produced it for his family to eat. Within hours they were all dead. Another man had a leaking tank from which he was spraying. He did not notice and soon died in the fields. Someone else had found that pouring the chemical into a river killed the fish there and brought them floating to the surface of the water – how much more simple than fishing with nets or lamps at night. As a result, a whole village was wiped out.

After a brief stop at the coastal town of Pare-pare, we turned inland from a rich, brilliant green belt of paddy fields up a road winding steeply away from the sea. From high up we had a magnificent view of the port and the harbour below, sheltered by a group of thickly palmed islands. Fishing boats were tiny dots in the distance and spidery bamboo fish traps spread out along the coast and stretched into the horizon.

The tarmac surface quickly deteriorated as we passed a dozen or more lorries which had broken down on the side of the road. It was not long before we joined them.

There was a sharp hiss of escaping air, a few moments of wild careering down a steep hill and then the sound of metal as a wheel rim hit the road and Asrad brought the jeep to a standstill.

We should have been warned by the resignation with which Asrad woke the boy and the two Indonesians jacked up the jeep, removed the spare tyre from under our luggage and began changing the wheel. We should have been equally suspicious about the careful mending of the burst inner tube which went on after the spare had been bolted in place, and by the way the holes in the tyre itself were carefully padded with folded pieces of torn-up inner tubing in places where it had worn bare. It was only then that we noticed that if Asrad had indeed changed the tyres in Makassar he had not changed them for ones any better than those there had been before.

It was obviously going to take some time for the boy to pump up the mended tyre with a small, leaking hand pump so Robin went for a walk and I sat on a stone beside the road, smoking and watching the insect life crawl through the grass around me. In just a few yards, I counted over a hundred different species, from minute spiders to large cricket-like creatures. I scrambled back into the jeep when I saw a thin black snake twisting its way through the grass towards me.

In about thirty-five minutes, we were on our way again and the boy was able to drift back to sleep, which he did at once, looking totally exhausted.

In the jeep's cabin the heat was almost suffocating and dust filtered through every crack as we drove through open rolling country. We flushed out a wild boar that shot across the road in front of us, short-legged and sturdy with coarse black bristles standing up like a comb along the back of its spine and vicious-looking tusks curving up from its snout.

Climbing higher again, we reached another plain thickly planted with rice through which a long straight road, lined with trees, led towards the town of Rappang where Asrad told us the tarmac would end altogether.

Beside the road a large patch of giant waterlilies grew in a shallow lake with salmon-pink flowers rising like clasped hands from thick, fleshy stems. They were being gathered up in armfuls by small children wading through the water. Slender white herons watched them unblinkingly from a safe distance. In rich paddy fields, women were gathering up armfuls of rice in neat bundles, their sarongs and wide hats reflected in the water, with shadows lengthening behind them as the sun began to go down. Beside the road, ears of rice, rich harvests turning to gold, were spread on woven mats to ripen. Outside little houses, more women were winnowing the grains by tossing them up from large shallow baskets, their movements sure and graceful, and the air around them was full of golden chaff, caught in the slight breeze and wafted away in a translucent cloud. A large iguana, armoured and prehistoric, scuttled across the road, stopping for a second to swing its head round and gaze at us from reptilian eyes.

Black and pink buffaloes, and occasionally black buffaloes with pink patches on their hides, grazed beside the roads or wallowed, hippopotamus-style, in muddy ponds, their huge heads topped by massive curving horns, lolling grotesquely, and their wide nostrils distended with the exquisite joy of the cool, black liquid. Sulawesi was the first country where we met this pink species of buffalo. To us, they had a rather unreal, anaemic look as though something had gone wrong with their pigmentation, but the Toraja prized them highly, especially the spotted ones, and they were the animals picked for sacrifice whenever possible. They struck me as being most curious creatures. The amount of grass they ate appeared to be extraordinarily little yet they grew to such an enormous size, dragged around staggering weights, and could be driven with metric precision through the rice paddies. They looked docile and yet they were said to be difficult to train and have the most vicious tempers.

Between sunset and the hours of total darkness, we had two more blow-outs, killed no less than four chickens, ran over two dogs lying in the middle of the road and not only narrowly missed countless goats but also strings of children who waved wildly when they saw our faces were white, shouting out words in high-pitched voices, their cries making Asrad smile, but we could not determine whether they were noises of friendship or abuse – they could have been either.

Driving was made even more difficult by heavy rainstorms and the road seemed to be never-ending. Sometimes I thought we had reached the top of a high belt of mountains as we began a frightening spiral downhill, skidding on bald wheels round hairpin bends, one wheel often missing the edge of the road and spinning in space, but then we would begin to climb again, each slope more perpendicular than the last. I could only imagine the precipices on either side – but I imagined them vividly.

We reached Makali at about nine and drew up in what seemed to be the centre of the dimly-lit town beside a large pond flanking a spacious mosque. High on a hill somewhere in the darkness, a cross, illuminated by red electric light bulbs, gave a ghostly pink glow.

It was easy to find the Bupati's, Dr Randa's, house but, to our disappointment, he was away and we were directed to the wisma (rest house) near the centre of the town, a spacious, one-storey building, barred and shuttered against the wet night and without any lights showing. The door was reluctantly opened and we were led through a clean, bare lounge-cum-dining room with one table, to a large bedroom with a washroom. It was clean and neat and there were sheets on the double bed, but the place had a cheerless air, and, after the humid heat we were accustomed to, was cold enough to make us shiver. The water, when I tried it, felt icy and, although I should have had a thorough wash, I did not, partly because of the temperature and partly because a spider, large as a coffee cup and an unattractive shade of muddy grey, glared at me from a corner. I glared back, ready to run for it if he moved an inch.

In the sweltering heat of Makassar, we had forgotten about the cold of the mountains. That night we went to bed with our shirts and our socks on, warmed by those and the excitement of knowing that outside, in the darkness, lay Toraja country.

The Toraja (the name means 'men from above') are one of the great romantic peoples of Indonesia; they are fiercely independent, highly intelligent, proud, and very hard working. Like the Bataks of Sumatra and the Dayaks of Kalimantan, they are thought to be of proto-Malay origin, descended from people who crossed into the island from Indo-China. They themselves have a more romantic idea of their origins . . . .

The first Toraja, so the legend goes, were a seafaring tribe until one day, long ago, a huge tidal wave swept up their ships, flinging them high onto the mountains in the centre of the island. There the people stayed and made a new life, living in houses built like the original craft they had once sailed in. They became farmers and when the Dutch colonized Celebes fought so strongly they succeeded in beating their invaders back from the mountains with a success so great the conquerers were forced to declare an independent province of Tana Toraja.

The religion, 'Aluk', of the Toraja is the worship of their dead ancestors. They believe souls continue to live in the world beyond as they did on earth. Sacrifices and offerings are made to their dead kinsmen as, unless the dead are materially well provided for, their souls will wander aimlessly forever, like the soul of the Wandering Jew. The bodies of the dead lie in state in their houses for anything from three months to a year, the corpse tightly encased in many yards of coloured cloth, neatly sealed with just a small hole remaining open to allow small driblets of water to be dropped through. Ritual mourning takes place every day while the body remains in the house and sacrifices are made at intervals during the interment. At the end the funeral is a fantastic affair attended by everyone who had contact or dealings in any way with the dead man. Mourners come from great distances to join in the feasting, to pay their respects, and to receive their rights.

Ceremonies of all kinds play a large part in the lives of the Toraja. Many sacrifices of pigs, buffalo and chickens take place during the ceremony when the gods are asked for a good harvest; ritual singing and dancing goes on for many days. In times of disease or epidemics (especially the dreaded small-pox) no pork or maize is eaten for a month, more chickens are slaughtered and the elders of the community go into trances as men and women perform ritual dances, handed down from generation to generation. They cut themselves with sharp knives and bind the flowing wounds in special red-coloured leaves to prevent scarring.

And as the Toraja believe in the spirits of their dead, so too do they believe in the spirits, evil as opposed to good, that live under their houses in between the thick piles. There are, I was told, literally thousands of these evil spirits, but the one which struck me as being the most nasty was the 'Pok Pok'. The 'Pok Pok' lies in wait for single or married women at night. When it finds a victim, it sucks out her entrails through the anus, enters her body and goes around its wicked business in the camouflage of a human frame. We heard one particularly cautionary tale about this revolting phenomen: a husband had reason to suspect his wife of infidelity, so instead of going to sleep one night he lay awake, watching her. After a time, she rose and crept up into the eaves of the house, followed by her husband who witnessed the 'Pok Pok' sucking out her entrails and entering her body. The change-over completed, she climbed onto the roof and flew away through the night. Her husband, with great presence of mind, quickly threw her entrails on the burning embers of the fire where they shrivelled with a blue flame. He waited until it was almost dawn for her return; when she came flying back, the 'Pok Pok' evacuated her beside the spot where her entrails should have been and the woman, who had been his wife, disappeared into thin air.

Today, missionaries have gained a stronghold in the midst of the Toraja. Already only sixty per cent of the people follow their own religion, Aluk. The rest are almost evenly divided between Protestant, Roman Catholic and Muslim. Today, too, the government of Indonesia plans to exploit the beauty of the country and the colourful traditions of the people in the interests of tourism. We were fortunate enough to see the Toraja while they still had pride in their adat and while both their houses and their culture were relatively 'unspoilt'; nevertheless, we were only too aware of the pressures being exerted on the people by those who wished to change or exploit them in various ways.

We had been told someone would come to see us from the Bupati's office first thing next morning but no-one turned up and, by nine, Robin was impatiently pacing up and down beside our packed bags when a young man of about twenty-five, sporting pointed, black city shoes, maroon socks and a rather short pair of tightly tapered trousers, arrived and introduced himself as 'Simon'.

He spoke in English as though making a well-rehearsed speech and announced proudly, 'I learn English at the Protestant school,' and handed Robin a scruffy piece of paper with the heading 'Official Guide' on it.

'I am from the Bupati's office, I am officially to accompany you. You pay me official charges and not more for anything.'

We must have looked unenthusiastic about the idea as he

said more firmly: 'It is forbidden to go without a guide and I am "official".' We accepted his offer as gracefully as we could and were rewarded by him saying that he knew of a funeral taking place that day, not far from Makali. We would have to walk there but it would be worth our while.

To have the chance to see a Toraja funeral during the brief time we were going to be in the area was an unbelievable bonus. We set off at once.

A path rose steeply above the rice paddies, up a high range of mountains curving in a stony track up which we scrambled in single file between jungle growth of bamboo and monumental teak trees laden with flowers that were fragile puffballs of cloudy yellow. Big butterflies, with a wingspan of at least six inches, black as demons or patterned in red and white, danced easily in front of us, moving with lazy grace while I puffed and panted.

High up the mountain, on a little plateau carved out of the grey rock, stood the village of Limbong Burake where the funeral was taking place. The village contained a cluster of four or five Toraja houses, the first we had seen, miniature copies beside each one for storing the harvest.

Toraja houses are built on a standard pattern and vary only in size and in the sophistication of the carved and painted patterns which cover the front of the house. Ornate patterns start below the sharply pointed eave of the roof and run down the sides, flanking the balcony which stretches the width of the building. The roofs, as are the whole buildings in fact, are made to last and many we saw were as much as three hundred years old. Layer upon layer of bamboo is built up into a complicated, curving structure running the length of the house and topped with a thatch of palm that weathers over the years to a sombre grey and, like the houses we saw in this village, eventually becomes covered with moss. In every village, the houses run from north to south, and are usually built in two long rows with a large, almost square community building at the end. This, however, was a relatively poor village. There was no community building and, although the houses still ran strictly north to south, they were built in layers, wherever the mountain would allow the space.

It was hard to imagine what the people live on high up on this harsh rocky mountain but, though they were obviously poor, they looked well-fed and very healthy and, as funerals go, it seemed to be an occasion for enjoyment rather than misery.

About fifty people were sitting around the village when we arrived, so news of our coming had obviously gone before us. They looked up with surprising unconcern, avoiding our eyes, but certainly were not hostile, and seemingly accepted us as part of the general scenery.

In the centre of the highest clearing, walled on one side by high grey-white rocks, a dozen or more young men sat cross-legged or lay stretched out on straw mats on a wooden platform covered by palm thatching. In the shade between the thick wooden piles supporting the body of the largest house, lounged the elders of the village, some talking idly together, some dozing and others asleep. Women and children occupied the balcony above with a grandstand view of the village and, on a slightly lower clearing, another crowd squatted under the shade of one of the miniature storage buildings.

The funeral itself, Simon said, was not going to start for some time, so he and Robin went to climb higher up the mountain to see where the corpse, the chief of the village, would be buried when the rituals were over. I decided to stay where I was, sitting with the lean-faced Toraja men who moved aside to make a small space for me, occasionally handing round my cigarettes which were politely and gravely accepted.

Most of the women wore black cotton sarongs and tight black blouses emphasizing the lines of their breasts. They sat divided, men and women in separate groups; country people with country peasant faces, though not the face of the plodding, pedestrian peasant. These were brighter and more intelligent, sharpened by hard living and hard work but also pleasantly open and alive. Young and old seemed in harmony and the young women, especially, had a fresh beauty about them, an innocent look one never sees in city people. Black suited them. It set off the pale, olive tones of their skin, their rounded oval faces, clear skin and thick black hair, parted in the centre and pulled back from their foreheads into a twist at the back. Many wore beads around their necks and bracelets of thinly beaten gold and silver.

The women chatted idly or picked lice from each other's heads as one sat and another knelt behind, sifting with well-practised fingers through the heavy tresses. Only the chewing of betel nut distorted their features, bulging a cheek, staining lips a harsh red and rotting teeth. The younger women had not yet picked up the habit but their elders continually plucked betel leaves from small pouches or from a bundle in their swept-back hair, pounding lime, cutting off slivers of brown nut as they slowly and automatically went through the ritual of making the small parcels which were chewed and spat out in a neatly directed stream of scarlet juice.

A man arrived with a squealing pig held tightly by one back foot. Other guests began filing up the mountain, large, flat straw hats on their heads, carrying gifts wrapped in banana leaves, in baskets or carried in long stems of green bamboo. The crowd shifted to make room as they settled in an ever-increasing crowd on the platform, where I sat under the shade of the largest house, or on the rocks surrounding the village.

An old man, a black sarong slung over one shoulder, leaning on a stick, appeared at the entrance to the village and stood for a moment, waiting to be recognized. He was obviously important. A space was made for him on the platform under the rice store as women moved aside and children were shooed down the steps to another house below. A retinue of servants helped him into a lounging position, unrolling a mat for him to sit on and offering him a drink from one of the lengths of bamboo.

The wailing began as Robin and Simon returned, a high-pitched volley of sound which reverberated down the valley, 'Eeeeeh, eeeeeh, oooah, oooah,' a racking cry of sadness to which no-one seemed to pay any attention at all. The body had been in the house for three months (it was not a very important funeral) and this wailing was part of custom and tradition, a way for the wife and relatives of the dead man to show their sorrow.

We climbed up the steps onto the balcony of the house where women and children hung over a balustrading of carved wood, chatting and smiling at their friends below. In a bare room leading off the balcony, the body lay like a large, trim bolster, neatly packaged in a carefully sewn-up striped cloth. To my surprise, there was not a trace of the smell I had expected, though inside the wrappings the body must have been distinctly rotten. Either they had some way of preserving the corpse or the mere fact of sealing out all air itself acted as antidote against decay. It rested on a simple bier of bamboo and beside it was an ever-growing heap of sarongs, cloth, plates of food and bamboo containers of drink to be buried with the body.

At each end, two women knelt on the bare floor, their heads bent over the body and their heads, faces and arms completely obscured by overlapping sarongs. They rocked as they wailed, making an unbelievable racket that came out in monotonous streams of vacillating lamentations. Irreverently, I could not help feeling they sounded rather like pigs having their throats cut or cats warring on a moonlit night.

Things began to happen. Most of the men wore sharp pangas in carved wooden sheaths hanging from their waists and these now came into use. Two boys appeared carrying the severed head of a large pink buffalo with the neck neatly parted from the body and its huge eyes, fringed with thick long lashes, still wide open, staring oblivious through a curtain of flies which came to settle on them. It was placed upright on a bed of palm leaves under the big house.

From below came a sound of pigs being slaughtered (I was right about the similarity of their squeals to the women wailing) and soon the dead carcasses were tied to long bamboo poles and carried up onto the rocks above the clearing. Here they were laid on more palm leaves and neatly carved up, the blood and entrails being placed in an enamel bowl which was set in front of the house. In the warm air the smell of warm blood mingled with the smells of pig, buffalo and tobacco.

People were still arriving and there was a general movement to begin drinking whatever it was they had in their bamboo flasks. Most of these flasks were about four or five feet long and often one man had to hold up the end while the other drank. The liquid seemed to be milky white and I imagine it was alcoholic for the men began laughing and joking with each other. Even young boy children had small versions of these flasks but the women and girls appeared to be tee-totallers. Watching all this liquid gurgling down throats made me unconscionably thirsty, but we were still being totally ignored. There did not seem to be any feeling against us – we just might as well have been invisible.

The body was brought down from the house and put carefully on the ground by the entrails, pointing due north. A soft khaki hat, which had obviously belonged to the deceased, was hung over one end of the bier and one of the mourning women took up her position and begun her wailing again, going into paroxysms of sorrow, leaning far over the bier, her body shaking with sobs. With one final long shriek her duty was over, she pushed the brightly patterned sarong back from her face and piled it turban fashion on her head. A second sarong was pulled over her shoulders and neatly twisted into a tight knot above her breasts. To my surprise, there was not a tear in her eyes and her face was a study of composure. She was a fairly old woman with lined, humorous features and a mouth distorted and scarlet. She took her place as part of a group sitting in the shade by the side of the house, under the watchful eyes of the buffalo head, chewing betel like mad and eagerly sifting through a pile of neatly wrapped packages laid at her feet. From a basket, she brought out more packages wrapped in finely woven straw-work and handed those round to the most honoured guests. On the rocks above, the pigs were still being carved up and a stream of men and women hurried up to get their rightful portions. Flies settled everywhere but, like us, were ignored.

A loud roll on a drum and seven men went to stand in a semi-circle around the body, linking arms. They began to dance, singing as they did so, stamping back and forth, raising one leg after another and swaying from side to side. When they stopped, the line parted in the middle and revealed a wizened old man dressed in dirty white shorts and a ragged shirt with a grubby white sarong slung over his shoulders and a tattered cap on grizzled white hair. A large wad of betel still bulging his cheek, he squatted on the ground, beat another rhythm on the drum and began singing a long and complicated incantation about the long life and good deeds of the dead man. Under his cap, the old man had a tight band of bamboo tied around his forehead. Our guide had quickly revealed that he, in fact, spoke only a few phrases of English (although he repeated those frequently and refused to acknowledge Robin's Indonesian) and he seemed to know disappointingly little about Toraja adat. But, at this point, Simon had something constructive to offer. 'That is the dead man's servant,' he whispered.

While the incantation went on, people around continued to chatter happily, exchanging gossip and laughing at stories. When it was over, everyone sat up and began to pay more attention. The seven men danced again and this time the crowd watched eagerly as they shuffled from side to side, performing a series of movements, each ending with a great leap into the air accompanied by loud cries, great shouting and energetic cheering from the audience. When they finished their performance, the party seemed to begin in earnest.

The women joined the men in a serious drinking bout as more bamboo flasks were passed round from person to person and the milky liquid flowed freely. Later, I found out it was Toraja palm wine called 'Vaduk'.

Parcels were unwrapped and the feast got under way as everyone tucked into pieces of pig baked in bamboo, small mounds of rice and grains of yellow maize. Parents picked out tender morsels for small children and occasionally a woman opened her blouse to breast-feed a baby, holding it loosely with one hand as she ate and drank with the other. Many of the women changed from their black into bright sarongs tied above their breasts, wrapping turbans of garishly coloured towels on their heads and exposing stumps of stained teeth as they laughed.

The morning had been hot and sunny, but now a black barrage of cloud swept across the sky, obscuring the sun, greying the air and bringing with it a cold, relentless wind. Within minutes it began to rain in large, heavy drops and it was not just a passing shower. The whole sky turned battleship grey and lowered sullenly with water.

Men and women began packing up their belongings and moved under the shelter of the prowlike overhanging roofs of the houses or huddled closer together than ever on the small platforms.

'No more ceremony now,' Simon said. The body was carried back to the house and the funeral procession, he told us, would probably not take place until the next day when they would kill another buffalo and dance outside the grave. He was vague about the timing. 'Perhaps it may not take place for another week. We should go.'

Neither of us was particularly eager to spend another night in Makali so we decided that, despite the rain, we would push on to the next town of Rantepao, the central market town of Toraja country. It was not all that far away, and from a faded, rough map we had been given at the wisma, it looked as though there was a Toraja burial cave we could see on the way.

Chapter 11

As we drove to Rantepao along a road beside a wide river that was partly tarmacked but mainly mud, the sky began to clear a little and we had our first real view of Toraja country. Even in the grey, cold light with clouds obscuring the tops of the mountains it was as magnificent as we had been led to believe. The mountains rose all around, harsh, jagged and topped by high, craggy peaks. Every inch of the valleys was planted in rice, curving terraces of green that formed rippling patterns in between the footholes of the hills. Where earth showed, it was richly red, the colour of ox blood. Small, miniature hills rose from the paddies, terraced in a complicated patchwork pattern and topped by an elegant plume of palms and bamboos.

The road was deeply rutted and here not long ago a Toraja girl had been driving in a truck with a man who had picked her up along the way. In the rain and darkness, the driver missed a corner, shot over the river bank and into the rapids below. Both were killed and now, the Toraja say, the spirit of the girl haunts the road at night, warning others who might make the same mistake.

A sign showed the way to the graves and we turned off the road and drove up a grassy track through arches of bamboo, coming to a halt by a pole padlocked across the path. Asrad tooted his horn which gave a pale, despairing peep and a band of young children trotted down a little path from above, accepted a few coins and lifted the barrier. They ran behind us, shrieking in excitement, clustered around the jeep, chattering like parakeets, when we came to the end of the path and led the way to the top of a small hillock overlooking a deep horseshoe valley facing a wall of sheer white cliffs.

Under an overhang of rock, about thirty feet high, a balcony of wood had been built. On it a spooky collection of wooden effigies stood in a stiff row, fully dressed and lifesize, faces painted brown with flat, large, round eyes, looking weirdly like a royal party standing to attention in an opera box or a Governor's assembly reviewing a march past. They were elegantly though strangely dressed in a mixture of Toraja and Western clothes. Some had elaborate turbans, some black pillbox hats and one an outsize toupeé. Most wore white cotton jackets and some had sarongs thrown across their shoulders. Stony-eyed, they stared unblinkingly across the small valley towards the curving paddy terraces.

Beside the balcony, a row of skulls were lined up on a narrow ledge, the bones weathered to a shining white. On the rocks beside them, food on plates, hats, sarongs and parangs had been put as offerings. Rotting wooden coffins with bones protruding from the broken slats were pushed into crevices in the cliff wall, and on the ground an ornately carved replica of a Toraja house, standing about twelve feet off the ground and very new from the look of it, had been left for one of the deceased to have a house to continue his after-life in.

Two of the children lighted wooden flares and led us down to the bottom of the cliff and into a damp cave entrance that smelt strongly of death and decay. Tunnels, carved by nature, or the Toraja, led in all directions into a series of curved vaults with walls that gleamed smooth and white in the flickering torchlight. Coffins were everywhere, some new and intact, most cracked open with age. They were stacked one on top of another, some simple and others carved with curious patterns. Occasionally, there was one in miniature, a reminder that small children die too. The floor was littered with plates, cloth decayed into dusty strips, knives and pangas. Everywhere there were bones of all shapes and sizes and skulls that grinned hollowly. Bats flew over our

144

A Dayak woman carries her child and her water-pot towards the long house

Offerings to the spirits are still law on the altar in the centre of a Dayak village

A traditional Dayak long house – these can have as many as sixty front doors inside

A Dayak lady tends her pigs – vital for the survival of peoples in the interior

A Toraja woman chews betel nut at a funeral

heads and spiders, scorpions and thick centipedes scuttled along the walls.

The sun came out again as we left this valley of death and we stopped to take photographs of a minute boy sitting on top of an enormous black buffalo and crowned by a hat of such enormous mushroom dimensions that it almost completely hid him. He sat rigidly still, frozen by the sight of our cameras levelled at him. The other children began shouting at him and dancing around, the buffalo tossed his head with an angry glare in his eye and the tiny boy shot as from a catapult through the air, landing with a loud thud on the ground a few feet away, upside down, with his hat sailing down behind him. It must have hurt considerably; he couldn't have been more than about six years old and he very nearly burst into tears, but he manfully dug his fists in his eyes and, with the other children cheering him on, caught hold of one of the buffalo's horns and pulled himself back onto its wide black spine.

It had been the most comical display. Asrad, Robin and I laughed ourselves silly, almost hysterically on my part, because it was a relief to be away from the smell of death and in the midst of the living again.

Early next morning we drove from Rantepao and crossed an incredible suspension bridge spanning the river. Spindly bamboo shoots swayed wildly as our wheels turned over wooden slats under the shade of a thatched canopy. People leant against the flimsy wooden sides to make way for us, protecting their strings of dried buffalo meat and bamboo poles of palm wine from the mud which spattered in a black shower from our wheels.

We were heading for a tiny village, well off the beaten track, called Rieuw, which Dr Meyer in Makassar had suggested we try to reach.

Up the mountain, on the other side, the road became a track once more, strewn with rocks and boulders, running with water and mud and a permanent threat to our fragile tyres. We had little idea which direction Rieuw lay and the track looked suspiciously 'unfit for motor vehicles' but Asrad, at least, was cheerful.

'If you want to go up here, we got to go,' he said to Robin as though indulging a spoilt child, and we swung crazily from side to side as the wheels spun on mud or smooth stones. We churned higher and higher into a light moving mist that made the bamboos look pale and larger than life, curving in an arched tunnel above us and giving everything a pale glow of unreality.

We stopped to look at circles of neolithic stones – miniature Stonehenges, covered in lichen, that stood twelve feet upright in a closely cropped grassy knoll – wondering how people ever got these massive chunks of rock into a standing position, how old they were and if the central flat rock was used for sacrifices. Many of them, we were told later, were still used for the sacrifices of buffalo when Toraja kings died or were enthroned.

Great groves of plumed bamboo dotted the mountainside, fanning out in all directions like pale green fountains, but we could not see much of the surrounding countryside for the thick mist still lay heavy in the valley and moved in undulating white waves across the hillslopes.

It took us a long time to reach the village at the top of the mountain. When we did we met one of those moments of rare magic that make the world seem very special.

Asrad stopped the car on the track, with the village itself on the right above us, and a square school building of plaited palm on a small plateau and a few yards below. For once, he dared to cut the engine and in the silence that followed we heard the haunting, floating, lighter-than-air music of pipes, thin but swelling, filling the plateau, filling the valley below, obscured by mist, and spreading out over the mountains. Soft music, the music of Pan, unforgettable, pure, fluting mountain sounds.

Slowly, we walked down the hill to the schoolhouse and a teacher came out to meet us and showed us into a bare wooden classroom filled with children of all ages, all playing strange

146

instruments made from a network of bamboo stems painted white with black tops. They stopped to stare, round-eyed, and then continued playing as the teacher sharply rapped a blackboard covered with simple notes.

'Would you like to hear more?' he asked, and when we nodded he waved a baton at the children and they began a different tune, this time a happy 'umpah, umpah' beat, reminiscent of a brass band. The children's enthusiasm for the music was catching, they puffed their cheeks and put their hearts into it, the more sophisticated teenagers at the back blowing complicated tonal chords on the larger pipes and small children sitting on benches in the front row keeping pace with high, reedy sounds from simple flutes.

Robin recorded a tune on the small pocket tape recorder he uses for taking notes and the excitement was intense as he played it back and, for the first time, they listened to the way their music sounded to an outsider's ears. Dismissed, the class disbanded with chattering, giggling children running across the playground, to tell their parents what had happened. The villagers came and joined us, friendly, and happy to show us around their magnificent carved and painted houses.

By mid-morning the mist suddenly, dramatically, disappeared and for the first time we saw the magnificence of the Toraja country unfolding below and around us.

Terraces of rice, some strips no wider than a couple of feet, had been moulded from the slopes and stretched down in ever-widening curves to the valley below where the mosque domes of Rantepao and Makali glinted in the far distance. The river was a curving silver ribbon; groves of bamboos, dark plumes of green, and small villages, perched on top of hills, like small fleets of proud galleons. On the horizon, all around us, a ring of magnificent, faintly-purpled mountains pointed their craggy spires towards the sky.

Most of the paddy fields had small holes in the centre, ringed by a fence of sticks and topped by a scarecrow in the shape of a large, carved wooden bird, painted black, hanging from a long pole and looking extremely lifelike as it moved in the breeze. For a long time, we could not determine what these holes were there for. The answer was simple but brilliant. They were fish ponds. When the paddies were flooded, the fish swam freely through the rice. When the water level was low for planting or ploughing, they retreated to the holes where there was always enough water for them to survive. These fish were an important source of protein for the Toraja and we found this method of farming them had been copied in other parts of Sulawesi.

Further up the track, the village teacher told us, were some more burial caves which were well worth seeing. We must be careful though, he warned, because they were also the homes of a particularly dangerous species of hornet which, if it stung, would cause instant death.

We could not go far in the jeep. I was still gazing at the view when Asrad slammed on the brakes and we teetered on the edge of a precipice caused by an enormous chunk of the path just dropping away down the mountainside and leaving a monumental chasm. Skirting it gingerly, we began walking up the other side, round the edge of the mountain, Robin striding out ahead as though he had a train to catch, me following at a more leisurely pace and Simon quite some way behind, still trying to keep his shoes clean as we crossed streams thickly growing with some sweet-smelling weed that filled the air with scent as our feet bruised it.

These burial chambers were square holes carved out of a towering lump of grey rock and had carved and painted doors sealing each entrance. Here again, some of the doors, especially those more than thirty feet above the ground, had deteriorated in the harsh weather of the mountains. The remains of coffins and the white pallor of bones showed through the gaps. From these, the hornets came pouring out, buzzing angrily and sending the swarm of small boys who had followed us scrambling back up the road.

Now often on the expedition I had trouble keeping up with Robin's pace and physically I was not feeling terribly well. It was not very serious and I could not put my finger on just what was wrong, but whatever it was it managed to slow me down more than usual.

Now at last I was able to show my exploring prowess. Although I am naturally and femininely averse to most insects, for some reason I am totally unafraid of bees, wasps or hornets and although these were the largest I had seen and an angry red in colour, they could not scare me. I walked nearer to examine the pile of offerings at the foot of the soaring rock and ostentatiously would not come back when Robin begged me to and even Simon got alarmed. Eventually, I strolled away with my self-confidence restored and my sense of humour returning. Exceptionally childish, probably quite dangerous, but, at that moment, very much to the point as far as I was concerned.

When we got back to Rieuw, a small crowd were waiting to beg lifts from us. A heavily pregnant woman wanted to have her child with a sister in Rantepao, a small boy wanted to go for the ride, some wanted to go to market, others had relatives they wanted to see and one or two wanted to catch up with the unfinished funeral we had been to the day before.

Asrad looked sad and got out to examine the springs, which as well as everything else on the jeep even I could see were showing signs of pressure. Since the argument was obviously going to go on forever, he sensibly compromised and about half a dozen of them climbed into the back. The pregnant woman sat up near the front, her arms pressed close to mine. She was so very near birth time (by her size, it would be triplets at least) that, with the inevitable bumping and jolting which took place as we began the downward journey, I wondered if she would make it. Asrad seemed to have the same apprehension. At first, he allowed us to stop and take photographs from places where the road curved out over the valley, then he ignored our gasps of excitement as view followed stupendous view, just made for a camera lens, and drove faster and faster so that we were too busy holding on to dare ask to stop. With some relief, we made it to the bottom and the woman climbed out, her internal burden still intact.

She had only gone into a relation's to change and soon came back resplendent in an outside sarong, clean from the wash, and followed by four more children to add to our load.

The road from Rantepao to Palopo in the east, our next destination, had a remarkably good surface that was almost tarmac. It led steeply up from the valley, out of Toraja country, to a high pass in the mountains. As we climbed upwards, the rice terraces grew narrower and narrower. In one or two the rice had already been harvested and the fields were now being ploughed. The skill with which oxen, drawing wooden ploughs, were driven along the curving terraces and turned in what was sometimes less than their own width was fascinating to watch; an inch off course and one of the narrow dykes would be broken.

After ploughing, the padding of bare human feet would smooth out and pack down the soil, more rice would be planted and the cycle would begin again with two rich crops being grown a year. The labour force involved was incredible and the importance of the dykes prodigious. Every drop of water that fell from the sky or streamed down the mountains must be measured and channelled through the terraces so that a perfect level was kept in every field all the time the rice was growing. Too much or too little water and the crop would be poor. There were channels everywhere and a constant plugging and unplugging of outlets in the dams so that water could flow in carefully regulated quantities from one terrace to another.

Where cultivation became impossible, a new kind of scenery began. Here, the tops of the mountains were heavily covered with a forest of fir trees and giant ferns giving a strange, wild contrast to the bamboos and the neatly curving vivid green strips below.

From the top of the pass we could see Palopo far away in the distance with a sweep of silver beyond that was the sea. We began the descent to the coast and had three punctures before we reached the bottom.

Evergreen forest gave way to evergreen tropical jungle.

Tall mahogany trees rose up to an enormous height and every now and then there was a group of spectacular giant fern trees, with feathered foliage sprouting from the top of a thick, tall trunk like a great bunch of bracken magnified a thousand times. Strange, high palm trees with narrow trunks spread out their leaves in layers of neat, identical fan shapes with a span of at least eight feet wide; others had scaly trunks like snakeskin and leaves spread horizontally and bending neatly down, each at exactly the same point, giving them a prim, tidy look. Near the road there were bright red and yellow flowers and occasionally a high bush covered with white blossom. Narrow waterfalls fell from the mountain above, catching the sunlight and tumbling to deep ravines where the water foamed as it cascaded down a gully over rounded boulders. To the east, the mountains dropped gradually away until their foothills almost touched the sea.

I had been feeling progressively more ill each day. When we reached Palopo I knew what the matter was at last. Somewhere, I had picked up a bug, my stomach felt like a lump of churning lead and I was alternately sick and made weak by violent bouts of diarrhoea. Robin, sympathetic, administered a strong dose of pills which we carried for just this complaint and then left me to search for the Palopo Bupati and the police headquarters. I dozed uncomfortably, hands holding my stomach, my feet cold but the rest of me soaked in warm sweat and mosquitoes having the meal of their life, but I was too miserable to care.

He came back depressed. The tribe we had hoped to visit further north were a good four days' walk into the interior, a journey it would be impossible for us to do if we were to get back to Makassar in time to meet Dr Meyer. Both of us held strongly to a maxim that when things went wrong, one impressed oneself with the belief that 'it could have been worse'. He did this now with a rather twisted grin.

'Still, it could have been worse. The rajah of the tribe happens to be in Palopo. He is visiting the Bupati this evening and the Bupati has asked us to meet him.' The Bupati had insisted on meeting me too, so I shakily dressed in clean clothes (not that anything was very clean by then but at least I had a reasonably respectable cotton skirt and a shirt that was less grubby than the other one) and prayed fervently as I went to the hole-in-the-floor lavatory built out from the back of the Palopo wisma and open to the elements on two sides, that I would get through the evening without disaster.

The Bupati was charming and expectionally kind and helpful. He was a good-looking, well-built man (I supposed him to be about forty-five) and I imagine he came from either Java or Sumatra. His eyes had a faint Chinese slanting aspect to them, his smile was friendly and he had a pleasant, firm handshake. He also spoke good English and we were told later that he was high on the list for being a future ambassador to the United Kingdom.

We sat in a cool, pleasant room at the front of his large house and were offered tea and a large bowl of langsams, a small, lychee-like fruit.

The old rajah and his son, the prince, arrived soon after we did. The son was only a little taller than his father who was slightly shorter than I am. Both had lively, intelligent faces, especially the rajah with whom every gesture was one of grace and dignity. He told us stories about his and other tribes, regretted we could not return with him and hoped we would be able to come back some time in the future.

His people, the rajah said, lived high in the mountains. In good weather, it took about two days to walk from the road but now, in the wet season, it would be a journey of at least seven days or more.

'Many of my people have been missionized now,' he told us. 'We were the last to hold out against the Dutch in 1906 when they wanted to destroy our adat and cut our hair but some of my people still keep to the old ways. Some still hunt the babirusa [the hog deer which has two pairs of horns, one like that of a wild boar and a top pair which curve up over its head], the wild buffalo and a wild goat found only in the mountains. They hunt with bows and arrows and blow-pipes.

'Some are still very primitive,' he said, smiling, a look on his face that was a mixture of embarrassment that his people should be so uncivilized and pride in their adat remaining strong. 'Some still have holes in their ears, they put on feathers to perform war dances and many of them have strange tattoos on their bodies.'

'How do your people live when they have given up hunting?' Robin asked him.

'We are fortunate. High up in the mountains we have good grazing on a large plateau. Long, long ago this was a lake, now it is fertile soil.'

He was pleased with our obvious interest and went on to tell us about the other tribes in the hills.

'One tribe used to remove all their teeth as soon as they were no longer children. Many, many centuries ago, they did something very bad and their king, as a punishment, made all his people pull out their teeth. Gradually, it became a habit and they went on doing it. Still today,' he said, smiling delightedly, 'you see many of their older people with empty mouths. That was part of their adat, you understand?'

Robin asked him if he knew anything about the nomadic tribe called the Bado and if he knew where we might find them.

'I have heard of the people. They live in boats like houses. There is a legend that they were making a boat by a river and a large tree they were cutting down fell into the water with such a splash that it created a big wave which destroyed their houses and swept them out to sea. Now they live in these boathouses so that if another wave comes, they will be able to sail on it.' We liked the story (rather like the Toraja legend but in reverse) but sadly he did not have much information as to where they might be. 'They move around,' he said vaguely.

The Bupati, who joined us again then, said he thought the Bado might be found across the water from Palopo, in the western, central finger of Sulawesi, a journey of only one day by boat.

'Could we hire a motor boat?' Robin asked.

'No, no. You must have my boat. It is very good and very

fast. I will arrange for it to be ready tomorrow morning and all you will have to pay for is the petrol and money for food for the boatmen.' He called for a servant and sent him off with Asrad to give a message to the boatmen. We were quite overwhelmed with gratitude at this great stroke of good fortune but this delightful man waved away our thanks and insisted he was only too pleased to be able to help us.

Our leave-taking seemed to take forever. There were now about fifteen men in the room and each one had to be shaken hands with, the Muslims putting their hands on their hearts, the old rajah bowing low and wishing us a happy journey.

In the morning, I felt better, though weak, until a boiled egg I had ordered for breakfast was cracked open to reveal an almost fully fledged chick inside. I had to rush to the wash-room once more.

'Perhaps it's a local delicacy,' Robin suggested, and I said I had had rotten eggs before now but a chicken on the point of hatching was ridiculous. He tried to get me to embark on another one or even just have some tea, but eggs were out and the ants crawling over the remains of our supper from the night before – still left on the side of the one table in the room – were too much for me. I just managed to swallow a couple more stomach pills and that was my lot.

Chapter 12

The boat was something of a disappointment. We had imagined a motor launch, something on a larger scale than the Dory we had at home, but it turned out to be a long narrow boat, only about three feet wide, which had once been painted blue, but was now faded to a pale grey. Flimsy outriggers of bamboo supported equally flimsy floats, and the centre of the craft was covered by a layer of foam plastic sheeting nailed to wooden boards. It had a sorry look of dilapidation about it. The Johnson engine on the back, however, did look new and in good working order.

Small canoes, all with outriggers, were bringing in the catch from a night's fishing. Large crabs from the skeletal traps out at sea were being unloaded beside whole boatloads of fish that looked like mackerel, silver and blue-grey, the colour of the sky above which threatened rain. One canoe wallowed deep in the water under a catch of still-leaping small fry. As we passed our luggage to a cheerful-looking boatman and climbed on board our fragile-looking craft, the inevitable crowd of children milled around, getting under everyone's feet, staring and whispering amongst themselves.

We had thought that Simon would leave us in Rantepao but he'd begged us to take him to Palopo where he had relatives, and once there insisted he went with us to Malili in his 'official capacity'. We were also joined by a policeman, a most attractive-looking man and, like so many Indonesians, exceptionally neatly dressed in a well-pressed uniform covered with black and gold epaulets. What was unusual about him was that he had a curving moustache and small goatee beard that must have been a great envy to a lot of his acquaintances. His broad smile showed a mouth of startlingly white and even teeth.

The afternoon was glorious. Robin had made friends with the driver and now steered the boat most of the time while the boatman went to sit with his mate on the prow. Our police guard was a friendly fellow and Simon spent all of the time in the cabin. The wind blew through our hair, rippling the waves gently and it felt good to be alive again as the mountains on the coast retreated and the shore we were heading for showed as a hazy blur on the horizon.

We reached the far shore at three, in what the policeman said was record time, and began, more slowly now, chugging up a wide river flanked by wide beds of low palms growing in the mud. They could have been sago but, I thought, were more probably nippons – the palms used for thatching houses; both had the same outlines and I never really did get to tell one from another at a distance.

On the river there was plenty of activity. People were fishing from little canoes, each with miniature floats of bamboo frames sticking out on either side of their craft. Larger boats, with sails patched so often they had become a maze of faded colours, tacked sideways across the water and, every now and then, we churned past the most extraordinary constructions moored at the side of the river. They were a sort of boat, but like nothing we had seen before, complicated frames of bamboo on catamaran floats that rose in a network of poles and had a small house suspended high in the air. They looked highly unstable and yet people obviously lived up there; washing hung from the rigging and spirals of smoke rose from cooking fires at the back.

The little town of Malili is some way up the river. Before we reached it we saw many reminders that fighting here had been fierce during the war. Landing craft wallowed like great rusted carts with three-quarters of their bellies below the surface of the water and what could have been a gunboat had now become a tangled heap of unmovable flotsam by the side of the muddy bank.

We hoped to stay at a mining camp some way away and as soon as we landed the Camat, who came to meet us, organized a lift for Robin on the back of a motorcycle to the camp.

The last I saw of him for some time was his back view, clutching a young man tightly round the waist, bouncing up and down as they roared up a mud track, with the wheels spinning and the machine taking off in kangaroo leaps as it ricocheted over stones and boulders.

To start with, Robin had rather a rough time at the mining camp. He was met by an accountant who said firmly that no-one except mining staff were allowed into the area and that, in any case, they had no guest accommodation for a woman. Robin, as far as I can make out, tried to explain that I was not really a woman – at least not that sort of a woman. Finally he saw the head of the camp and was more successful. We could stay, but Robin would have to watch over me while I had a shower because, although there were some wives and a female teacher stationed there, they had special bungalows and we would have to be given a room in a 'men only' barracks. Apart from the 'not really a woman' bit, I thought the prospect sounded delightful and told him I had no intention of letting him stand guard over me while I had a shower.

I had the sinister feeling of entering a concentration camp. Simon, who tried to come with us, was firmly turned away. Inside, the area looked as though a bomb had hit it. Bulldozers had scarred the earth and ripped up all the natural vegetation and, although a row of small prefabricated bungalows had little gardens in front of them, the rest of the compound was totally devoid of trees and baking in the strong sun. We drove past petrol stores, offices, and came to a stop beside a long hut opposite which, we were told, was the communal mess. An Indonesian servant showed us to a room with three beds and blessed air conditioning, and pointed out a bathroom down a corridor where a row of three showers stood beside a row of three lavatories. The lavatories had swing doors, four feet high and two feet off the ground, and the only privacy about the showers was a transparent plastic curtain which could be pulled across the opening. Opposite, notices pinned above a row of six washbasins reminded the inmates of the camp to take their anti-malaria pills every day.

Robin did guard me whilst I had a shower and I was rather touched by his bulldog stance as I stripped off and went behind the curtain.

There was hot water and soap, glorious soap, a real man-sized bar of it instead of the miniature squares we had pinched from the hotels in Jakarta, and had been making do with on our travels. I turned the hot tap all the way and felt fantastic, lusciously clean and deodorized all over.

The head of the mining company, a really nice character (Indonesian) called Benny, had asked us to join the audience watching a tennis tournament that evening. Tennis parties had not actually come into the category of 'clothes we might need out of Makassar', but I did the best I could, sponging down a grimy tee-shirt, putting on a mercifully unworn pair of flared jeans with silver studs and donning, for the first time for weeks, some gold chains which I had in my travelling bag.

I was quite pleased by the effect as we walked through the compound towards the soft putt-putt of tennis balls. The pleasure did not last long.

Three games of tennis were under way on spanking new courts, and watching them were an audience dressed to make Wimbledon on finals day seem pale in comparison. It was like a garden party, with chairs pulled up in rows beside the courts and on the steps of the clubhouse. Both Indonesian and European women were dressed to kill in colourful sarongs, cotton dresses or smart trouser suits. Young children, brown and saxon pink, played around them, drinking coca-cola through straws and dropping the empty bottles at their parents' feet.

The match, against the youths of Palopo, was in full swing with the home team of engineers, mechanics and geologists obviously at a disadvantage against skinny bouncing all-Pepsi-Cola boys.

Later, in Benny's bungalow we drank tankards of cold beer and talked about isolated tribes and our journeys up to date. He had good maps and an interesting collection of books, including an original edition of Wallace, for which I greatly envied him. To our dismay he told us the Bado had moved from the area many years before, but he also told us about a tribe to the north the miners had come across whilst on a survey. They were too far to try and reach on this trip, but that evening became the starting point of a later expedition for Robin.

Little was known about this tribe, the Toana. The prospectors had come across them deep in the jungle. About a thousand little men had come from the trees and converged on the helicopter. One had blown a dart at them which caught one man on the arm, but had not really harmed him and, apart from that incident, they seemed friendly. The miners met them on two more occasions when they dropped into jungle clearings from the sky, and they agreed that the men were exceptionally small. They wore bark loincloths and appeared to live in houses built in the trees. Benny had not seen them himself, but he had been trying to find out more about them.

'They seem to have some contact with the outside world,' he told Robin, 'and have a sort of trading route to the sea which they use for getting salt. By a guess, I would think they number around five thousand and, as far as I can make out, they seem to prefer the jungle to civilization.' I could see Robin's eyes lighting up. The whole Palopo journey had been a disappointment up until then, but hearing about these people almost made the trip worth while.

With the Bado nowhere to be found, the trip across the water at first seemed an abortive venture but, surprisingly, it turned out to be an interesting thirty-six hours. We had come to find an isolated tribe and in a way we did, for the people in that mining camp were far more isolated than any tribe could ever be. They were separated from the outside world by a high wire fence; they lived in a world of their own and, on the whole, they did not seem to like it one bit. The Indonesians were the exception. From a boy who did some washing for us, up to the chief, Benny, they all seemed to find fulfilment in their lives and in the jobs they did. They were pleasant and interesting to talk to. The white, mainly Australian, community were a different matter altogether. Never in my life have I heard such discontent and bitching; they were like a group of spoilt, soured, children.

Mr Ruru, however, who kindly offered to take us inland, up the mountains next morning to the main mining area, became a friend in a very short time. Mr Ruru was of Chinese descent and, although he was not fat, he had the most extraordinary spherical shape, like one of those rubber toys which bounces upright again every time you knock it flat. His life had not been happy. His parents were murdered in a Muslim rebellion on the farm they owned near Malili and, years later, their son had taken a job in mining in order to try and find their bodies amongst a heap of dead so that he could give them a proper funeral.

'Most rebellions,' he said sadly, 'have a touch of romance about them. That one did not. It was religious fanaticism gone mad, and the killing that went on was horrific as the Muslims tried to take over Celebes.'

He had other problems on his mind too. His wife was having her first baby rather late in life. She had developed complications and was now in hospital in Makassar where she had been for the last two months. Despite all this, he took endless pains to entertain us, chatting about this and that and pointing out places of interest.

'In many ways,' he said, 'I am a very fortunate man. I have

a lovely woman as my wife, in two weeks I hope to have a son and then we will be a real family. The ways of God are strange.'

We drove in an almost brand-new Landrover and, although the road was just a bulldozer slash across the countryside, it was a comfortable excursion in the comfort of a well-sprung vehicle.

Our route followed a river gorge, twisting and winding as we climbed up a high hillside, and the river became a series of spectacular waterfalls, glimpsed through thick jungle, dotted with trees that flamed with vivid scarlet blossom. Great tangled ropes of rattan looped from tree to tree and crept across the track as the forest tried to take back that which belonged to it. A gigantic yellow bulldozer looked ridiculously insignificant beside the great wild backcloth of jungle green.

At the top was a great plateau of open land, deserted except for a small settlement in the centre where two tracks crossed. Until the 1950s, before the rebellion, Mr Ruru told us, the area had been thickly populated with many small villages. They had all been burnt by the Muslims. Malili, too, had been razed to the ground three times, but houses had quickly sprung up again and now, because of mining, the town was prospering.

The opencast mine was up in another range of hills. The slopes were scarred by bulldozer tracks with great trees hurled to either side of wide muddy clearings. It was as though a hurricane had swept through, leaving havoc and destruction in its wake. Below it lay the long silver length of lake, only five kilometres wide but stretching thirty kilometres from east to west, with crystal-clear water that went down to seven hundred feet below sea level. In cliffs beside the lake there were ancient burial caves, Mr Ruru told us, which would probably interest Robin. To get there we would have to go some distance along the lake, and when we reached the small camp on its shores he arranged for a man to get a small motor boat ready.

We had lunch in a small dining room overlooking the water, and a geologist showed us some heavy bronze bracelets, some plain, others carved with intricate patterns, linked together to form a chain two yards in length. It was incredibly heavy.

'The prospector who found the graves took these out,' he said. 'I haven't been there yet. The place is very taboo and it is difficult to find anyone to take you, but luckily I have found a boy who agrees to come with us. The funny thing is I've asked him before and he always refused to talk about the graves. He wouldn't tell me why he'd changed his mind and he even refused to accept money.'

'What about the bracelets?' I asked. 'Didn't the people mind them being taken?'

'Nobody said anything,' he replied, 'but to tell you the truth, I don't really like seeing them here myself and I don't think I would personally dare to remove anything.'

The temperature in the room seemed to drop at that moment. I felt definitely spooked and even Mr Ruru stopped beaming. I had a quick sensation of dizziness and wished I was not there. The sun disappeared behind a thick grey cloud and the water lost its sparkle.

By the time we set off, the lake was an ugly petrol blue, and a surprisingly chill wind lashed small waves into white wings across the water. Black thunderclouds were massing like giant fists up behind the mountain giving everything a sickly tinge.

We were quite a party in the boat. Mr Ruru sat beside us and the geologist in front, dressed for the outing in orange slacks, thick-soled tennis shoes, a gaudily patterned Balinese shirt and a white cotton hat that was rather too small for him. In his hands he held a stout Toraja walking stick which he grasped firmly as he tried hard to look as though he were enjoying himself.

At the last minute we were joined by the chief of the villagers, from a settlement up the lake who bury their dead in the caves, who sat, still and silent, neither talking to us nor to the boatman beside him.

After about half an hour, grassland and slopes on the shore gave way to steep grey and white cliffs, rising in a high wall and lightly covered with hanging vines, twisting snake-like into cracks and fissures. This was our destination. We turned towards them and, with the engines cut, slid silently under an overhang of rock beneath a tangle of thickly entwined vegetation.

The water below the boat was crystalline and a curious translucent green blue. One could see for ever, down and down, a massive never-ending parapet of white rocks, tumbled one on top of another with centuries of dead tree trunks and black, curling, serpentine lengths of fallen vines scattered amongst them. Above, a network of roots hung down into the water and here, in the shadow of the cliff wall, it was dank and cold.

The boatman pointed to a cave that was a mere black slit from below. He and the chief sat firmly in the boat holding it steady whilst we pulled ourselves onto a platform of matted branches and clambered upwards over rocks and roots. It was not far, but the climb was an almost perpendicular one and the sheer drop below was magnified by the clarity of the water. One could imagine oneself sinking, weightless, for ever into that water.

We pulled ourselves up onto a ledge outside the narrow opening of the cave. Beneath our feet dead leaves had turned to a damp softness of peat; offerings and belongings of the dead were everywhere and rotten rags, bits of broken pots and bowls, crumbled beneath our feet. A rusted kris struck a rope of bronze bracelets, green with age, and gave off a deadened metallic thud.

There was the smell of death everywhere and, inside, the horrifying evidence of it. Human bones cascaded out of rotting coffins, skulls and fingers lay in a grim heap. Mortal remains were everywhere and the floor was strewn with bracelets, some carved from shells and glowing eerily pale in the dark dampness.

'They say the uncoffined bones are those of their enemies,' Mr Ruru whispered.

Robin switched on his torch and began to go down a steep

incline deeper into the cave. Mr Ruru called out: 'No. No. Don't go right inside. The chief of the village says it is full of snakes.' Robin walked on and I followed, hating it, loathing it, but filled with a kind of horrible fascination, stepping on human bones.

Looking upwards, I saw a thick black snake curled over the top of a rock ledge. My fingers dug into Robin's arm as, unable to speak, I just pointed. He swung the beam of the torch up, illuminating walls stacked with coffins in a faint gold light. The shape stayed immobile and, to make sure it was not a snake, Robin clapped his hands causing a bombardment of bats, their eyes glowing red in the torchlight, to flutter over our heads. When they had gone the black serpentine shape had vanished as though into thin air. I felt sick again.

One body had only recently been put there. Scraps of clothing still clung to the skeletal shape inside a coffin that had no top to it. The eye sockets and gash that had once been a mouth grinned insanely and large black ants scurried across bones not yet picked clean. Black ants were everywhere and I began gasping for breath in the fetid, rank and cloying air, stumbling back outside to join the geologist and Mr Ruru, who had his stick raised ready to attack if necessary. He looked wonderfully comical, and dearly alive, as he stood there bravely waiting to face the snakes.

Drawing in courage with deep gulps of air, I followed the geologist along the cliff face to another cave he discovered. We had to climb like monkeys, clinging onto rocks and digging our fingers in crevices. It was hard enough for us but how, I wondered, would one ever get a heavy wooden coffin and a human body up here. The geologist thought they must be thrown from above, down some kind of natural chute.

'It would explain why they are so broken,' he said reasonably, pointing out a tumbled heap of wood and bones which looked as though they had been crushed by giants' feet; it did not explain why some coffins remained almost intact and were stacked, one on top of another, in a side tunnel shafting upwards.

The second cave was larger than the first and, as Robin brought the torch and swung it round, we saw there were literally hundreds upon hundreds of corpses, bronze chains looped over them and hanging like manacles from cracks in the roof.

On the floor we found crude iron swords, primitively made but beaten to a slim and sharp shape; and amongst a pile of shattered pots lay a nautilus shell, the silvery lining gleaming dully through a film of verdure.

Mr Ruru still remaining firmly outside called that it was getting late and we must go, and slowly, almost reluctantly, we turned back towards the daylight. They were horrific, these caves, ominous and drear, but somehow morbidly compelling.

Outside he showed us a Dutch plate he'd picked up from the ground. The china was weathered by rain, but the pattern still showed up clearly with the date 1836 ringed by a wreath of flowers.

Back in the boat there was an atmosphere of relieved tension as though a great strain had been lifted from us all. To match our mood the sky changed too; thunderclouds scudded southwards and the expected rain moved in a grey curtain away from us. Sunlight came shafting down in rays of golden light onto the water and the engine started with one pull, sounding strong and firm. For the first time the chief spoke and Mr Ruru translated:

'He says the spirits are glad we visited the caves and they are in favour of us.' He, rotund little man, almost clapped his hands in delight and beamed at everyone, wiping his smooth forehead with a clean red handkerchief. We all talked at once, laughing excitedly, telling each other how brave we had been, and revelling in the fresh air and clean light.

We saw Benny briefly again before we left Malili early next morning, and I was rather alarmed by his concern about our travelling to Palopo in such a small boat.

'The crossing is surprisingly tricky. Only a few days ago a boat was picked up after drifting for seven days. The motor had broken down and the people in it were helpless. We had to fly one passenger to Makassar hospital. He was on the point of starving.'

In fact we had no problems (although I noticed rather nervously that we only had a single short pole and no oars in the boat if the engine did cause trouble); and it was a smooth, pleasant crossing.

Asrad was waiting for us on the jetty, smiling, and by now a good friend who behaved towards us rather like an indulgent Victorian nanny. He gave Simon, whom he did not like at all, a sour look.

Despite torrential rain and thunderstorms, we left Palopo at once, retracing our drive through Rantepao and reached Makali in the early hours of the next morning where Asrad readily agreed to leave after a rest of only four hours.

Waking up was no trouble. We were rudely woken by the wailing, echoing call from the nearby mosque, telling the Muslims it was time to pray to Mahomet. The call was so loud, and went on for so long, that sleep was impossible and we left without waiting for tea. As a result, we crossed the mountains in daylight, this time beginning the long mountain drive as the new day's sun was beginning to rise over the craggy peaks. The sun was a great orange ball that filled valleys and mountains with a warm golden glow, giving, with every sharp turning in the road, a view that seemed more spectacular than the one before.

The drive back to Makassar was one of unbelievable beauty but it was also long, inconceivably hot and very tiring. The heat, the thick clouds of flies and mosquitoes which surrounded us whenever we stopped to mend a puncture, or just mend a burst tyre, and the hours spent jolting around in the uncomfortable jeep succeeded in getting us both down. On top of that, there was the disappointment of Palopo and, for once, Robin's usual good temper, patience and ability to think 'it could have been worse' deserted him, as yet another tyre went with a bang. He stood in the middle of the road and swore – loudly, efficiently and with great feeling.

Chapter 13

In spite of everything, thanks to Asrad's fantastic driving, and the speed at which he and his sleepy grease-monkey changed and mended the tyres as they popped, we reached Makassar with a day in hand. It turned out to be an aimless twenty-four hours; we were like two pieces of driftwood floating until they hit a shore. Within twenty-four hours we would start travelling again – until then we were rudderless.

Dr Meyer was sitting on the balcony of his house waiting for us at the appointed time, and looked relaxed in a pair of lightweight trousers and a Batik shirt. With him was an exceptionally small bearded European, with longish hair and a scruffy shyness about him that was instantly attractive. He was introduced to us as Christian Pelras, a great chap, a Frenchman and the only anthropologist working on the island.

'I persuaded him to come with us to the south,' the doctor said proudly. 'He made noises about work, his wife and his car, but I said they were all nonsense. So he comes.'

For once there was no hurry; while Robin and Christian talked in French, Dr Meyer began to tell me stories of Makassar and his life there. He was to keep us amused for the whole of that journey with legends, tales and stories; he was to vastly increase our knowledge of Indonesia, of life, of learning and of mankind.

All that came later. Sitting beside him that morning, I was only aware of the magnetism of his voice and the stories he told and, for me, who soaked up the tales of Somerset Maugham, Guy de Maupassant and Saki like a dry sponge, it was like sitting at the feet of all three, listening to a voice that rasped from too many cigarettes, that spoke in a mixture of French and English with a Caucasian accent and who held one spellbound by the magic of his narratives about the island of Sulawesi, which he still determinedly called 'Celebes'.

'There is a story in the Celebes,' he told me, 'about the origin of white men. It goes something like this. Once there was a king of Palopo who had many children. One of the princes had a bad skin disease, all over him, like leprosy. The king decided this was a bad omen and would bring misfortune to his people so he put the prince on a raft, pushed him into the sea and watched him drift away.

'Strong currents took him to Bone in the east. Where he landed, there were no people, only forest stretching forever into the hills. The prince was inevitably lonely (apart from his skin disease, he was a virile, healthy young man) so he married a dog bitch he found wandering in the forest. Not long after, she gave birth to a large litter of white-skinned, blue-eyed and fair-haired people.

'The king, getting a conscience in his old age, decided his son must come home and sent a servant to fetch him. When he saw the strange, pale children, he was terrified and demanded a raft should be made to send the prince and his family away again at once so that they could not put the evil eye on the people of Palopo. His elder statesmen didn't agree; they begged the rajah to let the white family remain, but the old man was adamant. They were put on a large raft and pushed back into the sea once more and, as they sailed westwards and drifted away, the elders moaned and wept, telling the rajah that the white people would flourish in another country, they would return and make the people of Celebes slaves.

'And, of course, they did come,' Dr Meyer concluded.

'The omens of the old men came true with the arrival of the Dutch and their long rule over the islands.'

He told stories of Makassar and the colourful people he had met there in his many years on the island. He talked about the famous Daisy O'Keefe, daughter of the O'Keefe who had built an empire in the east. Daisy was old when he first met her, her days as a ballet dancer were long gone as were the days when she had been the mistress of princes and kings, but she was still a flamboyant creature with boundless charm.

'There used to be wild, drunken parties in those days and Daisy had a favourite trick she would play when everyone was nicely away. She would lay enormous bets to anyone that was interested (and most still were) that they couldn't guess the colour of her knickers. Men put hundreds of pounds on every colour they could think of. "Red," they would shout, "black, green, yellow" – all the colours under the sun. In the end, Daisy would roar with laughter and collect their money – she never wore any knickers so they were *all* wrong. If they didn't believe her, she had no qualms about showing them.'

We travelled south, along the western coast towards a small town called Tenate. Once more a whole new panorama opened up as we saw a new part of Sulawesi.

It was Friday again, mosque day, and also, on this occasion, a special holy day. Men were dressed in their best, their sarongs of silk and a blaze of purple, magenta and shocking pink checks, each carrying a prayer mat under his arm as they walked towards the nearest village.

A band of laughing girls walked two by two along the road; their tightly wrapped sarongs were topped by snug-fitting white lace jackets and a wide sash of green ran from their shoulders to their waists.

Those who had already said their prayers for the day rode along the dusty road on small, sturdy ponies piled high with bunches of harvested rice or with baskets of new plants to start off the cycle once more.

We had been driving for a long time when Dr Meyer asked Asrad to stop in the centre of a small colourful town and eased himself slowly from the back of the jeep with obvious pain.

'One of the petrol cans was leaking,' he said. 'It's gone all over my leg. I tried to ignore it but the stupid thing's hurting rather a lot.'

As the major doctor in the only large hospital in Sulawesi, Dr Meyer had friends all over the island. People began to recognize him; they came running out of a small shop, clutching at his hands, showering him with questions, treating him with a reverence that was almost godlike. Meyer looked desperately embarrassed by this treatment but answered their questions and greeted them with warmth before even mentioning his leg.

At once, we were all led through to a small living room at the back of a bakery shop; glasses of warm, sweet, pink lemonade were produced and, for once, the doctor was the patient as they all fussed round him. Great red streaks ran down his right leg where the petrol had seeped through his trousers and burnt his skin. It must have been extremely painful and he looked pale but he went on smiling gently, insisted that bathing the burns in cold water was all that was needed and then, dismissing the matter, asked how the woman he had recently operated on was feeling now and burrowed in his suitcase for some pills to give her husband who was suffering badly from arthritis.

We arrived in Tenate as the sun grew old, and drove up to a large bungalow, standing on a slight rise, surrounded by tall fir trees.

'The Camat here is a friend of mine,' Dr Meyer told us. 'He is away but we can stay here for the night. It is simple but quite comfortable.'

Until darkness fell and the mosquitoes became unbearable, we sat in sagging cane-chairs outside under the trees and listened to the doctor telling more stories of the Bugis, of the Toraja and of Makassar; of legends, myths and of people he had known in the island. Christian, opening up gradually, joined in with Bugi folklore and tales of his experiences working amongst them.

The Bugis – people who live south of Makassar – are seafaring men and fishermen; for most of them the sea is their life and their livelihood. For centuries, they had been building large wooden *praus* – deep-bellied sailing boats which still kept to a traditional pattern. Explorers and travellers, they were sailing thousands of miles long before the Portuguese discovered the East, and reaching Java from Celebes in only five days. From Java, they went further, to Madagascar and places beyond, trading in spices and cloth. In the south, Christian said, we would see these magnificent boats and watch them being built.

A large ring of children came to squat round us and were gently slapped at by the doctor when they came too near; they were unable to understand a word but were hypnotized by his voice and us.

We talked about the next day's proposed journey to Tana Towa, the sacred forest of the sect who wore indigo blue. Christian had been to the area before and spent three weeks or more in the vicinity of the outer edge of the sacred forest. He had not been allowed into the inner circle of the Tana Towa and was depressing about our chances of getting there: He shrugged his shoulders in that distinctive way the French have, his shoulders hunching up to his beard and the palms of his hands held outwards. The spiritual leader of the sect, the Ama Towa, is considered in Celebes to be the wisest man in the world, and the highest people from the government make pilgrimages to try to see him and ask for his advice. Christian told us:

'But they seldom get to see him. Tana Towa is a fortress without a wall, yet it is impregnable for strangers; those who live in the inner circle never go to the outside world and those who live outside the outer circle are seldom allowed in.'

Over a frugal supper, we learnt more about the doctor. He ate little; he could not take much food at a time, he told us, since having been interned as a German prisoner-of-war in Siberia.

'Sometimes we starved. Sometimes we had bread, hard as rocks, and water the colour of black mud. We caught mice and rats, eating them raw if we had to.'

He had been captured in 1944 and moved from camp to camp. The only reason he lived, where so many had died of disease or starvation, was because of his use as a doctor.

'The Rumanians,' he said, 'were the toughest of the lot; somehow they seemed to survive everything and they were the best thieves of all of us. Real ruffians but fair too. You had to be fair in those camps or your own people killed you instead of the Russians.'

He told of a Russian wardress who'd saved his life and made love to one of the guards in order to steal some medicine from the camp surgery. He was laughing now and showing teeth that were rotten through malnutrition.

'Tania, she was called. A great robust girl, strong as an ox, who'd have it off with anyone as speedily and lustily as an animal. The only time she drew the line was with anyone from Budapest. "Have you been in Budapest?" she'd ask every prospective lover and if they said yes she wouldn't touch them. She knew they'd have syphilis. She used to grab me under the grey blankets of the hospital ward and laugh because I was too weak to perform properly.'

We sat late into the night as the small kerosene lamp grew dim, drinking cup after cup of weak tea from a chipped enamel pot as he told us stories of his patients; of the problems of birth control in the island; of abortions caused by massaging, and of a man with elephantiasis of the scrotum who had balls so large they were like two water melons.

'He had them supported in a string basket, like a pair of exhibition marrows, carried by two men, one in front and one who walked behind him. I said I could operate (it wasn't a difficult operation) and made an appointment for him to come into hospital. He never turned up and when I saw him again he said those giant balls gave him status – if he lost them he would no longer hold the position he held then and so he'd decided not to have the operation.'

Christian, Robin and I were still laughing at the comical picture he had conjured up when we decided it was time to turn in.

The next few days were, looking back, some of the happiest we had on the whole of our travels. No-one could ever be such a delightful companion as the doctor. He made us laugh, at times he moved us to tears and he was unfailingly good-tempered and thoughtful despite the fact that most of the time he was in great pain. The next morning the burns on his legs looked frighteningly red and angry. In one place, the skin had been rubbed away and exposed an inflamed weeping sore. I offered him an antibiotic cream we had but he refused it, putting a disinfectant salve on the wounds.

'In the West I think the use of antibiotics is becoming sadly misused. They are being handed out like aspirins – for everything,' he said as we drove over hilly country along a slippery track through a forest of rubber trees that seemed to go on forever: a depressing dripping grid of straight lines stretching in every direction. When it ended we travelled through a more wild landscape where small valleys, terraced with rice paddies, fell below hills topped by barren scrubland. The houses, in the small villages we went through, were like those of the Bugis we had seen on the way out of Makassar, oblong wooden boxes, brightly painted, with thatched roofs, although here they were larger and more ornate, with the apex of each roof crowned with an intricate fretwork symbol of some pattern, animal or bird.

We reached Katjang, our first objective, a small town on the coast, at what would in England have been breakfast time. It was a pleasant-looking place with a small, central fountain and a narrow main street with one wooden stall that seemed to serve as the main store, beyond which was the Katjang Camat's house. The Camat ruled the province on the edge of Tana Towa and it was from him that we would have to get permission to go into the outer circle of the sacred country. His house was more grand than most, built of stone and cob, not wood, and the Camat, Christian told us, was the direct descendant of a rajah and a most powerful man.

It was a long, long morning. Christian and Dr Meyer were used to the waiting, the protocol, the endless exchange of compliments and seemingly pointless hanging about that was part of the Eastern way of life. We had not yet learnt the lesson of patience.

After half an hour, we were ushered up to a small room where plastic-strung chairs were grouped around low coffee tables and the Camat, resplendent in a spotless uniform with the Star of Indonesia on his chest and a black velvet hat on his head, emerged from an inner room. He looked more like a Javanese than a man from this region, quite a large man with a wide face, with deep-lidded dark brown eyes and thick lips that parted continually into a brilliant smile that revealed nothing. Three other men were with him and when he sat, we sat, though he settled himself comfortably whilst we perched on the edge of our chairs. I could feel the plastic strands digging through my skirt into my thighs and it was hot and airless in the little room.

For some time, the talk was purely polite about the history of his rajah descendancy and of local adat. Christian had been chosen as the one of us who should ask permission to enter Tana Towa but he did not mention the sacred forest for what seemed a never-ending length of time. When he did, he spoke in Bugi and then turned to us to translate the Camat's reply.

'We can only go to the sacred stones in the outer circle,' he said with another of those shrugging gestures. 'I dare not suggest we go further in.'

'Of course you can, Pelras,' the doctor urged. 'Ask. Ask. It can do no harm.' Christian shook his head pessimistically, but, nevertheless, he asked, bowing his head politely as he put the request. The Camat nodded gravely, glancing at the doctor, Robin and myself as though weighing us all up. Then he spoke to a young man sitting with us, who immediately rose and left the room. Outside there was the sound of a motorbicycle being gunned into action. We looked to Christian for enlightenment and he shrugged again.

'Someone has been sent off with a message. We just wait.'

We waited and the polite exchanges went on, as the room seemed to get hotter by the minute and buzzing flies gave a soporific effect. Finally, the talk came round again to the Tana Towa.

The Camat spoke in measured Bahasa Indonesian. 'At the moment the road is impassable with bad mud.' If we could come back on Tuesday, then perhaps something could be arranged. His son was to be married then, and there was going to be a big fiesta. We were welcome to attend and there would be people coming down from the outer circle of Tana Towa. Perhaps then something might be worked out. . . .

We could not wait until Tuesday. The doctor had to get back to his hospital and we had a plane to catch to the Moluccas.

The Camat rose and we thought that at last we might be moving, but he waved us back to our chairs and, bowing himself out with his entourage behind him, said he hoped we would join him a little later to eat. All four of us could hardly restrain ourselves from groaning and the minutes seemed to pass with immeasurable slowness. Twice, I looked at my watch after what I thought was a space of twenty minutes or more but which turned out to have been less than five.

Alone, Dr Meyer told us more stories of cases he had seen and ministered to. Among the Bugis men there was a universal terror of impotence. If a husband was suspected of infidelity, his wife would threaten to cut off his balls and that almost always brought him to heel. In one case it had not, and the woman actually had cut them off with a large pair of scissors while he was sleeping.

'Terrible mess,' said the doctor, 'but I suppose she was happy because one thing he wasn't going to do any more was to commit adultery.'

This same fear frequently caused incidents of what the doctor called 'castration complex'. Men would actually become physically ill with the conviction they were becoming impotent. One had even died from the conviction but most could be cured by a simple injection or a supply of harmless aspirin which he convinced them would work miracles.

He talked too of transvestites. How many priests of tribes or sects practised dual roles as men and women and how, as with the Dayaks in Kalimantan, it was not unusual, strange or thought amusing, for men or boys to dress as women when performing ritual dances.

By this time the room was like an oven, pre-set to a regulo for baking. Sweat ran down our faces, and bare feet (our shoes had been left outside the door in the customary fashion) left damp marks on the bare wooden floor. The heat was increased by the fires roaring in an area behind the room we sat in, where women and girls were busy preparing food for the coming wedding. Robin's eyelids continually drooped over his eyes and I kept having to kick him when he actually dozed off for a minute or two.

Children stared at us from the door and I caught a glimpse between them of an old woman walking slowly up the street. On top of a large banana leaf, covering her head, lay a long, fat fish a good four feet long. Its tail flapped up and down as she walked, making it appear to be still alive.

Even Dr Meyer ran out of stories and we slumped like four limp rags when the meal was announced. For the first time, the Camat's wife appeared, a plump, pleasant-looking woman, her face shining from cooking over an open fire. She clutched the doctor's hands and made as though to kiss them, which made him cringe in shy embarrassment. She, too, it turned out, had been a one-time patient.

We ate in what appeared to be the bridal chamber. In one corner, a wrought-iron, double four-poster bed was draped with curtains of virginal white cotton embroidered with blue flowers, so shiny it would have gladdened the heart of any soap manufacturer. Beside the bed, a portion of the room was screened off by arches of bamboo, decorated with palm leaves. It all looked very gay and festive.

The meal was gargantuan (no wonder it had been so long in coming) and the Camat beamed at us, encouraging us to tuck in. I was the only woman – the Camat's wife had once more disappeared.

A dignified, elderly servant served us with masses of dishes; small fried fish, a highly-spiced stew of chicken, slices of some sort of mackerel covered in a fiery sauce and fried eggs with vast quantities of rice. I noticed the doctor quail.

There was little conversation and none of it was about the Tana Towa. The subject seemed to have been forgotten; in fact, it might never have existed and I could sense in Robin a feeling I had too, that perhaps this trip, like the one to Palopo, was going to turn out to be abortive.

After the enormous meal we walked to the end of the town, where a long stone jetty led way out into the sea. In the distance, we could see large prau (called 'prau penis' because of the curving pointed shape of their prows), with huge sails billowing from tall masts. They were heading towards the harbour in a wide fan formation, and within only a few minutes it was clear why. With that sudden unexpected violence which still amazed me, the sky clouded in a matter of seconds, black clouds swept across the canopy of heaven, darkening the world around us. From nowhere a vicious wind whipped up, lashing the sea into foaming white horses, forcing out the sails of the fleet of ships until they leant sideways looking as though they were almost lying on the water. With the wind came rain, first great silver drops, then cascades of icy water that soaked us to the skin.

We ran back to the Camat's house and this time rainwater, not sweat, lay in puddles at our feet.

Since no-one seemed to know what was going to happen next, I pushed my way through the curtain screening off the kitchen from where fascinating noises of whisking, beating and stirring were going on. Earlier, I had been overcome by shyness and had thought perhaps it might be considered bad manners. Now I was overcome with curiosity to see what was going on.

The kitchen was like a cave, large and dark with a ceiling blackened by smoke. Beside two glowing fires, women were bent over large pots, stirring a thick heavy substance. Others were rolling the same treacly mass into long strings on mats of banana leaves laid on the floor, working swiftly as it began to harden and sprinkling the surface with sesame seeds. Two beautiful girls knelt geisha fashion near the door, beating huge bowls of eggs into a pale yellow froth with bamboo whisks. Each bowl must have held at least three dozen eggs. An old woman, her face elegant with age and wisdom, took my hands in hers and said something which sounded like a sort of blessing and the others smiled at me, stopping their work to giggle shyly.

At long last, a man arrived to say we were ready to leave for the sacred stones of the Tana Towa and a place they called the 'navel of the world' where man first touched the earth. In the jeep, we drove to a wide river and there left Asrad while we climbed precariously into a narrow canoe, carved from a tree trunk, and, with two men paddling hard against a strong current, reached the other side, to enter the outer circle of Tana Towa and to get our first glimpse of a place that was magic, enchantment and peace.

Chapter 14

Here in Tana Towa the people believe that the life of man on earth began. On the other side of the river, cut off from the rest of the world by a wide span of water, it seemed natural to accept the credibility of their beliefs. There was nothing tangible, nothing one could put one's finger right on, just a feeling that here there was an element of mysticism, a sense of timelessness.

Two men came into Tana Towa with us, an elderly Sergeant of the police force and a nice young man who was known as the 'Jaksa' who, we were told, held the important position of local judge.

We trudged up the path, under wide spreading trees, for a short time and then were met by a group of men, galloping bare-backed towards us on small ponies, with their sarongs swung over their shoulders and flying out behind them. They dismounted and offered the ponies to us. Only Christian refused. He, he said, loathed both riding and horses.

The animals were small but quite sparky, and mounting mine in a skirt was not easy, especially as they had saddle cloths consisting of a quilted sack filled with kapok balancing on their backbones without the support of any girth to keep it in place. Their bridles were a simple length of rope, vaguely fashioned into a rough halter, and having only one rein.

We dismounted by a house that was larger, and had more carving, than the usual buildings of the area and Doctor Meyer pointed out that above the windows of the carved balustrading on the verandah there was a second set of three shuttered windows with two smaller ones on yet another floor above. As we removed our shoes, he told us:

'Three storeys like that shows a noble family of importance. The Camat of the outer circle of Tana Towa lives here and now we will ask him for permission to visit the forest and the Ama Towa.'

We trooped up steps and into a large central room. We were an untidy group of ill-assorted Europeans, generously caked in mud, who were made to feel even more dishevelled by the neat severity of the little man who rose to greet us. He was even smaller than Christian, but he radiated dignity and presence. He looked about eighty or more and leant heavily on a highly polished stick of twisted sea-tree branch, but a pair of very sharp discerning eyes looked at us acutely from behind a pair of circular silver-framed spectacles as he gave us an eloquent speech of welcome.

To Christian's request that we might be allowed to visit the sacred stones, the Camat bowed graciously and waved us back to the horses. To Christian's further nervous request that we might be allowed to enter the sacred forest, he was totally noncommittal.

Despite the slipping kapok cushion, which slid further and further along my pony's back until I was almost sitting on his tail, I was glad to be mounted and not on foot as the path we followed up a steep incline to the top of a ridge wound through bushes barbed with sharp, spiked thorns. On top of the shoulder we paused to let the ponies recover their wind, taking deep breaths of the fresh, slightly cooler, air and gazed at the spectacular view on either side.

Had it been a painting, one would have said: 'Ridiculous. Nothing can look so perfect as that.' It wasn't a painting. Here was a living landscape, freshly washed by rain and now sparkling in full sunshine once more, that would have defied any human art of paint or photography.

To the right lay groves of tall coconut palms, their tops thickly bunched with green fruit, their feathery leaves moving gently in a light breeze. Beyond, rolled a gentle switchback of small hills, fringing the wide expanse of sapphire sea, now dotted again with ships. The air was so clear that even at this great distance one could see each boat as though through a telescope, picking out their colours and the haphazard patterns of their finely mended sails. To the left, the ground fell away in gentle curving sweeps of bamboos, coconut plantations and viridescent rice paddies.

We climbed higher through undergrowth of wild chillies, spattered with little red fruits, and arrived at the top of another ridge, where we stopped under a clump of twisted trees. Here we dismounted and were met by two men wearing indigo blue sarongs and shirts, dark as the midnight blue of night, and strange twisted turbans, tied so that they formed two medieval twists at either end and fashioned from the same cloth as their sarongs. These were the first Tana Towans we saw and between them they acted as guardians of the 'navel of the world' where the first man from above slid down from a rainbow to the earth and the first woman came up from the sea.

There was a curious silence on the top of that hill and the men who led us towards a circular fence of closely knit bamboo stakes, were grave faced as the old Camat joined them, leaning on his serpentine stick. We had come on horses yet he, who was at least an octogenarian, had got there just as quickly on foot over the steep and rocky ground. He shook his head as we brought out cameras and said something to Doctor Meyer in a low voice.

'The Camat asks you not to take photographs,' Doctor Meyer translated in a whisper. 'This is a sacred place and the spirits might be angry.' In a way I was glad; there was too much to take in besides using a camera too.

Inside the fence the ground had been carefully cleared. In the centre, side by side, were two large flat stones, one traced with faint engraving. In a way, they were not all that spectacular, and yet there was that strange feeling all around as we stood motionless beside the small men in midnight blue, for once oblivious to large red ants that mounted one's legs and arms, shooting out stings of formic acid.

Beneath the stones a large hole, hundreds of feet deep, they said, fell to below the level of the sea and here, not so long ago, human sacrifices and the bodies of goats and sheep were flung alive to appease the gods. To move aside those rock masses must have been a feat of unbelievable strength, and how the great stones had been cut into symmetrical shapes was inconceivable.

We moved away from the shrine, out of the shadows of the trees surrounding it and further along the shoulder of the hill to see other strange stones – great rounded boulders forming monuments that were of a totally different substance to the terrain around.

One was the grave of the woman guilty of committing the first incest in the world – Tana Towa's Eve. She had been encased in the large stone, and on the side the Camat pointed out long scratches below a narrow crack. A few strands of her hair, he told us, had hung through the crack and the marks had been made by the fingernails of her incestuous brother as he tried to pull her back from death.

A tall, sturdy lump of rock identified the place where one of the first kings of the world, a man who spoke with a forked tongue, had gone up to heaven. Another, under a clump of tall bowed bamboos, marked the spot where another king had slid down from heaven on a bamboo pole. Further away, slightly below the spine of the hill, a reclining chunk of stone was the shrine of the man who had first taught the people to catch fish and grow rice.

I suppose I am as sceptical as most people of my generation, yet there I found it easy to believe in the reality of these legends, and not in the least strange that high on this hill, with the curious clarity of the air that surrounded us and the beauty that lay on all sides, man should have begun life on earth. Even now, thousands of miles away, looking back to that moment I still do not find it strange.

As we moved away from the sacred area, people began to talk again and we were joined by a group of young men all wearing blue sarongs and by girls in Bugis adat costumes.

The girls were bright as birds of paradise in cloth of brilliant yellows and reds, with tight sashes bound round their waists, lace jackets moulded to ripening, swelling breasts, and black hair crowned by turbans of fringed silk.

Except for one woman, they were a gay bunch. She, older than the others, had practically no face. Sad eyes looked at the world from a purpled, misshapen visage, with only holes where once a nose had been. She was a grim sight, a spectre at the feast, suffering, Doctor Meyer said, from a very advanced stage of yaws. I am ashamed to say I would have found it hard to talk normally to that mask of eaten flesh, but the others chatted gaily to her, treating her with a respectful normality.

The young girls giggled shyly at us four Europeans, glancing at the men from lowered lashes, their heads tilted slightly sideways. The boys teased them with obvious vulgarity and the golden-skinned face of one, more beautiful and colourful than the others, flushed as she hid her face in her hands. Doctor Meyer was laughing delightedly as we rode back to the Camat's house.

'The boys are teasing them. They say: "Look at those white men, they have giant 'things'." Many of the Bugis believe that myth for some reason, rather as many white men believe the same about Negroes.'

After another traditional, vast and highly spiced meal we thanked the Camat for his hospitality and Christian, urged on by the doctor, asked again whether we could visit the sacred forest the next day. He sat motionless and I had the extraordinary feeling he was examining our souls. I found it hard to stand still. Finally he nodded his head and quite curtly, leaving the room, dismissed us.

'I think it will be all right,' the Jaksa said as we began walking back through the darkness. 'I will accompany you.'

'And the Ama Towa?' Doctor Meyer asked. 'Will we meet him?'

The Jaksa shook his head.' It is unlikely. The Ama Towa does not see many men, but it is for him and his elders to decide.'

The doctor and Christian wanted us to see a part on the east coast called Bira and although it was late when we crossed the river out of Tana Towa again we set off immediately.

We seemed to drive forever – in fact the journey took two and a half hours – but by now stiffness from the ride was setting in and the hard seats and bucking, jolting motion of the jeep, through the night, along tracks that were just rutted cartways of mud or rough stone, made every mile a slow, grinding torture.

We came to a halt finally outside a large house with a tiled porch covering the steps leading up over high stilts and the Jaksa who had come with us quickly had our hosts awake and dressed (although the husband was still yawning as he came to greet us) and the family turfed out of their respective beds in the main room.

By local standards these people must have been extremely well off; there were comfortable chairs and sofas in the room and an air of general prosperity. We relaxed after the drive and children played around us on the floor with smooth shining shells.

Their kindness, considering we had descended on them in the middle of the night without warning, was boundless. Where the family slept, or if in fact they did at all, I never knew. Asrad and the boy went back to the jeep after yet another meal and the doctor, Christian, Robin and I were left to sort ourselves out between a double bed in a half-curtained-off cubicle in the main room, and a second double bed with a small truckle cot beside it.

When we woke, the doctor suggested we should swim and then come back to the house for breakfast before setting off for Tana Towa once more.

'The Bugis are some of the most hospitable people in the world,' he said as we got into the jeep, explaining why, in our short stay, we had been pressed to so many meals. 'It is part of their custom to offer a guest everything in the house. Not to accept gracefully is the height of rudeness. The amount of food they produce for guests indicates their wealth.'

A stony track led towards the sea between a row of houses similar to the one we had slept in. Each was surrounded by a high fence and lay in a sizeable garden, rich with fruit trees and a surprising contrast to the poor, rocky land around, where there was no sign of cultivation on any scale.

'These people,' Christian said, 'have a good life. They live and make their livelihoods from the sea, building their great praus and trading. All their raw materials are here, the wood for their boats is local and there is just enough farming land to produce the food they need. Here, in the south, everyone builds boats.'

The rough path, lined with tall trees, dropped steeply through outcrops of coral rocks, twisting and curving as it dropped and, skidding around one corner, we came to a brake-screeching stop within only a few yards of a family of black apes.

I held my breath in excitement, as this was the nearest I had ever been to large wild animals before. They were an amazing sight; there were about twenty in the family, black hairy creatures with long arms, no tails and surprisingly human faces. They looked far more like eighteenth-century drawings of 'primitive man' than they did animals and one, a large male, who seemed to be boss of the community, stood over four feet tall when he rose from a sitting position. He looked remarkably like someone we knew.

The apes appeared totally unconcerned by our presence, and it was only when Asrad began tooting his horn that the boss gave some kind of signal to the others. They bounded quickly away, on all fours, up into a patch of scrub below some caves in a cliff of white coral. There they sat in a group, chattering and looking down at us with cool curiosity. Already my day was made.

The bay at Bira was a wide curving semi-circle, fringed by white coral sand, with a row of tiny, brightly painted houses shaded by tall coconut palms on the edge of the beach. It formed a perfect setting for the dozen or more towering, solid Bugis praus moored in the water. Great tall ships with curving pointed prows, high squared-off sterns and a massive depth for storing cargo, topped by a windowless cabin on the deck. Two tall masts rose from every boat and each had two large steering rudders at the back shaped like giant paddles.

The sun was coming up straight ahead of us across the water, sending the shadows of the ships slanting out behind them across a sea that, this early, was still a sheet of mirrored silver, so calm that only a few gentle ripples disturbed the images. These were the same ships that had explored the world as far back as the fifteenth century, carrying cargoes of gold, spices and silks. Even in 1973, more Bugis praus, as large and splendid as those in the water, were being built along the shore.

'Under sail, which they are designed for, these are the strongest ships in the world,' Christian told me. 'Once someone tried attaching an engine to one to make it go faster. It was a disaster. As long as they keep to the old pattern, the prau will hold its own in any water and any weather. Add an engine and the juddering of the mechanical motion causes cracks in the wood and, pauf, that is the end of your ship.'

A curving line of shells lay on the sand by the edge of the water and, almost immediately, I found two perfect cowries. It was Easter Sunday and already I had seen no less than twenty wild apes. I also had two cowries too, for luck, and though we all looked further, they appeared to be the only two on the shore.

When we left Bira it seemed as though the whole village had come to see us off. People rushed from their houses to wave, and children ran shouting beside the jeep.

We did not talk much. All of us were wondering whether today we really would be allowed to enter the sacred land of Tana Towa or whether, which seemed more likely, we would like the day before, be fobbed off, spending the day hanging around until it was too late to cross into the 'old country'.

I do not think any of us were too hopeful. The Jaksa was silent and the subject was not mentioned as we drove back along the coast, and then inland towards Katjang on the other side of the isthmus.

Here, in the south, the Bugis have little communication except by boat. The road we drove on was little more than a narrow stone path, and the springs of the jeep hit the ground with ominous moans as we lurched over large rocks and through hollows filled with mud. The only other vehicles we saw that morning were two small motor-bicycles, and a little wooden cart pulled by a small pony.

We drove back to Katjang to drop off the Jaksa's wife and child, and pick up the police sergeant. Inevitably, she offered us food and looked hurt when we refused, too anxious now to get on our way to be meticulously polite, sitting nervously on the edge of our chairs, waiting for something to be said about Tana Towa.

The sergeant appeared on a motor-bicycle and had to be given coffee. We waited with what patience we could muster. At last we were asked to follow him. We still had no idea what was going to happen.

Following the sergeant, we drove up the road inland to a small village about eight miles away and waited again until, half an hour later, five boys on ponies appeared at a gallop and jumped off their mounts. Christian, looking pained, was told that this time he would have to ride as we were going to cover too long a distance for walking. The Jaksa climbed gingerly onto the back of a spirited horse they said was just broken, and sat behind a boy in indigo blue who managed the wild-eyed creature – its eyes rolling and flanks flecked with foam – with extraordinary skill.

Robin heaved me ignominiously onto the back of a small grey creature, but my legs were almost unbearably stiff from the day before, the kapok saddle cloth slipped and I rolled to the ground on the other side. The crowd watching us roared with delight and I swore roundly. A second attempt was more successful. This time I bent my knee and with a 'one, two, three' was lifted off the ground and plonked down on the horse's back, to an accompanying cheer from the spectators.

Gradually, the ponies calmed down and settled into a fast walk as we turned off the track into a narrow path that wound up and down small steep, almost perpendicular, hills under a canopy of branches that met over our heads, forming a cool green tunnel.

We crossed a shallow river forming the boundary of Outer Tana Towa, and came at length to a high arch of bamboo. Through this, we passed into the magic that was Inner Tana Towa, the 'old country', As far as we know, we were the first white people to do so.

Chapter 15

We entered a strange new world with a cool, green light from sun that filtered softly through the leaves of tall trees and the gently moving fronds of arching bamboos. There was a sense of timelessness, of silence and of peace. We had passed into a land where nothing had changed for five hundred years and I knew that this was really magic, that this was surely an enchanted land. The sense of sanctity I had experienced at the sacred stones was intensified and here leavened by this emotion of enchantment. I was no longer a clumsy rider on a bony horse with saddle sores beneath its kapok cover. I was as light as air and he a proud steed with arched neck and flowing mane.

Behind each massive tree, I could imagine a unicorn grazing, pools of molten gold were reflected in the tumbling water of small streams and God and mysticism were everywhere. For this was Easter Sunday and, with every stride of our horses' hooves, we entered deeper into Tana Towa.

The few houses that existed were simpler, plainer versions of the Bugis habitations, almost hidden by large trees. Beside one, a carpenter worked with simple tools on lengths of wood, a muffled regular thudding came from his workshop and outside there was a smell of clean wood and resin. On the steps of another house, indigo sarong pulled down over a breast, a young woman fed an almost sleeping child. She answered our greeting with a wave but without speaking. Beside the houses, high in the tall trees were small platforms with miniature replicas of the structures below, built in the branches. In these, when fruit was ripening, guards would spend the nights frightening away flying foxes and bats that came to steal the fruit.

As we rode, our horses' hooves the only sound around us, Dr Meyer told me what he knew about the Tana Towa and their customs.

For the sake of convenience, the Tana Towa are known to the outside world as a sect of Muslims but this is not truly so. Their religion goes back far into the mists of time, they worship their sacred stones and have a spiritual leader – the Ama Towa, who is virtual king of all his people. Politically, since the seventeenth century, they had come under the jurisdiction of the Rajah of Katjang, and it was from these rajahs that the Camat had been descended. He himself was installed at a ceremony by the sacred stones, he respected and honoured the 'Old Country' and the Ama Towa but he was cognizant with the problem of their future. The Jaksa was his titular heir and had actually been born in Tana Towa, but if for some reason he was deposed, there was always the possibility of a less sympathetic official taking over the post and trouble resulting.

In this world of peace and sanctity, no outside elements of noise or destruction are allowed and time stood still three hundred years ago. No machines of any kind are allowed within the Inner Circle; no torches, radios, motor-bicycles or twentieth-century tools or articles of any kind. Those who live in the Inner Circle seldom venture into the world outside. They are not prevented from doing so but if they do they are not allowed to live in Tana Towa again. A strict pattern of birth control keeps their numbers at an even figure.

Money is seldom used in Tana Towa, there are no shops and nothing to spend it on. On the rare occasions when coins do change hands they are mostly in the form of seventeenth-century Portuguese silver, handed down from generation to generation from the time when the Portuguese first arrived in the area. Their language is not Bugis and neither is their blood. They are said to be Makassarese by origin and speak an ancient form of Makassar dialect called 'Makassar Conjon'. As neither the doctor nor Christian spoke this language, our interpreter on the journey was the Jaksa.

The Ama Towa is chosen by a series of celestial, ritualistic ceremonies with rules so stringent that for fourteen years before the investiture of the present spiritual leader the people of Tana Towa had been without a divine superior.

Often as many as eighteen men pass the original tests which put them into the category of standing as a future Ama Towa. They must be fully versed in all the legends, myths, traditions and complicated rites of their religion and be totally conversant with all the ancient adat of their people. Potential Ama Towa have to be able to foretell the future and be proved correct before they have the right to stand for leadership. When they sleep, the candidates must be seen to levitate some way above their beds at all times. Having passed all those tests, the candidates go through yet another series of trials before the leader is chosen.

A white buffalo is set loose in the forest a week before the ceremony. The candidates are arranged in a circle and the buffalo must walk from the forest straight up to the chosen man. The buffalo is sacrificed, his head laid on a fire and the smoke from that fire should blow distinctly towards that same man. When one of the Tana Towa has passed these two tests, a small mound of rice is put on the ground in front of each aspirant and a chicken released in the centre of the circle must go straight to the future leader and peck from the grains at his feet.

Only when all these requirements are fulfilled is an Ama Towa chosen, a holy man who will lead his people until he dies.

As with the Toraja, the funerals of their dead play an extensive role in Tana Towan religion. Feasts take place at intervals after the death, culminating in a big finale where many buffaloes are slaughtered and much rice is shared amongst the people. Many of their trees are sacred and so too are the krises each man wears at his waist. These, like human beings, have spirits; they have to be treated correctly and consulted and if a kris is misused it will fly away and kill of its own accord.

The people of Tana Towa are not totally a peaceful sect. If necessary, they are prepared to fight for their freedom. During the rebel troubles, a band of well-armed bandits came and violated the country, stealing chickens and buffalo. Out of roughly a thousand Tana Towa, over two hundred attacked back with bamboo spears, successfully recapturing their animals and sending the outsiders running for their lives.

On the whole, their own lives are quiet and a great excitement comes on feast days when ritual dances play a major role. Their dancing is studied with complicated and often exciting music played on flutes, gongs with great beating of a drum. The women, on occasions, danced with the men with formal, studied steps, but it was really the men who excelled, whirling with complicated movements to the stirring music of an ancient war dance.

All this the doctor told me about as we rode through that strangely silent land, up and down hills, across streams of silvered water tumbling over smooth stones, through the pale green-tinged sunlight that filtered coolly through the trees and towards the heart of Tana Towa, climbing always higher until we reached a large wood of vaulted bamboos.

They say that bamboos grow so fast in the tropics, one can almost watch them growing. These were colossal, tall, spraying fountain heads, making graceful patterns of dark green and faded yellow stems topped by ever-moving, slender-pointed leaves. It began to rain heavily with one of those storms that came from nowhere and departed as suddenly, so we sheltered under one of these great arches and although the rain fell in heavy sheets, there, under the canopy of leaves and curving poles, we remained relatively dry.

The Jaksa, his companion and Robin, who had gone ahead, were waiting for us by a small clearing, their horses tied under a slender construction of bamboo. It was a relief to dismount and use one's legs again to climb a narrow ladder up into a single spacious room running the length of the building. Here, about ten feet above the ground, there was a gentle breeze coming through the open sides between three-foot-high walls of wood and a vaulted ceiling.

The room was empty except for two women, sitting on the floor of split bamboo beside baskets of pale yellow langsams and green vegetables. One was young, the other ageless, both had unlined faces, gentle smiles and sarongs wound up around their waists to show firm brown legs and bare feet. They had been sheltering from the rain and, now it was over, picked up their baskets and moved away, leaving us alone in the simple building with the only furnishings a few rolls of rattan matting, one beautifully patterned in pink and black and the others plain, stacked on a narrow, slightly raised platform at the end of the room. The Jaksa unrolled the plain mats and laid them on the floor for us to sit on.

There was an air of expectancy and anticipation. We talked in whispers and outside the only sound was of the wind rustling the leaves of bamboo and the occasional burst of song from a hidden bird. From below, a slight haze of steam came from the horses who sometimes snorted gently or pawed the soft ground, also waiting but for what we were not sure.

The Jaksa, noticing the doctor's bare legs, motioned to him to put on his sarong.

'Do you believe we will see the Ama Towa?' the doctor asked, and the Jaksa shrugged. He did not know. This was the rest house for guests coming to the Inner Circle to see the leader of the Tana Towa and sometimes they remained here for days or weeks without seeing him. It was his decision. Many came but few were privileged. Not so long ago, an important General with widespread powers had come to seek advice from the Ama Towa. He had waited for three weeks and had to leave without having had an audience.

I do not know how long or how short a time it was we waited before two Tana Towans – elderly, dignified men – came up the ladder and crossed the room to sit opposite us. The elder of them sat beside the central pillar of the house, his white hair covered by a flattened turban which fell into a peak over the side of a wise, deeply lined face. His eyes were large and round, his cheeks high and slightly distended from chewing betel and he had the unusual feature of a moustache as silver white as his hair. Faint cataracts glazed his eyes, yet, even through the haze, they had that same sharp, intelligent light peculiar to all the sect. The other man, similarly dressed, sat behind and a little to one side of him. We shook hands gravely with them both and went on waiting.

'The old man,' the Jaksa whispered, 'is the master of the dance, an important man and even older than he appears.'

Did people here live a lifespan of a century or more? I wondered. Nothing seemed impossible or improbable. Miming a request to photograph him and receiving a slight nod of acquiescence, I clicked the shutter. His large, deep-set eyes avoided the lens as he leant back with his weight on one arm and his legs crossed one knee above the other.

A fanfare could have heralded the arrival of the Ama Towa, his entrance was so impressive. He appeared in silence and we still did not know he was coming until he mounted the steps and swept smoothly into the room, followed by an entourage of ten men all dressed in indigo blue, with krises by their sides and turbans on their heads. With the Ama Towa slightly in the lead, the party came towards us; they seemed to float silently across the bamboo slatted floor in a dignified, graceful procession. We rose, half crouching, to greet them. The Jaksa unrolled the coloured, woven mat in the corner against the sleeping platform. The dance leader and the man with him bowed their heads low as did the Jaksa and the sergeant and we did the same as the Ama Towa sank, in a movement of total fluidity, into a cross-legged position on the floor. The hand he offered us was neatly narrow, pale, cool and smooth with a touch that was almost that of a woman.

The Ama Towa sat alone and every movement he made was one of grace as he leant back against the corner with one slim arm extended along the top of the wooden wall. His cortège sat cross-legged behind us in a semi-circle, a group of mainly elderly men with the small, sharp, curiously unlined faces of hill people.

It was his eyes that I remember most about this strange man sitting so tranquilly in the midst of his kingdom. The irises were totally, unbelievably, black with a curious light that seemed to come from behind, giving them a piercing, almost supernatural beam. They were impossible to meet. In a way, those eyes were calmly detached, yet if he looked towards us I noticed that we all, with one accord, lowered our own to the floor.

If the land of Tana Towa was magic, so even more was its leader. Does it sound fanciful to say that the Ama Towa seemed to me like a magician, another Merlin? His dark blue turban, the colour of the dark night-sky, was tied into a complicated oriental format, rising high from his forehead and culminating in two sharp twisted points; curious small ears with no lobes slanted back and ended close to his head; a small, pointed beard, a narrow fringe of hair above his lips and straight, thick eyebrows gave his face a symmetrical facet, and although he was a small man, every feature was so perfectly formed, his every movement gave him stature. He sat against the bare boards as though in the luxurious comfort of a cushioned throne in an attitude of total relaxation.

Still no-one talked as large dishes of oval ripe langsans were placed on the floor and the Ama Towa waved a hand giving permission to eat. A silver ring with a flat white stone gleamed from one finger and a narrow wrist was encompassed by a thin, twisted bracelet of shining black seaweed. His shirt was silk, almost as black as his eyes, with a high, mandarin collar and small silver buttons. Around his shoulders, material hung like a cloak, similar in colour to the sarong which fell in flowing folds from his waist. The other men were all similarly dressed though their turbans were not tied in points so high as that of the Ama Towa and an occasional bleached shirt relieved the sombre darkness of their costume.

One by one, the men brought silver betel containers from the folds of their sarongs, glowing dully with age and much use, and intently pounded the nuts and made up the little packages. The Ama Towa too had his own equipment, a curiously carved wooden pipe and a small silver knife that he used with ritualistic gestures, producing a tightly packed small wad of betel which he kept high under a cheekbone as he began to talk.

His voice was the most extraordinary thing of all about him. I have never heard a voice in any way like that before. The tones were high and fluting like the piping, reedy notes of a bird. Quietly measured, yet penetrating and with a clear ringing quality. It was the unbroken voice of a boy or the sound of a eunuch, yet again it was powerful and totally compelling. He spoke in Makassar Conjon and the tones vibrated in the air. This man, I thought, knows everything that is good or evil in the world, and yet he has never been outside the small world of Tana Towa and he speaks only a forgotten language.

The Jaksa translated to Bugis, and Christian into Bahasa Indonesian. The doctor, Robin and I were silent, awed and marvelling. Something here was like nothing else on earth that I had ever experienced before. The nearest I can come to describing the feeling is to say it was what I imagined a truly religious experience to be like. I remembered that it was Easter Sunday.

'The Ama Towa asks why you are here,' the Jaksa whispered. 'Do you come from your governments, have your people sent you to see him or do you come of your own accord?'

'We come of our own accord.'

'Where do you come from and why do you travel to see him?'

'We come from three lands, countries far away. We come to learn from your wisdom, to seek guidance on how it can be that here in Tana Towa you have no violence or discontent.' The Ama Towa inclined his head with a slight movement; he had heard of Germany and England but not of France. Was France, he asked, part of Holland? Robin now leant forward eagerly:

'How is it,' he asked, 'that in your country the people still respect your adat and your customs?' Dark eyebrows raised and black eyes turned to study him.

196

'It is above all things necessary that adat be truly followed in all things. Without adat, there is no Father and no Mother, for adat is both those. Without adat there is no country.' He considered for a moment and then asked Robin:

'Is this not so in your country? Do you not have an adat the people respect and a king they follow?'

'In our country, the adat has been destroyed. Young people have forgotten it and do not wish to remember.'

'But have you no elders they respect?'

'Yes, we have elders but the young no longer respect them. How, Ama Towa, does a country regain its adat?'

'Your government and your king should enforce it. They should encourage adat at all times for that is the life of the people.'

'And if the young will not listen?'

'Then they should be punished or sent away.' He knew he was right; the words in those unearthly bird-like tones rang sharply into the listening silence and his own elders nodded their agreement. He turned to the doctor, bowed and said he had heard of the doctor's fame and good works.

'You are a good man and your adat is strong,' the Jaksa translated.

'Is it true that the Americans have sent men to the moon?' he asked, and when we nodded, he said, 'For what purpose do they send men to the light in the sky? For what reasons do they go there? Is it for good or for evil causes?' It was a difficult question, and all three European men looked dazed as they tried to evaluate what exactly was the answer to this.

He went as suddenly and as silently as he had come. Food, he said, had been prepared for us in one of his houses and we were welcome. Then he waved a slender, pale mahogany-coloured hand and, with those extraordinary floating movements that within fleeting seconds took him out of the room, disappeared. The elders followed and we watched in total silence again as they walked away through the bamboos and the thin shafts of golden green light – thirteen dark, shadowy and transient figures.

We sat for some time unmoving, unable at that moment to even discuss or talk of what we had experienced. Gradually normality came back as we let out breath in sharp gasps and the full impact of our audience with the Ama Towa began to sink in. Limply, stunned, we looked at each other, four people who had shared something miraculous, an experience that none of us would forget.

We mounted our horses again and rode deeper into Tana Towa, up a wide sweep of stone cobbled track and into a village, the Jaksa leading the way. At the last house, we stopped, turned in through a wooden fence and tied up our horses. At the top of the steps of the house, two women stood waiting. Ceremonially, the eldest one welcomed us and led us into a cool, well-shaded room that was bare of furniture. Mats were unrolled on the floor and small, hard pillows set against the wall for us to lean on. The mats were of such finely woven rattan that they felt smooth to the touch, with a silken sheen, and despite acute saddle sores and sitting still for so long in the bamboo house without moving, it was easy to lounge against the pillows in complete relaxation. Mats were laid across the floor and the women busied themselves putting round trays of beaten pewter in front of us and cooking over a red-embered fire, built at about waist level on a stone fireplace near the door.

We drank pale, aromatic tea and ate cooked banana flowers and langsans that were fuller and sweeter than any we had tasted before. The Jaksa said again and again how strange it was that the Ama Towa should have granted us an audience. No-one knew or seemed to know why he had agreed to see us, and eventually we agreed that it must have been the doctor's presence, for Christian, after all, had tried before without success.

The day had been long, I kept forgetting to look at my watch and we would all, I think, have been happy to remain where we were for some time. But, as evening had come and darkness was falling swiftly, we reluctantly and stiffly rose to our feet.

We had one more place to see in Tana Towa. This time we

rode into the edge of the sacred forest itself, where every tree has a spirit. Great, massive branches radiated high above us, forming a canopy of dark foliage and here, after a precipitous ride up and down almost perpendicular, moss-covered paths, we came to the 'original house'; the first house on earth that was sent down from above for man to live in and the building used as a pattern for all the houses in Tana Towa. Inside it, a very old man and his equally old wife who still had those strange, unlined features despite having shrunk through old age, asked us to sit and brought more baskets of langsans for us to eat.

The one-roomed house was extremely large. Unfortunately, it was almost dark and the only feature I could really make out was the enormous central pillar which they said had been made from a chilli tree, the only one ever used because, after that had been cut down, the chilli plant ceased to grow higher than a bush of a few feet. The wood was almost black and hard as steel with a strange, cold feel to it. The rest of the house, they said, had been repaired and rebuilt in places over the centuries, only this central navel remaining completely untouched. I ran my hand down its side and could feel no marks of an axe or knife; the wood was smooth and perfectly rounded.

It was totally dark when we left the 'original house' and the sacred forest where a single night bird called out softly again and again. With the tread of our horses' hoofbeats muffled on grassy stones, we followed the road away from the heart of Tana Towa, passing under the bamboo arch and to the outer circle. As we left the sacred Inner Circle, a long roll of thunder crashed through the sky and streaks of forked lightning broke up the sky with forked tongues of silver outlined in blue. After the third crash, the heavens opened and released torrential curtains of heavy black rain as we rode hour after hour through almost total darkness out of the 'old country'.

It took two days to get back to Makassar. About halfway, in a town called Bone, we stopped to eat and to see the remnants of a former rajah's palace now inhabited by Bupati officials. Once more, we had to check with the authorities. Men in sombre uniforms sat in rooms painted gold and white, split by flimsy partitions. After waving the Governor's letter around in an authoritative manner, we were taken to see the remains of the rajah's treasures. It took a long time to find the key of the room they were kept in and when they found it the smell of mildew in the room was almost overpowering. Faded silks of one-time finery were now embroidered by the tracks of moths; a ceremonial umbrella in dusty pink and gold had a sad, forlorn air of bygone days; a skull cap threaded with human hair and a basket holding the shrivelled remnants of the first rajah's umbilical cord were positively sinister. By far the best pieces in the collection were two gold krises and a heavy gold chain which alone could be untouched by time or decay.

We had a good Chinese lunch in Bone and, while we had it, Asrad asked for permission to go off with the boy to the other end of the town. The doctor grinned delightedly and said a few lewd things in Indonesian. Apparently, they both had girlfriends here in the town and they hoped to spend their lunch-hour doing something more energetic than eating.

'We take it in turns,' Asrad said, showing all his teeth in a broad smile. 'One guards the jeep, the other has fun.'

The doctor pointed to a village set back off the main road soon after we got going again.

'That is a leper colony,' he told us. 'All the people who live here are lepers. They go out only on horses and they marry amongst themselves.' They were very rich, he said, they farmed well, had big houses and kept their money within family groups. If they would only send the children out, they could be cured, but they preferred to keep within the colony and the disease spread to every child born.

In the fields, lepers were ploughing behind oxen, bending over the rice with the reflections of their coloured sarongs spreading across the water and riding horses behind plump cattle with shining golden hides. From a distance, they looked strong, healthy people; close to, the ravages of the disease were of nightmare proportions.

Again, the doctor made a fascinating companion, telling us the names of trees and flowers; rattling out stories about the countryside and the people who lived in it.

When we neared the high central mountains, Asrad began having considerable trouble with the brakes, so we stopped by a row of transport cafés beyond a long suspension bridge spanning a wide river. After ordering coffee at the least filthy of the wooden shacks, we wandered down to the river and stood in a row along the bridge staring down into whirling water heavy with sediment. Inevitably, the doctor said:

'There is a story about this river. Many crocodiles live here and once one of them ate a child playing on the bank. The people were terrified and called a strong medicine man to their aid. He walked down the river a little way and then called all the crocodiles of the river onto a grass field beside it. "You are bad crocodiles," he berated them. "It is wrong to eat people. Now own up, who did it?" The one who had eaten the child owned up and the medicine man killed him on the spot. "That," he said to the others, "is what happens if you eat people again." From then on, the children by this river have been able to swim in the water without fear, none of them are ever hurt.

'Some Sulawesi people talk crocodile language. In this river, the people say, there is a crocodile so large it can lie with its head on one bank and its tail touching the other. Before they built the bridge and a ferry had to be used, those people who talked with a crocodile tongue could call to this huge beast and walk across the water on his back to reach the other bank.'

Later we sat on packing cases in an open side room built on an unlevel dirt floor. Along one wall, a double bed took pride of place, made up with sheets of a pristine whiteness.

Over nauseating coffee that was full of bitter grounds and only lukewarm, the doctor told us more of the crocodile legends of Sulawesi, while Asrad still tried to mend the brakes of the mud-spattered jeep.

Crocodiles, he said, were considered important and often sacred animals. Once there was a woman who had given birth to twins, a human child and a baby crocodile. People had come from far and wide to see her, bringing gifts of money and food so that she grew immeasurably rich. The doctor had come across cases where his patients had tried to repeat this miracle.

'I had a maternity case once. The woman who came to see me was so vast I thought maybe she was going to have quins. Then I examined her and found this was not the case – she was merely horrifically constipated and blown up by a barrage balloon of wind. I discovered the cause; she had stuck a crocodile's egg up her arse, hoping it would hatch at the same time as her baby and that she, like the other woman, would grow rich. The egg, by the way,' he added, 'had gone rotten and it was a nasty business altogether.' We listened entranced, like children hearing a bedtime story.

Asrad appeared to be having no luck with the brakes. With a snort of annoyance, he wiped oily hands on his trousers and poured water into the brake cylinders.

'You can't do that,' Robin shouted, racing across the road to stop him, but Asrad had other ideas.

'No brake fluid here so we use water,' he said calmly. It did not mean a thing to me but the three men looked horrified and Robin distinctly nervous.

'How high did you say these mountains are?' he asked the doctor.

Going up was all right but the drive down the other side to a high plain was a nightmare. The water had not worked. There was a strong smell of burning and as we started the steep descent, it was all too obvious we had not a brake to our name. Precipices lay on all sides with sheer drops of hundreds and hundreds of feet and the road ran between in a thin tarmac line of hairpin bends. Luckily, there was only one other vehicle in our path; that one nearly killed us. It was a small red truck, wheezing along on one cylinder, making a noise that totally drowned out our horn and being driven firmly and relentlessly in the middle of the road; we were going too fast for Asrad to change gear. Just as we were on the point of ramming the truck right up its backside, Asrad decided to try and pass it regardless. For a moment, one back wheel turned in thin air, the jeep lurched and rocked sideways over the abyss, righted itself and somehow squeezed past the truck back onto the road again. For a quarter of a mile, we went faster and faster, with the tyres squealing and what springs there were desperately trying to catch up with themselves as one sickening curve followed another. The luggage in the back shot from one side to the other and, for once, the boy's eternal sleep was interrupted. The only thing that brought us to a halt was a heaven-sent rise in the road. If that had not been there . . . pouff, as Christian would say, it would have been the end of us all.

From there on, we crawled down hills in second gear with the red truck now hard on our tail and tooting angrily to make us get out of the way or go faster. On the flat or going uphill, we had far more power than him but going downhill was a tortuous process. Each time he hooted, Asrad put his tongue out and waved a hand languidly out of the window, grinning cheekily.

If it had not been for the brake situation, the drive down the other side of the mountains, on the Makassar side beyond the high fertile plain, would have been a rewarding one. As it was, the grandeur and beauty of the mountains we drove through could not help but impress, whatever the circumstances. Jagged gorges of black and white coral rock had been eroded and weathered into the shapes of magnificent pinnacles and crenellations until they resembled a painted backcloth to a romantic German opera. What looked like the ruins of fairy castles and medieval fortresses were festooned with luxuriant lianas. Pockets of jungle rampaged through the narrow valleys beside spectacular waterfalls, Flame of the Forest trees glowed scarlet against the greenery, hornbills flew lazily along the cliffs and occasionally we caught a glimpse of large black apes sitting on the rocks.

One of the reasons we had raced back to Makassar was because we had a plane to catch for the Moluccas early the next morning. We needn't have bothered. The flight, for no apparent reason, had been cancelled and we spent another desultory day in Makassar, though we did stir ourselves enough to drive a short way out of the town and visit the grave of Sheik Joseph. I never discovered who he was, but his resting place was worth seeing and a popular pilgrimage.

A short, tiled passageway leading to a miniature mosque was lined with cripples of every description, standing, lying or squatting against the walls with their hands outstretched. Some men had no legs, others were dwarfs or hunchbacks, one or two had open, suppurating sores and a few were blind. They were silent, their eyes beseeching and their hands shaking with helpless expectancy; we passed slowly along the row, handing out small handfuls of coins and receiving looks of pathetic gratitude.

Inside, it was dark and cool. The Sheik's grave was protected by an iron balustrade and guarded at each end by two squatting men, their sarongs wrapped tightly around them. In the centre of the grave stood a fine Chinese vase of pale blue, exquisite in shape and design and, like the rest of the grave, festooned with flowers and petals. The smell of scented blossoms lay heavy in the air and at each end a phallic shape in bronze shone dully, touched by thousands upon thousands of women's hands. Legend has it that if you touch and massage these figures with hands soaked in oil your reward will be instant fertility, and barren women will come from all over the island to try their luck. (Apparently, the Sheik was a very prolific gentleman sexually.) One or two were there now, kneeling on the floor, rubbing the figures with little moaning cries and almost frenzied concentration. I was careful not to go anywhere near them.

In the afternoon, we called on the orchid grower, Carl Bundt, to report on the success of our journey and to get advice on Ceram, an island to the west of the Moluccas, where he had been brought up and which was, in theory, to be our next destination.

He was depressing about our chances of getting there. There

was no regular transport to the island, he said, and on no account should we risk our lives trying to cross on one of the Chinese tramp steamers which trade through the islands.

'Ten or twenty of those boats sink without trace every year. Always they are overloaded and, as life is cheap, no-one bothers to enquire what happened.' Until late that night Robin and Christian talked anthropology over almost untouched glasses of beer in the dismal bar of the hotel. The doctor and I swilled down vodkas and tonic and talked of simpler things – tales of bechak drivers, striptease dancers and the women you can buy in Java.

'A man has to be careful there if he is alone, staying at a hotel. Late at night there is a loud knock at the door. The proprietor stands there smiling at you and offering a string of beautiful girls for massage and relaxation and all on the house because you are an honoured guest under his roof. Of course, you accept, but before you have time to get any benefit of this generous offer there is another knock on the door. You open it and this time there stands the chief of police. "How dare you treat Indonesian women like this!" he says, "you are violating everything we hold sacred." Well, of course, you can't afford to have trouble and, in the end, you beg him to accept the most enormous bribe to prevent the shame and disgrace of your actions being made public.'

As always, I was entranced and we said goodbye with great sadness.

'Don't write to me,' he said, 'because I never answer letters. But perhaps we will meet sometime again.' I hoped so very much.

Chapter 16

Our adventures in southern Sulawesi had left me exhausted, battered, and so stiff that every movement was extremely painful. On the day we flew to the Moluccas I awoke in a miserably depressed state of mind, overwhelmed by home-sickness and a longing to be back at Maidenwell with my own things around me. We had been travelling non-stop for two months, our clothes were ingrained with greyish dirt that washing made little difference to, mosquito bites marked my flesh like pock marks and I was still miserably stiff from our ride to Tana Towa.

Our destination, Ambon, is the capital of the large group of islands called the Moluccas. The island of Ambon itself is a small one, situated off the south-western tip of Ceram and, as we flew towards it, I found it hard to believe there could possibly be an airstrip here; mountains seemed to come right to the edge of the water and there did not seem to be a flat area in sight. As it was, the airport was a long way from the city, on the main body of the island, opposite a second smaller peninsula on which the city is built. The strip joining these two almost parallel fingers of land is so narrow they are connected by a mere mile-wide strip of sandy soil making a long sheltered harbour for the island. We saw little of Ambon except the town and the immediate surroundings, but I found it an attractive place and the people colourful, with the women all wearing a traditional costume derived from the mother hubbards forced on them when missionaries first landed there; neat sarongs of pink and white checks with cotton over-blouses that fall long and loose, from rounded shoulders, like full maternity shirts. On Sundays they all wear black with a wide crossed sash of bright emerald green over their shoulders.

We were travelling east and the people here were considerably darker than those we had seen on other islands, although their features were similar to the Makassarans and their hair was still thickly straight and heavy.

The airport building was little more than a rough shack and, while we waited for our luggage, we looked with horror at large numbers of parakeets, parrots and cockatoos crammed in miserably small cages, hardly high enough for them to stand upright in. The traffic in birds in this part of the world is a profitable one and someone must have been doing a roaring trade. In one box alone, no larger than a bottle crate, we counted over fifty birds, chattering in terror, with two or three lying dead in the thick layer of droppings around them. They stood, unsheltered, in the burning sun without water or food. Most pathetic of all were the fine cockatoos, their bright colours dull and their wings matted with filth. If ever I saw a case for the RSPCA, this was it. The sight was sickening.

Once again, we had little idea what lay before us. We had Carl's introduction to the Catholic priest, Father Rutges, and we had heard of an Italian anthropologist working in the interior of Ceram. Ceram was where we were aiming to go, though how we would get there remained to be seen.

We stayed at a central Hotel, once a pillar of Dutch society but now run down, shabby, but expensive. From there, we managed to contact Father Rutges and practically the first words the old priest said when he arrived an hour early were 'Why are you staying in this terrible place? You should have come straight to me from the airport and I could have advised you where to go.'

The Father looked about seventy with silver-white hair, a round bespectacled face and a hearty energetic manner. He talked very fast in broken English heavy with a Dutch accent.

'Well,' he said, 'you are here. I heard about you from the mission.' (Robin had written to the Catholics in Ambon from England.) 'But we never expected you to come; your programme was so ambitious. Still, you are here, so welcome to Ambon. You have come to the right person. I know everyone in Ambon and everyone knows Father Rutges. They all come to me and I do my best to help everyone, in between doing my own duties and going my rounds to help the people of Ambon. Now I will help you too. Without me you could do nothing.'

He was delighted with the bottle of whisky we produced for him. Politely, Robin brought the conversation round to the Italian anthropologist, Valerio Valeri, a friend of Christian Pelras, who was reported to be working in Ceram.

'Is there any hope of getting to Ceram to see him?' he asked.

'Ah, Valerio. Of course, I know him well. When he and his wife first came to Ceram I was the one who helped them. Without me they would never have got to Ceram at all. They stayed in my house. They had no money. I fed them and fixed for their papers, which was not easy, not easy at all. Now Valerio is working far in the interior of Ceram with a tribe of headhunters. It is very difficult to get there, boats go seldom to the island and he is a long walk inland. It is very dangerous and there are no roads in Ceram you must understand.' He paused and then, just when our spirits were sinking, went on again at a rattling pace:

'However, you are lucky. Father Rutges will fix everything for you. Valerio's wife, a Swedish girl, is here in Ambon at the moment. I think she leaves tomorrow. If we go to her perhaps you will be able to go to Ceram with her. She came for a new police permit and to do some shopping. Of course, I am helping her as I help everyone who comes to Ambon.'

On that first occasion of meeting the Father I was a little suspicious of this permanent insistence that he was all things to all men. It did not take long to discover it was true. It was

A wooden carving outside a Toraja grave

A Toraja village on Sulawesi

Toraja children play their bamboo pipes high in the mountains of Sulawesi

A reception committee watches the *Honi Moki* dock at Sawai

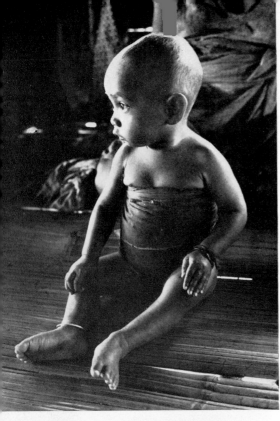

A Hua Ulu baby has its stomach wrapped in bark to help ease a stomach pain

The Hua Ulu boy who accompanied Robin and Marika into the mountains of Ceram. The bamboo band around his forehead shows that he is unmarried

to him that the Valeris owed the entire success of their two-year stay in the Moluccas. He did indeed know everyone in Ambon and the town and its environ were his whole life.

He was a man of action as well as words.

'We will go and find Renée, Valerio's wife. She is staying at a small family hotel much better than here.'

He bounded out of his chair, donned an ancient black jacket, opened a large black umbrella and led us through pouring rain to a bechak stand about a hundred yards away. While we drove through a stream of water in a wooden bechak, decorated with a primitive painting of a fierce-looking tiger on the back, the elderly priest bicycled beside us, one hand on the handlebars and the other holding up the umbrella.

At first, when we met Renée, the anthropologist's wife was reserved and unforthcoming, eyeing us with a suspicion that bordered on hostility, not surprising as we had burst in on her unannounced and Father Rutges subjected her to a barrage of rather hazy comments about us. Then he left, saying he had to go and see to his duties, but we were all three to call on him at nine the next morning and he would lend us his car and 'do everything' for us. After Robin explained why we were there, what we had done in Indonesia so far and what we hoped to do for the rest of our time in the country, she relaxed and it was not long before Robin found they shared many of the same ideas and interests.

Renée Valeri was a student of ethnology. She had a grant to work in Indonesia and study the practices of the tribe she and her husband were living with, the Hua Ulu. This was the first time in eighteen months that she had left Ceram and it was almost a miracle that our arrival happened to coincide with her being there. She was planning to leave on a Chinese tramp steamer due to sail for Ceram the next day.

I remembered Carl Bundt's comments on Chinese tramp ships and his warnings to avoid them at all costs, but Robin was carried away with excitement.

'Will we be able to come too?' he asked. 'It's so fantastic to find you here and if we all travel together we could come with you into the interior. I think we would somehow have made our way there by ourselves, but this is a really heaven-sent opportunity.'

'You will have to get permits,' Renée answered, 'but I also have to go to the police tomorrow morning and the boats never object to extra passengers. The problem is finding out when they plan to leave; they don't run on schedule and they often go when they please. It's so long since I saw any other Europeans that I'd be only too glad of the company, but I must warn you it isn't a very comfortable trip: getting to the mountains to the Hua Ulu isn't like the sort of walk you'd take at home.'

At nine sharp the next morning, we arrived at the Father's house. He was sitting in a plastic garden chair by a small table inside the door.

'Read this,' he said. 'This is the story of my life. I want to get it published and I sent it to the *Reader's Digest*, but they said it was not of interest. You, who are my friends, will surely find it interesting.' It was a moving story.

Father Rutges had been in the Moluccas for something like forty years, most of the time in Ambon. When the Japanese invaded the islands eleven other priests, including the Bishop of that time, had been shot on the spot. Father Rutges had been visiting another island and escaped death, but was interned in a Japanese prisoner-of-war camp. The degradations he underwent, the horrors he saw, the starvation, the privations, the pain and the torture he endured were unbelievable, and it is amazing he survived them. At the end of the war he was released, a pitiful wreck that had once been a priest.

He was sent back to Holland to recover and there discovered that he had lost all his faith and belief in religion. He was like a thing of wood with no feeling and no piety left. For a time, he lived in a desperate limbo until one day, when a child of his brother's was to receive her first sacrament. A visiting Bishop had been going to perform the confirmation celebration, but, for some reason, he was unable to attend and

Father Rutges was asked to do it instead. At first, he refused, then, when he saw the child was almost overcome with misery, he agreed to hold the service. He felt nothing whilst he performed it, no glimmer of piousness or sanctity. Then the child came to take the sacrament and as he held the cup to her lips a tear formed in her eye and rolled down her face like, he said, a single silvered pearl. Something inside him broke, he rushed from the church and for the first time tears began to roll down his own cheeks. For three days he shut himself in his room, sobbing as though he would cry himself to death. It was a catharsis; he felt he had witnessed a miracle in that small child's tear and that he had been reborn. Before long he returned to the Moluccas to continue his work there.

Late that afternoon the Father took us to meet the Bishop of the Moluccas, an erudite Dutchman with a large collection of old books on the history of the islands, and a fund of fascinating stories about the area. He also had a fine collection of Chinese and Dutch ceramics.

'The Chinese have traded with the Moluccas for centuries,' he said, showing us some elegant, almost transparent, plates. 'They were bringing Ming and Tang pottery here at the time when it was being made and it's amazing how many pieces there are, used as everyday household equipment by the poorest of families. Still, you can pick it up for almost nothing, but now the government have got wise to the trafficking that was beginning to go on through the islands and they have prohibited any antiques going out of the country. In fact,' he smiled in a delightfully naughty way that I felt was very unlike a Bishop, 'a man who helps us with the mission was caught trying to smuggle some out not long ago and had to spend two months in prison before the Customs officer settled for half the loot and no questions asked.'

Most of the day had been spent trying to get police, government and military permits to enter Ceram. It was a nerve-wracking performance and we spent hours in office waiting rooms, answering question after question or filling up forms. Often such permits take a month or two to go through all the channels. Ours by some miracle (and Father Rutges) were ready that evening but at the dock we found the tramp steamer had been delayed for twenty-four hours.

Walking down the main street of Ambon with Renée next afternoon we came face to face with one of the most extra-ordinary animals I have ever seen. Wandering around in a rather aimless fashion, pecking at a pile of cement, poking its nose into a shop doorway and apparently ignored by anyone but us. It was the most enormous bird, about the size and the shape of a fully grown ostrich, with its head towering high above mine. The feathers on its back were a rather dull shade of blackish brown and more like coarse horse-hair than feathers, but what was most extraordinary about this creature was its neck and head. It was crowned by a sort of helmet of almost armoured horniness and the long skinny neck was coloured with the most startling combination of bright red and blue. The whole effect was so strange that, at first, both Robin and I thought someone must have painted the skin, but we found out it really was natural. This was the cassowary, a bird with no wings, a kick that can break a man's leg, and meat highly prized for its flavour; a most curious creature.

In a crowded market where walkways were ankle-deep piles of black slime, we went to the docks to see our boat and find out what time it was finally sailing. I had naïvely imagined that nothing could have been worse than the boat we sailed on to Siberut in the early stages of our journey, but the *Honi Moki* (well, that's what it looked like: most of the letters had been rubbed off) was an unpleasant revelation. It was tied up on the far side of four other boats which we had to cross to reach it. Each one was smaller than the last and the *Honi Moki*, when we finally reached it, was horrifyingly small and only riding about four feet above the surface of the water.

The hold was already piled with a mountain of luggage, and a crowd of men, women and children sat, lay or squatted on top of or beside rolls of bedding, baskets, wooden crates and tin containers of food. More goods were being loaded all the time, and with each addition the little craft seemed to sink still further into the sea. The very sight made me feel green.

We had naïvely suggested getting a taxi to take our luggage to the docks. In Ambon, it seemed, there were no taxis, only bechaks, and, again, the good Father came to our rescue, ringing up the Catholic mission to ask if one of the priests there would drive us to the boat. They said they would.

Robin went on ahead with the luggage while Renée and I walked back to the main street to buy some bread, beer and chocolate for the journey. If we were lucky, she said, they might give us some tea on board but that would be all. It took some time to find a shop open that sold bread and when we got to the harbour Robin came to meet us on the dock, his face a caricature of mixed amusement and dismay.

'I'm afraid you're in for rather a shock,' he said, and told us that the boat appeared to be even more crowded than before.

The docks were badly lit, though well guarded at the entrance by soldiers, armed to the teeth with sten guns held in front of them, who examined our papers each time we passed. On the gangplanks spanning the water between the three boats we had to cross to get to the *Honi Moki*, black shapes scuttled to and fro, their shadows grotesquely distorted by the pale lights coming from swinging lanterns hanging on the boats. I nearly slipped into the filthy water below when I realized they were cockroaches, mammoth ones and in such vast numbers one or two would scrunch under one's feet with every step. Whether they, too, were boarding the boat or whether they were leaving a sinking ship, I could not determine.

If ever I saw a boat more likely to sink it was that one. Baggage was now piled up to the roof over the hold with astonishing numbers of people sitting and lying on top or around it. At that moment I would have been happy to remove our baggage and scrap the whole trip.

'We'll have to make the best of it,' Robin said gaily. 'I've got us the only two bunks on the boat, in the wheelhouse, and they say they are now going to leave at ten.'

It occurred to me that if we really were to spend a night on that boat the only way to make it bearable would be to take a handful of librium and get pleasantly, paralytically drunk and, having seen an open café just outside the dock gates, I had an intuition where we could do just that. We had an hour to spare before ten o'clock when the boat was now due to leave.

In a Muslim country it's often difficult to find any alcohol, but my intuition had been foolproof (I have a sort of unerring instinct where food and drink are concerned). The small café, surprisingly clean and as usual run by a Chinaman, served coffee, jam sandwiches and, unbelievably, there were rows of exciting-looking bottles lined up in a glass-fronted cupboard. One of them contained brandy of a kind. The Chinaman poured us out three huge slugs of amber liquid into tumblers and brought us cups of delicious coffee. The brandy smelt strongly of vanilla and tasted of fire, but it went down incredibly painlessly and obviously had a kick like a mule because within seconds the cloud of depression we had been under lifted and things suddenly did not seem too bad at all. After a second glassful the world looked quite rosy, even Renée began to have some colour in her cheeks and when one of the *Honi Moki*'s crew came to tell us we need not hurry back because sailing time had now been put back two hours, we merely shrugged with Eastern resignation.

Back on the *Honi Moki* things improved as well. The bare wood of the bunks in the eight-by-five-foot wheelhouse had been laid with two unsavoury-looking inch-thick mattresses and one of the crew was busy covering these with two pieces of coloured cotton material, and he had even managed to dig up two miniature cushions from somewhere. It was impossible for four of us to squeeze, standing up, into the wheelhouse together so we left him to it and climbed onto the roof where a few men lay stretched out on the deck with their sarongs wrapped around them.

It was pleasantly cool up there and the town and harbour looked attractive with lights twinkling and a clear starlit sky reflected in the water. Far away, on the horizon, a yellow moon was rising slowly from the water.

While we waited for the *Honi Moki* to sail Renée told us about their life with the Hua Ulu.

'When we reached Ambon we had no idea where Valerio was going to work for his thesis. Like you, we found it impossible to find out anything about the tribes in this part of the world in France, where he was at a university studying anthropology.We travelled round the islands with the Catholic mission boat and then left it on the south coast of Seram where the Nua Ulu live. They were difficult people, living mainly along the coast and slightly degenerated by a sort of half touch of civilization. We heard from them of the Hua Ulu living almost in the centre of the island in the mountains. They warned us not to go up there and said the Hua Ulu, whom they were terrified of, would be sure to kill us because they were still headhunters.

'It was a terrible journey. I got ill and the going was frightful. Swamp first, and then these great mountains, one after another. Finally, we found the village we now live in.' She laughed, brushing back the hair that fell over her forehead and was still damp from the many soakings we had had that day. 'As you see,' she went on, 'they didn't kill us but it was a bit frightening at first. Even the missionaries are terrified of these people. They swore they will kill any missionary going into the village and I'm sure they would too, anyway the missionaries certainly believe they would. Soon after we got there a rumour got around that they had killed Valerio. It got back somehow to Ambon and the Father nearly went mad. Finally, a Bupati was sent over to the island. Of course he didn't come up into the mountains, he just threatened to send troops in so Valerio had to go down (two days there and back) to prove he was alive.

'Anyway, for some reason, they accepted us and built us a beautiful house at the end of their village. They seem to think we are some kind of talisman, and they're terribly proud of us. We have a brother and sister in the tribe, and after a time they began to trust us enough to sing us their songs and begin telling us their legends. They don't, of course, trust us completely and I can't honestly say I trust them entirely either. In fact, to tell you the truth I'm worried about Valerio at the moment.'

The Hua Ulu, she told us, were jealous and hated the Nua Ulu. While she was in Ambon, Valerio had decided to go for a walk over the mountains to another village where he could compare the culture and rituals of the people he was studying with those of another sector of the tribe. This other tribe apparently were equally jealous of the Hua Ulu and the prestige they had gained by having white men living in their village. Renée was terrified that if he had gone there something terrible might have happened.

I shivered. Ambon may not have been Paris or New York but, despite the dirt and the squalor, it was a reasonably civilized place, and even sitting on the crowded *Honi Moki* in the harbour there was a relative air of order about things. Soon we would be leaving that behind with no idea how we might return and a goal that meant climbing mountains, walking through jungle swamp and finding our way to a tribe who had accepted one white couple but who we had no reason to believe might accept another two; a tribe who need heads for their rituals and ceremonies and who still hunt for them.

Finding the heads in the twentieth century had become a bit of a problem, for if they killed and left a headless body the police immediately suspected them of the murder and arrested any of their tribe who went to trade on the coast.

Now, the elders had overcome this problem by saying the gods would not object to only some hair or the fingernails of a dead man being used instead of the whole head. In this case, the murderers would not immediately be labelled 'Hua Ulu'.

'You know,' Renée said before we decided to go down and discover the worst about the discomfort of the bunks, 'we read the letter you sent to the mission in Ambon when we were there last time. I'm afraid we laughed rather rudely at your proposed itinerary. "Fools," we said, "they sit on the other side of the world and make these ridiculous plans, just wait till they get to Jakarta and try getting permits to go to all those places, let alone try to cope with the difficulties of getting from one place to another in this country. One thing that's sure is that we won't see them in Ceram." And now here you are.'

Chapter 17

The walls of the cabin were crawling with a steady stream of large red ants and it was claustrophobically hot in the bottom bunk. There was not room to stretch out properly and, although both Robin and I are small, the space was so confined that half of me (I was on the outside) overflowed over the edge.

The sea was not in the least rough – that would have been all we needed – but there was quite a swell and as soon as we got round the western point of Ambon and started heading north, the *Honi Moki* began rolling in earnest with a creaking of wood that was distinctly alarming. Almost at once, I felt sick. I opened one of the doors, reviewing the possibility of making my way to the stinking little lavatory jutting out over the back of the boat, a tiny little box with a round hole cut in the wood only inches above sea level. I had managed to get into a nightdress under cover of darkness before we set sail and I did not relish the idea of stumbling past the crew looking like a Victorian matron, but I wanted to investigate the situation in case things got desperate. I saw at once that there was not a hope. The two-foot-wide deck both sides of the wheelhouse was jammed with bodies, sleeping head to feet, in rows on the wooden planks and the only way to get to the stern would have been to walk on top of them.

We slept little that night, only falling now and then into a fitful doze, both unpleasantly sticky from the heat. Robin, I think, had a touch of fever; his head was hotter than the temperature in the wheelhouse could account for, and he tossed restlessly, frequently trying to turn round, which was not physically possible without pushing me out of the bunk altogether. Morning and the end of the hours of darkness always comes as a great relief after nights like this.

We had our breakfast of bread, butter and jam, sharing a pint-sized mug of tea brought to us by one of the crew, sitting on the metal roof of the boat. It was a beautiful morning, sparkling clear and fresh with not a cloud in the sky. Ambon was a hazy speck behind us, Buru a clear mass of green to our left and the south coast of Ceram lay in front. The sea was dotted with small islands, ringed with yellow sand and thickly clad with palm trees and jungle. Ceram looked like one giant mountain rising straight from the sea with no sign of habitation and, at this end of it, there seemed to be less jungle than barren, lightly grassed slopes.

Before long it grew too hot to stay up above. As soon as the sun rose high, the metal of the roof became unbearable, burning to the touch, and we were forced back to the suffocation of the wheelhouse, alternately dozing and reading books we had borrowed from Father Rutges, who had an astonishing mixture of literature from the *Reader's Digest* to crime paperbacks. We lunched on our bunks off the last of the bread and some tinned cheese, waiting for the cool of the evening to come so that we could go back on top for some fresh air, as the smell of bodies and sweat in that small enclosure was almost unbearable.

The *Honi Moki* was to stop first at a small port called Sawai on the north coast of the island, then it would chug slowly on to a second township of Wahai about thirty miles further on, and finally round to Bula in the north-east where the mining camp was. The nearest point from which to walk in from the coast to the Hua Ulu was about halfway between the first two towns. From there, it would take about an easy day's walk to get to the village, but to go from either of the towns we would have to sleep in the jungle on the way, and would also find problems in getting anyone to go with us as a guide.

Robin had talked to the captain about his picking us up on the way back. If we waited for him at Wahai or Sawai he would do that, he said, but he was vague about the day on which he was likely to be at either of those places. The *Honi Moki*, it seemed, ran to no regular schedule, coming and going as it pleased. Robin gave him an extra five pounds on top of our two-pound fares and finally he did say vaguely that he would wait for us until mid-day in five days' time at Wahai. He was not sure, he said, that he would be stopping in Sawai on the way back, it depended on the cargo he picked up along the coast. It was difficult for us to know whether we could trust him to keep this promise, as his face was completely inscrutable, even for a Chinaman, the eyes narrow and the features expressionless. Renée thought not.

We decided to risk it since there was not an alternative. The four days we had on Ceram would be spent with the first taken up by walking up to the Hua Ulu, the two days and three nights there and the fourth walking back down again. At least that would give us time to see the tribe and for Robin to learn about their lives, problems and future from Valerio.

We arrived in Sawai at five in the morning and as soon as it was light small children encircled the boat, climbing over the rails and running along the decks under everyone's feet. When they saw us their mouths fell open in astonishment, they stood still, with lozenge eyes widening rooted to the spot and apparently completely mesmerized.

Those little towns along the north coast of Ceram are unparalleled for their attraction and setting. Behind Sawai rose an almost perpendicular wall of grey mountain, half clad with tumbling jungle, curving round to make a narrow sheltered harbour. Many of the little wooden houses of the town are built on stilts over the water, the rest cluster around a small square flanking the pretty red and white mosque sporting little pointed minarets, and a large onion dome. Beside it a large clear freshwater pool, carved out of the rocks, doubles as the public washing and bathing area for the town.

Already people were sweeping the paths outside their houses, pounding spices in tall wooden mortars and laying cloves out on mats in the street to dry in the sun. There was a fresh clean look about everything and a delicious aromatic smell coming from the green and yellow heaps of cloves.

Our next problem was how we were to get round the coast halfway to Wahai where Renée would leave some of her baggage until she could arrange for a party of Hua Ulu to come down from the mountains to fetch it at an isolated house belonging to a policeman. No-one showed any enthusiasm to take us and there did not appear to be any boat with an engine in the little harbour. Small canoes and larger boats with patched sails were moored in the harbour by their dozens, but no motors. It was nine before we found a couple of strong-looking youths who agreed, after a lot of tough bargaining, to take us for a journey of a matter of hours for almost what it had cost for a trip of two nights and a day on the *Honi Mokt*. They had the edge over us – we had to get up the coast.

They raised a sail, but soon lowered it again, as there was not the faintest of faint breezes, and began rowing slowly and rather lazily against strong currents alongside a stretch of ugly-looking mangrove swamp, jutting out in a flat finger of land into the sea. A tangled matrix web of roots sticking from the water made an impenetrable mesh of slimy sinister growth and I could see now why Robin's suggestion that we should walk up the coast had not been taken very seriously by Renée. Beyond the swamp were sandy bays, groves of coconuts and a wild backcloth of jungle rising up the steep mountains behind. We moved at a snail's pace and I soon felt my skin beginning to burn as fierce yellow sun rays reflected up from the blue water.

Luckily, amongst the presents Renée had bought for the Hua Ulu were a number of umbrellas, and she now unearthed these and opened up two of them. We must have made an extraordinary sight, slowly moving along the coast. Robin rowed, the two boys, a heavy rope over their shoulders, walked along the sand, pulling the boat along and Renée and I sat primly under the shade of our black umbrellas.

After hours we saw a fan of brown water spreading into the astonishing blue clarity of the sea. This was where a large river split the coast. East of it, on the farthest bank, was the policeman's house and about two miles west a small wooden house had been built just off the beach. Some relatives of the Hua Ulu lived here, Renée said, at the nearest point for walking inland to get to the mountain village. With luck, there might be someone staying there who would be willing to come with us into the interior. She went to see while I remained in the boat sheltering from the burning sun under my umbrellas as best I could. Her face was long as she walked back along the beach. Most of the Hua Ulu were in the jungle cutting sago and until they returned, which might be in days or weeks, there was little chance of anyone agreeing to take us to the village.

'There is one last chance,' she said. 'Further along is another house, maybe we will find some there.' This time I followed her. We climbed monkey fashion up a steep high ladder made from a rough, narrow tree trunk with grooved notches cut into the bark and entered an airy, half-open verandah. With what must have been a rather obvious start of surprise I saw my first Hua Ulu.

I had expected them to look like the Mentawai in Siberut or the Bugis people and it came as quite a shock to find they were completely different from anyone we had seen in Indonesia so far. For one thing, the Hua Ulu were much darker, the colour of rich bitter chocolate. Their faces were long and their eyes had only a hint of that tilting slant we had grown used to, but the most marked difference of all was in their hair, especially the hair of the men. Like all Indonesians the hair of the Hua Ulu was black and the men wore it long and almost down to their shoulders, but instead of being straight and heavy it stood from their heads in a coarse wiry shock that would have been the envy of many a Western pop star trying to imitate an Afro hairstyle.

There were about half a dozen people sitting on the verandah, men, women and one of those special sort of babies that make any woman feel broody. It was a little boy, just beginning to walk, with enormous eyes and an endearing lurching gait. He was naked except for a wrapping of bark around his plump little tummy, tightly strapped to cure a stomach ache. Round his chubby wrists and ankles were bracelets of shiny silver.

The women were chewing betel and making baskets from woven rattan and bark; the men just lounged around. One of them wore a turban of scarlet cloth, tied in a high peak, and the amazing explosion of hair fanning out from the head of another younger boy was held back from his face by a tight bamboo around his forehead. They were small people with fierce wild eyes, and the men had a tangle of facial hair, drooping moustaches, small beards and long fuzzy sideburns.

This time we were fortunate. These people were cousins of the Hua Ulu living up the mountain and with them was a young man, a comic character with a wide smile and unbelievably crossed eyes, who had fled from the hills. He was, it seemed, a veritable Romeo and was in trouble for wanting to marry a girl from another village. He and the girl had eloped and for a few days had 'lived in sin' – in the eyes of the Hua Ulu a heinous crime. Now the girl had been dragged home and her family had issued an ultimatum: if she was to marry her cross-eyed lover their village must be given a replacement girl from the Hua Ulu tribe as girls were short and childbearing women at a premium. The Hua Ulu elders were not particularly in favour of this exchange as they themselves were rather short of young girls and, for some reason, it seemed that the tribe were beginning to die out; only one child had been born in the last year and it seemed likely that, due to some genetic strain, intermarriage or some dietary lack of one sort or another, the women were becoming barren. All they would offer in return for the lovelorn lass was an elderly, well-weathered widow. So, while the argument and bargaining went on, the cross-eyed Casanova stayed on the coast, keeping out of trouble. He and two others agreed to take us up the mountain.

After settling that we would leave at the crack of dawn next morning we pushed on to the policeman's house, fighting across the fast current flowing with the river and landing at last on the far bank. Our two boatmen were now thoroughly bored with the whole trip and eager to get home. They threw the baggage onto the sand and left, rowing off with a lot more enthusiasm and effort than they had put into the outgoing journey.

The policeman's wife was at the door of her small house. She was a tall Javanese woman, with a fine face that would have been beautiful if it had not been for a large black mole in the middle of her forehead. Beside her stood a ten-year-old boy with what I first thought was a goitre and popping eyes that gave him a slightly loopy look. There were also two lumpish girls around eighteen and twenty, one with hair hanging down her back to her calves; both had a sickly greenish white substance plastered over their faces. What with the black mole, the distortion of the boy's features and the masks of the girls the whole family had an anomalous appearance that bordered on the nightmarish. They were, however, exceptionally hospitable. The policeman's wife greeted us with enthusiasm and begged Renée to stay down with her on the coast and not to go up into the mountains, to 'those savages'. She told me to call her 'Ibu' (Mother) and called me 'little white foreigner'.

Considering the isolation of the place there seemed to be a lot going on. Various people appeared from the trees surrounding the house and came to stand on the wooden, slatted steps leading up to the door, staring at us with open curiosity. A woman with a young body, but a frighteningly old face, pure white hair and blank, blind eyes, her hand held lightly in the fingers of a raggedly dressed little girl, stumbled across the sandy yard with a bundle wrapped up in a piece of cotton cloth. The little girl led her up the steps through the growing crowd and into the room, and she felt for the edge of the table and then laid her bundle in front of us. A dozen turtle eggs were inside, soft-shelled, grey-white and round like ping-pong balls. They were still warm from boiling and Renée showed us how to bite a small hole in the top and suck out the insides, squeezing the soft, pliable skin. They were strong tasting and delicious, like ordinary eggs but with much more flavour. The bearer of this gift, Renée told us, had seen something more than nasty in some local woodshed and had gone white-haired and blind overnight.

A storm which had been raging in the mountains now hit the shore with a dramatic crashing roll of thunder and veins of startling, jagged, electric blue lightning. A strong wind screamed through the palm trees, bending them into hoops and tearing at their leaves, and ice-cold rain slanted sideways from a black sky with the force of a jet spray from a high-power hose.

The three of us slept badly, head to feet, on the dirty wood floor of the front room. In the morning, we meant to leave at sunrise but, as usual, things did not work out that way. The Hua Ulu who were to come with us didn't appear and soon Robin was bursting with impatience.

'Marika and I will start walking along the shore to the place where we turn in,' he told Renée. 'You follow as soon as the Hua Ulu arrive.' Most of her luggage was to be left with the Ibu and Renée was now sorting out those things which were the most important to take up to the village in the first load.

Robin slung our rucksacks, still heavy despite the stringent paring we had done in Ambon, onto his shoulders and picked up our camera case; my stuff was in a nasty plastic shoulder bag which already seemed to weigh a ton. Off we went, getting a lift across the river in a tiny narrow canoe that tipped terrifyingly as the current caught it and we were spun out to sea with Robin and a fisherman paddling like mad to get us round in a half circle and back to the shore.

We walked side by side along the palm-fringed beach, our feet sinking in wet sand that dragged at our shoes and made each step an effort. We stopped to rest after a time on a tree trunk that had fallen across the beach. After scaring off a dozen or so crabs, swatting at the mosquitoes which now encircled our heads, we sat on the trunk, sucking in the welcome fumes of a couple of cigarettes. Before I was halfway through mine, Robin was chuntering again.

'You stay here with the things,' he ordered, 'and I'll run back and see if I can get the others moving.' He did not wait for an answer but really did begin running in the direction we had come from, his new footprints making a parallel line to the ones we had already left. I eased myself into a more comfortable position under the shade of a large branch and watched him fade into a dot along the sand.

The party that arrived about an hour later made me laugh, so incongruous did they look. Robin strode out in front, Renée followed more slowly, a basket on her back held in place by a band round her forehead, carrying a string of highly smelling salt fish in one hand and a small black briefcase and a basket in the other. She was barefooted and wearing a creased short skirt and a shirt that had both faded and shrunk through washing. Bringing up the rear were the two Hua Ulu; 'lover boy' with his eyes grotesquely crossed and his mop of hair crowned by a red turban tied in a conical shape with one end falling, like a jester's, over one ear; the younger boy, Hari, with the strip of bamboo still encircling his forehead, wearing a torn singlet and a brief, extremely ragged pair of once white shorts. He had a light fuzz of black hair, fringed wide thick lips and a wild untamed look about him. Both were carrying poles over their shoulders from which numerous packages were hanging and lover boy, who was very good with his hands, had tied the things up neatly in quickly woven baskets of bamboo and rattan. The third man had failed to turn up. We turned inland and set off for what was going to be the most unpleasant journey I had ever had in my life, and certainly the toughest, walking in single file with lover boy in front, Robin next, then me followed by Renée and finally the wild boy bringing up the rear.

We skirted a high stockade fence protecting an area of slash and burn garden where gourd vines rampaged over burnt tree stumps and small patches of maize and manioc had been carefully tended, and crossed a long fallen tree trunk to begin a wearying trek through a wide belt of swamp.

Ancient rotted trees, fallen centuries ago, wallowed in dark brackish water, twisted roots entwined in and out in a matted network and everything was slippery or filmed with a layer of brown-green slime. The water was thick like the worst of brown Windsor soup and it was impossible to tell how deep or how venomous it was from above as we stepped warily from one prone log to another.

It was not long before I found out exactly how deep the mire was. The Hua Ulu, Robin and the barefooted Renée balanced gracefully on the often narrow branches that swayed and frequently rolled under our feet; I tried to do the same but lost my footing within the first few hundred yards, slipping sideways and slithering into that evil-looking morass to discover the water stank with a sour, rotting and gaseous odour, but at least it was only waist deep and the bottom was reasonably solid. After that first fall, I stumbled frequently, throwing up my arms each time to protect my camera and bag with my jeans now saturated with water and the smell of the swamp impregnating everything. It was hot and airless. A light haze of steam rose from the water and coronets of large mosquitoes encircled our heads.

The swamp was a sinister insalubrious place. Large trees, with long roots reaching out of the water like octopus tentacles, looked primeval; trailing vines had the shape of flexuous snakes and many of the half-sunken logs were facsimiles of silent, evilly waiting crocodiles. As there were snakes and crocodiles around it was difficult to know where imagination was running riot and where there was real cause for caution. It was ominously silent with no bird song or animal noise of any kind. I disliked it intensely and the only thing that cheered me was that everyone else slipped too, even the Hua Ulu, at one time or another, and by the time we emerged at the other end we were all soaked through and stinking from the layer of evil mud that encased us like an extra skin.

A belt of jungle lay at the foot of the mountains and here walking was easier. The trees were of an incredible height, with silver bark and almost bare of branches until they reached the light far above. The undergrowth was light and the ground dry and springy underfoot and now there was plenty of evidence of animal life.

We stopped as lover boy put up his hand and froze. With a heavy crashing a couple of wild boar, large, black and with vicious curving tusks, stampeded past us only a few yards away. At the base of a tree was a hollow of bare earth where they had been rooting.

The chatter of parrots reverberated through the air, parakeets screeched at each other hidden in the foliage, and with a heavy flapping and whirling of wings a flock of clumsy hornbills rose from the ground, their great painted beaks curiously unreal, and flew lazily through the trees.

At the foot of the mountains we followed a fast-running, shallow river with clear water tumbling over rounded stones, wading through about three feet of water and treading carefully to avoid sudden holes. On the banks the jungle rampaged, a Rousseau picture of thick-fleshed leaves, exotic palms and tumbling rattan vines. Some of the trees had sharp barbed thorns protruding from their barks, here and there were the vivid orange trunks of hardwood trees and pointed palms.

After a long trek along the river, the water flowed through a sharply peaked protruding mass of grey-white rock and a long twisting and curving tunnel, almost dark in the centre with a faint glimmer of light showing at the other end. This, Renée said, was the quarter-way mark.

'Do you want to stop here,' she asked, 'or shall we press on to the halfway point?' We agreed to go on. Both Robin and I were worried about the Swedish girl. She had complained of a headache that morning and her face was unhealthily pale and blotched with angry red patches in places, though she said stoutly she was quite all right.

From the river we began the climb uphill over steep and

rough ground, pushing our way through scrub, scrambling across and sometimes along rivers, and seemingly following no kind of path or track. It was hard going. The stones were sharp beneath our feet and I was amazed that Renée could walk barefoot. I found it painful even with sneakers on and it was difficult not to trip over vines and roots that snaked in and out of fissures in the rocks. My bag was a problem, bouncing at my side, and eventually I put the strap round my head and carried it on my back. It was hot too. Sweat rolled down our faces, salty and tinged with dust, the mountains seem to rise for ever above us and straggling branches with hooked barbs caught in our clothes or whipped against our faces drawing blood that the mosquitoes enjoyed immensely. My breath was coming in short harsh rasps when we reached the small plateau that was the halfway mark to the village.

It was an eerie place. At some time there had been a fire there and now the trunks of huge trees, charred and blackened, lay in an untidy heap over the ground like the twisted framework of a burnt-out skyscraper. Already the jungle was creeping back.

We sat on a log, smoking, and around us the sounds of the jungle were a noisome chorus of bird song and insect buzzing. Renée had a water flask and, as we were thirsty and dry throated, we took small sips, but drank sparingly and were careful not to take more than our own share. Her shirt was damp with sweat, her hair hung in lank strands and her pallor seemed worse. Even Robin looked as though the pace was telling and for once he was content to sit still for a few minutes without immediately wanting to move on. The two Hua Ulu boys, on the other hand, were as fresh as daisies. They sat a little bit apart from us and lover boy carefully unwound his turban, letting a cascade of frizzy hair fall down his shoulders. He shook his head vigorously from side to side, ran his fingers through the tresses to remove any nits, and then swept it back on top, tied it in a tight knot and replaced his turban, this time tying it in a new and even more complicated series of knots.

'The Hua Ulu men are all so vain,' Renée told us. 'Always

they are primping and preening themselves. Sadly, so many of them have this skin disease, which I think is ringworm, but now that I have the medicine to cure it I hope we may be able to eradicate it from the village.' She pointed out dry scabby whirls that encrusted the legs and arms of the boy in the singlet and shorts. From a distance they did not show much on his dark brown skin but from up close it was an unpleasant sight.

While I was dragging on a cigarette, and gradually feeling the pressure that had been building up in my ears diminish, I glanced down and saw on my legs the thing I had been dreading most since coming East. A long thin, almost transparent, rubbery creature was hooping its way up my leg with a sinuous silent movement. I froze as I saw three more groping their way upwards, and then I screamed.

'Robin, leeches. Oh God, what do I do?' He looked, and nonchalantly flicked them off with a thumbnail.

'Roll up your trousers and see if any have got in under.' I did and two revoltingly repulsive dark bloated blobs were stuck fast to my flesh. Looking at them made me feel faint.

Again Robin flicked them off. 'Don't try to pull or even burn them. It doesn't work. A quick flick is the best method.'

I had dreamed of leeches. I had dreaded leeches. Now I was experiencing them and the reality was every bit as unpleasant as my imaginings had been, although I was surprised they were so small before they actually found flesh to suck.

From my leg two streams of blood ran from small bites and I saw then that Renée's bare legs were pinpricked with spots of blood too.

'I used to loathe them too,' she told me, 'but it's only in this part of the jungle and the swamp. They don't come higher up the mountain.'

From then on it was a miserable, uncomfortable and frightening trek, up and down steep slopes, stumbling on slippery rocks and often pushing through dense undergrowth. Lover boy was ahead, Robin forging behind him doing one of his marathon bits and me hurrying to try and keep them in sight. Renée and Hari had fallen back and were out of sight and sound, not that one could have heard much anyway above the flushing, splashing cascade of the water which filled our immediate world as another storm raged over the mountains.

When she caught up, poor Renée looked even rougher than I felt, her bare feet bruised and bleeding, water streaming off her and, like me, tears of exhaustion in her eyes. I tried to take her basket from her to relieve her of at least a bit of her load, but like all of us she had got to the snapping stage and said she could manage perfectly well.

'Never mind,' she said after a short rest as she pulled herself shakily upright again, 'we are nearly there. In a minute we will get to the river and then there is just one more hill to climb to the village.'

In a quarter of an hour we did reach the river, pushing our way through prickly, fleshy plants that looked like giant rhubarb and were bigger even than that sinister stuff gunnera, and stood in thick squelching mud on the banks of the barrier that separated us from our goal. We were only a few miles from the village but it looked as though we might just as well have been a hundred miles from our objective.

The rain had swollen the river to horrific proportions. It swept past us in a crazy, fast whirling spate of dark brown water filled with a swirling gallimaufry of tree trunks, branches and forest debris. We could see a large wooden hut on the opposite bank about a hundred and fifty yards away, but getting there seemed as though it would be impossible. We stood and looked at it in silence and went on looking at it, for once not smoking for we had not a dry match or lighter between us.

Lover boy decided that standing there doing nothing was not getting us anywhere. He disappeared a little way upriver, stripped off his ragged shorts and singlet and jumped into the water. Immediately the current grabbed him and swept him at a horrifying pace past. A few hundred yards further down he managed to reach the bank, grab at an overhanging branch and pull himself up. For a moment he lay prone on the bank, then he jumped up and we could see him running towards the hut, his parents' home, his turban a limp rag but still in place. The next time we saw him he was carrying a burning torch of wood and holding it in one hand high above his head as he re-entered the water upstream again and was swept back to our side of the river just below us. Triumphantly, he produced the still glowing length of wood and lit cigarettes for us all. It was one of the most friendly gestures anyone has ever made in my experience.

Robin was the next to attempt the swim. He decided to try to cross the river, climb up to the village and see if, with Valerio, he could get hold of some kind of a rope to span the water.

'Here goes,' he said and jumped into the water. Like lover boy he was immediately swept downstream, his head disappearing under the water as he desperately tried to dip the pole into the bottom and get some purchase. He looked small and helpless and I held my breath as the force of the water carried him away. Somehow he made the far bank a few hundred yards further down, and disappeared into the jungle on the far side.

Renée and I stood shivering miserably under the dripping greenery. Hari said something to her and she translated for me.

'The boys say that now it has stopped raining the water level of the river will soon fall enough for us to get across, but we will have to leave the bags here for some time.' We crouched on the muddy ground, huddling together for warmth, in a cloud of flies and mosquitoes and waited for about an hour until lover boy gave a signal and jumped back into the water again, followed by Hari. Renée followed and, taking a deep breath, I also plunged into the river and, like the others, swirled away in a panic-filled few minutes of confusion, mud-filled lungs and ineffectual threshing dog paddle. A whirlpool of current pushed me sideways, my hands, like claws, clung desperately to some overhanging bushes and with a last almost despairing effort I pulled myself into a tangle of fleshy plants that were, themselves, a head-high mini-jungle.

The others were crouched round the fire in the hut when I

arrived, muddy water flowing off me in a chocolate brown stream. They, and about a dozen Hua Ulu, moved over to make room on a low wooden platform on a wide verandah where a blissful glow came from a fire burning on a flat slab of stone.

Lover boy's mother was an elderly lady with an ancient, faded and patched sarong above sagging breasts. Her face was lined and monkeyish, dark brown like her son's, and her arms were thin as sticks. She was steadily chewing betel, spitting out the scarlet juice through the floor of slatted bamboo. Opposite us was a thin palm-woven screen behind which another fire glowed in the room that served both as a kitchen and sleeping area. Everything was swept and clean. Baskets hung from the wall beside spears, bows and quivers of arrows. Outside, two brightly coloured parakeets and a cockatoo chattered on a wooden perch.

The woman's husband, Renée said, was out hunting for wild boar and soon he arrived back carrying a vicious-looking spear in his hand that had five long, extremely sharp, barbs of iron on its head for spiking the dangerous wild pig.

'Has he got anything?' I asked.

'I don't know,' Renée said. 'It is not the done thing to ever ask if anyone has had any success hunting.' She spoke their language fluently and seemed better now, chatting easily and squatting in a relaxed position that I envied.

The other Hua Ulu were as dark as the two boys who had accompanied us. The women wore sarongs tied above their breasts or twisted in a roll around their waists and their hair was heavy with the palm oil they combed through it to try and straighten out the kinks. Most of the men wore red turbans tied in those strange conical or twin pointed shapes; those that did not had strips of bamboo holding back great haloes of tightly frizzed black hair as a sign they were unmarried. They were all small and wiry with tight hard muscles showing through spare bodies and many had the wavering, curling patterns of ringworm on their bodies.

We were high in the mountains here and it was damp and

extremely cold. My teeth still chattered uncontrollably, and to try and counteract an overwhelming longing for a cigarette or food I accepted an offering of a piece of betel nut wrapped in its green-leafed packing. It was the first time I had tried any. The first chew soured my mouth and the second, as I sank my teeth into the lime centre, sent a fiery burning sensation shooting through my jaw and gums. I spat it out regardless of manners, the stream of scarlet looking like the bloody phlegm of a far-gone tubercular case.

The Hua Ulu looked at me with reservation but without that blatant staring we had become so used to in more civilized places. As Renée's friend they seemed to be prepared to accept me but it was easy, looking at the sharp, fierce faces of the men, to believe the stories we had heard of their head-hunting exploits.

After what seemed an age, Robin arrived with Valerio carrying a long length of leander vine, coiled like a rope, between them.

The anthropologist looked as wild as the Hua Ulu he was living amongst. Two years is a long time to live far from the twentieth-century Western world with a tribe isolated miles from anywhere in a village almost impossible to reach. He was incredibly tall and so thin he looked as though he was suffering badly from malnutrition, with bones showing clearly through sun-weathered skin. A shaggy beard covered his chin; he wore a faded torn sweat-shirt and a pair of dirty shorts and his eyes were almost hidden by strong glasses tied in place by a piece of red string.

I had a distinct feeling that his reaction to Robin and me was one of slight hostility, but realized then that it must, in fact, have been a considerable shock for him to find us there. Also, he had every right to feel a touch of resentment at two other Europeans blundering uninvited into what he might naturally feel was his territory.

The river had by this time fallen considerably and Robin, Valerio and one of the Hua Ulu were able to wade back across, with the water only up to their necks, to fetch the rest of our bags. After a bit more polite chatting between the Valeris and the Hua Ulu, we left the hut to trek the last mile and a half to the village.

At last, side by side, the four of us walked slowly up the muddy, rain-washed central area of the naturally fortified village to the Valeris' hut at the far end, the Hua Ulu hanging over the verandahs of their houses to watch our progress.

Twelve hours after leaving the coast, we pulled ourselves up the single, thin notched log and collapsed onto the verandah of Chez Valeri, our journey into the interior at last over. Slowly we began to revive.

Chapter 18

The Valeris' house had been built for them by the Hua Ulu on the identical model of all the others in the village. The only exception to the pattern were two small huts at either end, where the women of the village stayed during their menstruation period, and the large community house in the centre which has four human heads buried under the large supporting pillars.

Their home was clean and airy with the long verandah screened off on one side to make a room. There were two cooking fires inside with wood tripods for supporting cooking pots at one end and a slightly raised platform at the other on which they kept their belongings and where they slept on two sagging camp beds under mosquito netting.

Renée was excited to be back, exclaiming over the small orange kittens that a wild cat they had tamed had produced whilst she had been away, and checking through the contents of what she called her 'treasure chest', pulling out of a metal trunk superb celadon and Ming plates which she had exchanged with the villagers for rice or tea. The Hua Ulu bride price, she told me, included the exchange of around thirty of these almost priceless plates, traded for centuries by Chinese visiting the coastal towns of Sawai and Wahai. The amount of plates a family owned indicated their wealth, although they themselves had not the faintest idea of their intrinsic value in the outside world and, in order to protect them, these treasures were buried deep in secret hiding places in the jungle. She had changed into a sarong worn like the Hua Ulu women.

One by one we climbed back down the perilous log (the stilts of the house were about ten feet high or so) and went to wash. From the jungle, rampaging on the mountain side behind the village, water had been cleverly piped along an aqueduct of split bamboo supported on forked sticks. It ended halfway down the village, sending a fountain of water into a shallow pool, but each family were able to tap the flow outside their houses by damming the pole with a bundle of leaves, thereby sending out a jet of water that overflowed just where they wanted it to. It was sparkling clear, ice cold and very refreshing, and seemed a most efficient system as the river was quite a distance below.

Five houses on both sides of the village were separated by a wide central strip of open ground with the larger community house halfway down on our left. Beyond the slope of the village stretched the mountains we had climbed, pale shadows now as night fell with their peaks wreathed in twisted spirals of mist.

A woman, Renée's Hua Ulu blood sister, arrived at the house with palm-wrapped parcels and the two of them disappeared through a door in the palm screen to cook. From the other houses came the sound of voices calling to each other, the twittering chatter of children, and of an occasional bird-like singing that echoed in the distance. When the meal was ready the woman disappeared and the four of us sat cross-legged in a circle on rattan matting by the cooking fires. We ate rice, salt fish and a thin soup seasoned with harsh salt dried from sea water, shared two tins of beer Robin found in the bottom of our knapsack, and then drank more whisky.

The Hua Ulu, Valerio said, drank only water and did not make palm wine like so many of the other tribes we had met. Two generations ago they used to imbibe frequently with the result that the men often became argumentative, fought amongst themselves and went in bands down the mountains killing anyone who came in their path. Then an old woman of the tribe put a curse on them and to break it they stopped drinking. Now even the word alcohol frightens them, and we

237

swallowed our beer and whisky like secret alcoholics, with the door closed, hiding the bottle when we had finished.

Outside, on the verandah, a group of Hua Ulu had come to visit, and sat gossiping amongst themselves on the raised platform at one end where the fire glowed sending up a spiral of strange-smelling smoke from the burning embers of the wood. There must have been over a dozen of them, men with those intricately tied turbans of red cloth and women in sarongs of pale muted colours, the heavy oil on their hair shining in the firelight. Robin and Valerio sat at one end with the men and Robin laid out the presents we had brought with us in the centre of the room, bundles of tobacco, a couple of torches, some razor blades and some sweets. Nobody actually grabbed at the small hoard, but they disappeared immediately with a mutual sharing out that involved no argument or discussion.

The women sat gracefully, legs crossed, one knee flat on the ground and the other bent, an elbow resting lightly on it. A few had babies, dark curly-haired children with enormous eyes that were bright and curious. If one cried it was hushed immediately, rocked into silence or quickly pressed to a bared breast swollen with milk, for if a baby cries the Hua Ulu believe that somewhere, someone dies; it is bad luck and a noise to be avoided as much as possible.

At about eleven Renée said she must go to bed. She brought out mats for us to sleep on, unrolled them onto the platform of the verandah and then she and Valerio left us to go to bed in their narrow camp beds under the covering of their mosquito netting.

It was cold on the verandah and the mosquitoes were out in force, but I was far too tired to care about those or our audience of half a dozen Hua Ulu men still sitting around. Our mosquito netting had been jettisoned a long time ago, along with our lilos and other pieces of equipment, and we curled up in our sleeping bags, stretching out on the hard floor by the dying fire, neither of us bothering to wash again or change from the sarongs we were both wearing. The sounds of the men talking in low, fluting voices went on and on, and from the village people still called to each other from one house to another. We slept at last, restless and tossing with one or other of us waking frequently to build up the fire when the cold became unbearable and the damp chill coming from the mountains brought on a fit of shivering.

Renée had brought up a package of porridge from Ambon and together, next morning, we lit the two fires on the kitchen hearth and brewed up the oats with water and tinned milk, sweetening it lavishly with sugar.

Renée collapsed back into bed and I wandered out alone into the sunlit village while Robin and Valerio went towards the jungle.

The houses were built on a narrow spur of ground which dropped sharply on both sides. Small gardens of manioc, bananas and fruit trees had been planted on the almost sheer slopes below where the ground fell away to a rushing, cascading torrent of water. Beyond that the jungle took over again in a thick tangled richness of matted greenery through which parakeets darted with sudden flashes of bright colour.

Beyond the Valeris' house, the last in the line of huts, the menstruation house was set apart in a small clearing. I went to see what it would be like to be imprisoned in the building where every woman of the tribe must spend the days of her menstruation cycle, where any contact with the men of the village was taboo and where food was brought in by their female relations.

Unlike the rest of the houses, this one was without a verandah, just one room, cool and pleasantly dim after the brilliant light outside, with the only light filtering in narrow shafts through chinks in the palm-plaited walls. At the end of the room were the usual two fires built on stone slabs and two women were busy washing down the floor of split bamboo with water thrown from large gourd containers. It was meticulously clean and the floor was easily washed as the water rolled over the bamboo poles and fell through the gaps between them onto the ground below. A couple of other women sat on a platform spanning one end of the room, weaving baskets and chattering happily together, giving me a smile but otherwise paying no attention to me whatsoever.

Life in the menstruation hut, Renée had told me, was really rather pleasant. She joined them when it was her turn, living as they did and sleeping on the rattan mat. During the day they were visited by other women and, apart from keeping the house clean, they had no work or cooking to do as all their food was brought in. Their children were looked after by other women and on the whole they all seemed to regard the days they spent there as a pleasant rest and a good opportunity to have a real, long-drawn-out gossip.

During the months the Valeris had spent with the Hua Ulu they had lived almost entirely in the way of the people, eating what they ate and doing what they did during the normal course of the days that passed. Renée had learnt to weave baskets, to walk barefooted and wear only a sarong; Valerio went hunting with the men and listened to tales told of the ancestors by the elders. It had taken time for them to be fully accepted and even now they were careful not to tell Valerio too much about their headhunting activities, but they had managed to win the trust and the respect of the people and also to help them medicinally in a limited capacity.

Sadly, Valerio was pessimistic about the future of the tribe. There was pressure from the authorities on the coast to get the Hua Ulu to move down into more populated areas; their birth rate was falling badly and, with a population of only about a hundred and fifty and little marriage outside their own people, it looked as if this state would continue to deteriorate. At the moment they were protected by their isolation and the natural barrier of mountains and jungle and by the fear with which outsiders regarded them – a fear which had been increased by the wounding of a policeman who had, not long before, been sent up from the coast to order them off the mountain. No-one had tried a second time so far. It was difficult to see how long these defences could be upheld.

All during the day women arrived with little offerings of

food which Valerio paid for in sugar, tea or coffee; a small banana-leaf-wrapped package of four freshwater prawns, a bunch of bananas, some sago, a few sprigs of green leaves and a parcel of wild pig that could be smelt a mile away. I could not help turning up my nose at this last offering and was soundly ticked off by Valerio, who said it was a rare gift and a sacrifice on their part to produce it for the guests of the village.

Renée crawled out of bed and together we prepared the evening meal. Most of the pig, the prawns and the green leaves she packed tightly into a tube of green bamboo, stopping up the top with a cork made of twisted coconut husk and then propping up this jungle casserole over one of the glowing fires. The sago she made into a whitish grey gruel-like substance and then collapsed under the mosquito netting again leaving me to do the best I could with the rest of the pork.

Readers of my weekly column in the *Sunday Telegraph* would have thrown a thousand fits had they seen me at work in that remote kitchen in the mountains of a small island called Ceram in the Moluccas. I cut the meat with a rusty panga trying to block my nose to the smell of rotting flesh, and not to investigate too closely the quantities of thick white maggots which crawled through its fibres. To cover the smell, and try and eradicate some of the greasy slime, I soaked it in a little whisky, doused it with lime juice and sprinkled it with red peppers and then dumped the whole revolting mess into a blackened cooking pot and hoped for the best.

We had sago gruel first, eating it with three-pronged wooden forks made from one twig of wood, finely smoothed and split at one end with the three prongs splayed out. Like spaghetti, the sago was wound round and round these forks and then sucked up.

We ate off Ming plates which I do not suppose I had ever done before and which, to the Hua Ulu, took the place of currency. With them, brides were bought and debts paid and they even, I was told, were of a high enough value to wipe out the stigma of adultery. If a Hua Ulu man or woman committed adultery the offended party was paid in Ming or celadon plates by the family of the partner committing the crime and all sins were at once forgiven and forgotten.

The plates, indeed, were of a rare and delicate beauty but, as far as I was concerned, the same could not be said of the pork. Not only did it stink, but no amount of disguising flavourings could cover up the taste of the rotten meat or hide the plump whiteness of the maggots which still lurked in the flesh and which, even though they must have been suffocated by the heat of cooking, still looked as though they might crawl across our plates at any minute.

The woman who had brought it to us with such pride was peering round the side of the door watching us eat. Valerio was eyeing me with a frown, daring me to turn up my nose, and Robin had turned a paler shade of green. But we ate. Somehow we got a decent amount down (in my case unashamedly helped by liberal nips of the whisky we had brought for Valerio). At last the meal finished and the greasy dishes were washed up and the smell began to dispel. Only Renée, still prone in her bed, was allowed to be excused from the meal.

Since we had to leave the next morning early to go back down the mountain to try and rendezvous with the *Honi Moki*, and both of us were still desperately tired and feeling pretty ill and feverish, we decided to turn in early.

Renée was a little better next morning and I was glad to see the unhealthy pallor of her face had nearly gone. I on the other hand seemed to be getting worse and I had spent most of the night being violently sick. I swallowed a handful of pills picked at random from our medicine bag and managed to keep down some tea although my legs felt like jellied-eels and my insides like a revolving butter churn. Robin, however, had completely recovered from his bout of whatever-it-was from the night before and seemed to be having no ill effects from the maggot-ridden wild pig.

We had been supposed to leave at six-thirty, but once more things went at a Hua Ulu pace. Originally, the plan had been that two men would come with us down the mountain. When we reached the halfway mark it was decided that Robin would hurry on ahead to the policeman's house with one of the Hua Ulu to try and fix a lift in some craft round the coast to Sawai or Wahai, and I would follow, at my rather slower pace, with the second boy.

We finally left at about nine with a fairly elderly looking Hua Ulu carrying our rucksack, and a second younger man carrying only a large bunch of bananas given to us as a parting gift by Renée.

But first, the older man, whose name sounded something like Tikele, had to say his farewells to his family and especially to his baby grandson who was obviously his pride and joy. Travelling to the coast meant danger on the way and possibly danger on the coast, and the whole of his large family clustered round as he sat on his verandah with the baby on his knee, the old man strong and tough looking despite the fact that he must have been well over fifty. His frizzled black hair fell almost to his shoulders from under a red turban that, this time, was tied with three points, eyes dark and deep-set under high cheekbones, jaw slightly protruding with his mouth a little distorted from chewing betel. A heavy moustache and short fringe of beard gave him the look of a rakish bandit. Tough he may certainly have looked, but with the baby he was as gentle as a young mother, tickling it to make it laugh, hugging it with great soft-hearted love.

At last he dragged himself away and we were ready to go. With a last bear-like hug he put the baby softly on the ground, picked up a bamboo pole plugged at both ends with holes in the top through which the faces and beaks of a family of young parakeets peered out, their feathers still pale and fluffy. Then he heaved our rucksack onto his shoulders and we left the house.

With a last wave we dropped down the slope out of sight of the village – the isolated people who lived there and the Swedish girl who, with her Italian husband, had made the village their home for nearly two years, and who had been accepted as friends by these people whom those on the coast considered murderous savages, but who, to us too, had seemed gentle, friendly and extremely civilized.

We followed roughly the same route we had come up by, Tikele in the lead, Robin going next with me following and the younger boy bringing up the rear. Within the first half hour the boy and our large bunch of bananas disappeared and that was the last we saw of them. He had looked sour when we set off and obviously even the promise of fairly considerable financial reward when we reached the coast was not enough to compensate for the rough journey. The three of us went on alone.

Robin, I knew, was desperately worried about catching up with the *Honi Moki*, and he was also worried about me as I seemed to be going more and more slowly, finding the terrain almost impossible. When I stopped just before we were about to enter the swamps, saying that I must rest for a little and I could not go on, he agreed immediately, calling to Tikele and making signs to show I must sit down.

Tikele led us onto a patch of reasonably firm ground and pantomimed for us to sit down. I sank onto a fallen tree trunk, the old man put down his parakeets and our rucksack beside us and then, with a slight wave of his hand, he strode off into the swamp again, disappearing quickly in the maze of water-logged, tangled and slimy roots.

'Do you think he is abandoning us?' I asked Robin nervously, and he too looked worried for a minute. Beyond us stretched the swamp and, although it was not all that far from the coast, unless one knew the way it would be almost impossible to cross that dangerous stinking morass which lay between us and the sea. Then his face cleared.

'He'll be back,' he reassured me. 'Look, he's left his parakeets here and, even if he'd abandon us, he wouldn't go without those.'

A few minutes later the Hua Ulu returned, jog-trotting through the swamp, balancing across logs and branches with a lightness and ease that I envied. In his arms he carried three long sticks of sugar cane dripping with liquid sweetness.

Quickly, he stripped off the outer layers and handed them to us.

With the first few voracious sucks of the sweet stalks, I felt strength returning. Where he had found the cane I could not imagine, but it had been a stroke of inspired genius on Tikele's part to know it was exactly what we both needed. I could have hugged him, instead I grabbed his free hand and shook it almost violently and, although he seemed a little surprised at this display of feeling, he gave a wide smile of gratification that I should be so pleased, and shook my hand in return, his brown hand horny and dry in my sweaty palm.

It was evening again by the time we finally got to the policeman's house. To our amazement and excitement we saw a fairly sizable canoe with, unbelievably where motors were one in a thousand, a twenty-five horsepower Johnson on the back. In the house we found its owner, a young Chinese trader.

'Will you take us to Sawai first thing in the morning?' Robin asked him, suggesting a fairly sizable fee for the journey. He did not accept immediately, countering the question with another.

'Do you know anything about motor engines?' he asked. Robin said he knew a certain amount. He had travelled alone 6000 miles through the rivers of South America in a rubber boat with an Evinrude and Johnson engine on the back so he'd had plenty of experience of the capriciousness of two-stroke outboards.

'In that case, I will take you to Wahai, not Sawai, for nothing, providing you look at a new engine I have there which I cannot get to work properly,' the Chinese man told him. The deal was finally settled to everyone's satisfaction.

The Ibu was full of chat. She was one of those people who believe that the best way to get foreigners to understand an alien language is to speak it louder and louder. Her tales of the problems of the various births of her eighteen-odd children were screeched to me at the top of her rather harsh voice, but it was easy to forgive as her generosity and hospitality again were without bounds.

A strange assorted foursome boarded the little pale blue and green painted boat next morning. Both Robin and I looked incredibly scruffy, the Chinese man wore a white plastic solar topee and his boatman, an Indonesian, sported a green jungle cap of faded denim. It was a tight squeeze as the boat was loaded with a large drum of petrol, a roll of distinctly pongy deer skins, a stack of antlers that had presumably come from the same animals, a pile of that dreaded fruit, the durian, a pile of cooking equipment and a heap of tangled fishing equipment.

We set off at a good pace with a couple of fishing lines strung out behind us, the sun beating down and soon burning hot. This time we did not have the welcome shade of Renée's umbrellas and, as I felt myself beginning to burn from the blinding glare reflected from the water, I had to put on my anorak, pulling the hood over my head again and drawing the strings together so that as little as possible of my face was exposed to the elements.

The fishing was a success though a rather terrifying experience as the first two mackerel-like fish caught (streaked bright blue and silver and gleaming as they fought against the lines pulling them towards the boat) were well over three feet long and thrashed about with astonishing power. Getting them into the boat nearly proved disastrous as both the Chinese man and his mate had to lean over one side, nearly upsetting us all into the water. For a time they went on moving and gasping between the rolls of deer skins and the antlers in the bow of the boat, and for myself I was relieved when they caught nothing else for the rest of the journey.

The small town of Wahai, built around the curve of a deeply indented natural harbour, was hidden from the coastline as we chugged along. Our Chinese friend pointed it out from a distance, saying it was just round the corner of a stretch of mangrove beside which a row of four huge praus were moored, their sails furled, each with a chequerboard pattern of bright blue and red exaggerating the height of their tall masts.

We reached Wahai, but was the *Honi Moki* there? As we got nearer and nearer, both of us almost held our breaths; I kept my fingers crossed and sat on a dirty handkerchief. (Sitting on a handkerchief was a good luck symbol I learnt from my Welsh nanny when I was about four, and I still firmly believe in its magic powers.)

Then we saw it. Before we rounded the corner into the bay, Robin spotted a large dot coming towards us, smoke pouring from its funnel.

'There she is,' he shouted excitedly, rocking the boat as he grabbed my arm to point along the coast. 'She's coming. We've actually beaten her to it. Oh, bless the *Honi Moki*.'

As a matter of fact, at that distance, even the best of nautical experts could not have been sure that the boat coming steaming towards us really was our steamer and not some other craft, but there was something familiar about the way the black smoke poured from her funnel and neither of us had the slightest doubt that we had actually achieved the almost impossible and successfully made our rendezvous. The captain had promised to wait for us at Wahai until mid-day, and as it was now eleven in the morning, we had arrived with an hour to spare.

'First,' the Chinese reminded us firmly, 'you must see to my engine. The *Honi Moki* will stay here for hours. She has first to unload and then to load up again.'

Wahai, in its own way, was as pretty as Sawai, but softer, without the towering rock cliffs that almost encircle the eastern town. A long stone-built jetty stuck out into the bay and behind it a cluster of whitewashed, palm-thatched little houses sat smugly basking in the sun like a children's model village.

The crew of the *Honi Moki* gave us a great welcome, heaved up our battered, damp baggage from the little boat and, automatically now, stowed it back in the wheelhouse. Within minutes of our arrival an Indonesian in uniform arrived on the jetty and asked us to accompany him to the police office and, as we followed him, our Chinese boatman ran along beside us, reminding Robin again and again about his engine.

Round the balcony of the police post dozens of children crowded to stare at us, hanging over the fence, jostling each other to get as close as they could.

'Isn't there a school here?' I asked one of the officials.

'Oh yes,' he said proudly. 'All the children go to school each day.'

'Then why aren't they there now?'

'How could they be?' he said, smiling. 'You have arrived in Wahai so naturally the school is released so that they can see you.'

The Chinese man was still waiting determinedly on the path outside and we followed him to his warehouse, through a dark room smelling strongly of sickly coconut oil and stinking salt fish and into a whitewashed courtyard where the temperature must have been well over a hundred and the brightness of the sun, beating off the walls, made it almost impossible to see. The offending engine was perched on the side of a tin drum filled with water.

Poor Robin. He is good with engines but this was an unknown make to him and had some strange fault that he was quite unable to discover. Apparently, it juddered badly at high speeds out at sea but when it ran in the confined space of the drum, it seemed perfectly all right.

He worked methodically through the parts, stripping down the carburettor and doing a whole lot of things that were unknown to me. He sweated profusely as he worked, while the Chinese and I sat in a two-foot patch of shade under an overhanging roof.

At the end of two hours, he had come up with nothing constructive to say about the motor except that, as far as he could see, it was in perfect condition. Then it occurred to him to ask the Chinese what sort of boat he used it on. When he told Robin it was the same boat he had used to bring us to Wahai, the problem was at last resolved. Robin mopped a dripping brow and heaved a sigh of relief.

'No wonder it judders at high speeds. This motor is far too heavy and powerful for that small boat, you must just attach it to something larger.' With that, we were at last allowed to leave.

Once more, we found the *Honi Moki* was almost unbelievably crowded when we made our way back to it through the crowds of children and grown-ups who had come to get a glimpse of these strange white people. Five chickens and a cock were tied by strings from their feet to the railing near the kitchen. In the front were crates of parakeets and cockatoos, screeching from perches swinging above the hold. As well as the usual crowd of people, bedding rolls and baggage, there were a set of four chairs and a wooden table blocking part of the deck and loading was still going on of more and more highly smelling salt fish, small golden-brown things the shape of mini-swordfish packed in rows between slats of bamboo.

The smell and the noise on the small steamer were shattering, the heat was of exhausting burning furnace proportions and, to our dismay, we were not, as we had supposed, going to have a bunk each for the return journey. Obviously, the captain thought we enjoyed sharing a two-foot bed for the bottom bunk was already occupied by the prosperous Indo-Chinese trader we had seen in the town. He was fat, corpulent and stretched out already asleep, snoring contentedly with loud, burbling expellations of rather garlicky breath.

My Ceram tummy, or whatever it was I had, was still playing havoc with my insides and I made my way over squatting humans, between cackling chickens and past piles of dried fish, to the primitive box-like lavatory at the back, next to an open fire where one of the crew was brewing up a large saucepan of rice. The wall of the 'smallest room' on the boat was only about two feet high and it certainly had not been cleaned out since we had left, but the relief of being there was, at that moment, so intense I was oblivious to everything but bracing myself against the roll of the ship and the job of the moment.

Shouts and yells from behind me made me look round. There, close behind the *Honi Moki*, towed from three short lines, were about a dozen small boats, hitching a lift, their occupants having the laugh of their lives at my obvious embarrassment at being almost totally exposed.

When we arrived in Sawai for an overnight stop the shopkeeper there (who seemed to be the head man of the village) asked about our journey to the Hua Ulu.

'Why did you go up there?' he inquired. 'The other white man and his wife are almost certainly mad but you seem quite sensible. What are the people like?'

'Marvellous,' we said.

The Indonesian looked at us as though he had discovered we were mad too.

'But they are filthy pagans. They still kill people, never wash and their houses are like the pens of pigs.'

'Not at all,' Robin said firmly. 'They are very clean people and their houses are just as good as yours. Their village is very beautiful.' The shopkeeper laughed, showing rows of gleaming, overlarge, china false teeth.

'I know you are joking,' he said and repeated the joke to the crowd around who laughed with him. 'You have a good sense of humour but the Mr and Mrs Valeri really must be mad. He is a professor and yet they go and live like pigs with those killers and even eat pigs with them like the Chinese. The Hua Ulu should be wiped out by the police.' We kept silence, realizing there was nothing to be gained by arguing with him.

We had hoped and expected that the boat would leave Sawai at the crack of dawn the next morning, but by seven they were still loading yet more of that revolting dried fish into every corner of the hold and deck. Most of the crew were lazily hanging over the rail and chattering to the townsfolk who were spreading small piles of sugar cane and green tomatoes on the wooden walkways.

After a meagre breakfast, Robin located the captain and asked him how long it would take us to get back to Ambon. The tiny wizened Chinese man, with a clean white strip of towelling wound round his forehead, shrugged vaguely. He had a number of villages to visit along the coast on the way, he said, picking up cargo; it might be three days or it might be four or five.

The fortnightly flight for Irian left in three days' time, and if we missed it our schedule would be ruined. To have caught up with the *Honi Moki* and then discovered there was little chance of getting back to Ambon in time to catch the flight was almost too much. Despite the glory of the scenery and the magnificence of the high, jungle-topped cliffs and small secluded bays we chugged past after leaving Sawai, we were both miserably depressed. And it was not only the thought of missing the plane; it was also the dread of having to spend as many as four days cramped up in that suffocating, little, over-loaded boat, surrounded by the rancid smell of high, smoked and salted fish. The *Honi Moki* rode even lower in the water than she had on the way out and I could hear the Prussian orchid grower's warnings of travelling on Chinese steamers ringing in my ears, as steam poured from the funnel and we chugged slowly past the policeman's house and looked up at the mountains we had climbed.

Soon after mid-day, we dropped anchor in the middle of a wide, sweeping bay opposite a small village, with a row of small, wooden, palm-thatched huts that clustered around a tiny, miniature, brown slatted mosque. There was no jetty and cargo had to be loaded and unloaded by canoe in frequent trips to the shore where about a hundred children stood in a row, watching.

Despite the fact we had been on or near the sea for so much of our journey in Indonesia, this was only the second time we had either the time or the inclination to take a dip.

We dived together off the roof, and went down and down through delicious salty coolness, rising with grins of delight on our faces, feelings years shed from us, and we played around like porpoises.

From the shore, a roar of excitement came from the children and by the time we reached the curve of sand beyond the washing pool, they were there waiting for us. This bunch were more shy than the children of the larger towns, keeping their distance nervously and following in a long, silent line as we wandered along the soft, warm sand. We stopped to pick up a shell here and there from a waving line that would surely have been a conchologist's dream, a strip about a foot wide that was thick with shells of all shapes, sizes and colours, many of them unworn and shining in shades of purples, pinks and yellows and browns. I crammed as many as I could into the top and bottom of my bikini, persuaded Robin to do the same, although he objected strongly to the rather strange bulge they gave his swimming trunks and, terrified of holding up the *Honi Moki* in any way, we swam back to the boat.

Diving in had been easy enough. Getting back on board was not such a sinecure. Although she rode so low in the water, the deck of the boat was still above our reach and it was not until one of the crew realized our difficulty and produced an old car tyre fender tied on the end of a rope, that we were able to get back onto the boat. Robin managed to scramble up the rope, monkey fashion; I did not have the strength for that and was finally hauled up by the crew in the most undignified way, straddling on my stomach across the tyre. As I rose, another great roar of delight echoed across the water from the massed children on the shore.

We went back on the roof and for the first and surely the only time in my life shared the experience of pop singers when a crowd of hysterical teenyboppers mobs them, screaming in mass hysteria. Luckily for us, this particular mob was, except for a few of the older boys who swam out to the boat and the prau, kept at a safe distance by the water. Every time we moved (even to lift a hand or leg) they burst into an echoing shriek of crazy excitement.

The crew found it hysterical and laughed too, but I began to feel a bit ashamed of our exhibitionism when I saw the Islamite passengers on the deck below craning their heads over the railings to see what we were doing and casting looks of the most extreme disapproval as they looked up at us. But the power of being able to turn on those screams was infantilely intoxicating and, until the boat's engines churned again, we kept them going with the occasional wave of a hand or raising of a leg. The half a dozen boys who had clambered onto the *Honi Moki*, naked or clad in strips of ragged bathing trunks, stayed on the boat until we had almost rounded the corner out of the bay; then they jumped over the side, launching themselves with almost suicidal bravery into space and swimming like frogs, with an exaggerated breast stroke, back towards the shore.

'If we stop for that long at every small village on the coast, we certainly won't make Ambon in time to catch the flight,' Robin said almost despairingly, and decided to try and encourage the captain to go faster and perhaps miss out some of his calls. He disappeared into the wheelhouse and came back looking more hopeful.

'It's almost impossible to know what the old boy's thinking,' he admitted. 'But I've offered him five pounds and, as far as I can make out, he has agreed to get us to Ambon by noon the next day.'

We chugged on stolidly through the night, through the narrow passage between islands that to most sailors, with the help of navigating charts (of which there were none) would have been a nightmare in the daylight, and were woken in the early morning by the captain giving us more weak tea, grinning delightedly.

We tied up at the dock in Ambon harbour at exactly eleven-thirty and never has a debt been more promptly or happily paid. I was still slightly dizzy with lack of sleep and food (the last night had been almost unbearable and Robin, who had a badly infected foot, had tossed and turned, in tune with the tossing and turning I was also doing from the effects of sunburn and fever). Despite everything, we were almost sad to leave the *Honi Moki* and the farewells we got from the crew and their captain were something I will always remember.

Chapter 19

That evening, we met up again with the good Father Rutges who was invigoratingly excited about our adventures and full of enthusiasm for our exploits.

'You must both be people of great determination,' he said, patting both of us on the head with as much pride as if we had been two of the prize pupils at the Catholic school in the town.

Several people in the Moluccas had asked us about birth control, so I asked Father Rutges what his feelings were about the pill.

'Is it, in fact, so necessary?' I asked him. 'This is such a large country, surely there is room for everyone?'

Father Rutges shook his head. It was true there was only a population of one million in the islands, but the number was increasing rapidly. With a world-wide shortage of timber, lumber companies were moving in at an alarming rate and quickly decimating vast areas of land making them useless for anything. Under a government plan, people from Java were being moved to Ceram and Ambon to grow rice paddies and thousands of hopeful immigrants from the overcrowded Celebes were arriving every day in the hope of finding work.

'As you know,' he said, 'the Catholic policy is against birth control, but I personally think the time is not far away when this will be changed. As you have already found, the people here are crying out for the pill but, as the people told you in Ceram, it is only possible for the well-off to buy it. UNO had a birth control programme here but the pills never got further than the Bupati's offices, or are sold in the *apotiks* for large sums which the poor can't afford. Many of the pills go to doctors but they too sell them instead of giving them away free.' He sighed, looking tired, and, for once, showing his age. 'You can't blame the doctors. The only place they are well paid is Java; here their salary is miserably low.'

'Perhaps,' he went on, 'it is anyway not so good for the poor not to have children. Often the people here have nothing but their babies. They live from day to day. They have no transistors or bicycles. Nothing at all except that each year they have another small baby to hold in their arms and rejoice over.'

It was an idealistic idea, but on the whole I thought the pill seemed more practical. In Indonesia one could see hundreds of people living in almost unbelievable squalor, fighting to live and scavenging in the filth of the rubbish-filled canals, existing at a far lower level than the Hua Ulu in their isolated mountain kingdom.

I was glad to leave Ambon. In many ways, the town was beautiful in its idyllic situation with the sheltered bay spreading out before it, crowded with ships of every shape and size; the Ambonese were an attractive race, tall and graceful, the women decorative in their pink-checked sarongs and voluminous *kabayas* often held together by the status symbols of huge safety pins; but the climate, at this time of the year anyway, was humidly suffocating and the sooner we moved on the sooner we would be home.

Coming out of our hotel, on the way to meet Father Rutges, we stopped in the street to wait for a passing bechak. Behind the first boy who came bicycling slowly up the hill, sat a large, pink-faced European, wearing a jungle hat and long shorts. There were few enough Europeans (apart from the missionaries) in Ambon for him to show surprise at seeing us, stop the bechak and want to talk. He had a slightly American accent and his face was that of a heavy drinker, fleshy and shot with broken red/purple veins. For a total stranger, he seemed just a little too friendly and, within five minutes, had told us a lot about himself.

He was the kind of man who had to be called Sam. He owned a

large white motor yacht we had noticed that morning in the harbour, a shining gin palace affair that reeked of dry martinis clinking with ice and dolly birds in mini bikinis. He had been travelling around the Far East with his wife and twenty-year-old son, doing a bit of 'this and that' and had planned to stay in the Moluccas, doing a bit of business, for another few weeks, mostly exploring the many wrecks around the coast. This morning, out of the blue, with no explanation, the authorities had terminated his visa and told him to get out by mid-day the next day.

'So I'm taking the boat back to Singapore,' he said finally, 'and if either of you'd like a lift you're welcome to come along for the ride. I've had Indonesia, frankly, in a big way.'

For just a moment, the thought of those iced martinis, an obviously comfortable boat and a quick flight home from Singapore tempted me, but I quickly came down to earth. It was not just that, despite my running nose, still green complexion and inevitably travel-stained appearance. He gave me a look of such lechery that I had a strong suspicion his 'wife' might not be joining him for the journey, but there was something that I can only describe as reeking of corruption about this smugly smiling, overweight man, I found it easy to believe the Ambon authorities had good reason to send him packing.

'Here's my card,' he said as he went on his way. 'If you change your mind before tomorrow morning, you know where the boat is.'

As we trundled down into the main part of the town behind a puffing bechak boy, Robin and I speculated on his business and 'bit of this and that'. Drug-running, we hazarded, pillaging wrecks or perhaps diamond smuggling.

'Probably the whole lot,' Robin concluded. 'I've seldom met anyone more fishy and if you think I'd ever have let you go off alone with that character, you must be out of your mind.'

We flew into the island of Biak, a halfway point to Irian, just as the sun was beginning to set, coming in over the sea to make a bumpy landing on a large runway. The island had played a big part in the last war and had, for a time, been a stronghold for the Japanese. Behind the airport rose sheer white cliffs where they had hidden their munitions. Apparently, the rocks were riddled with natural caves and tunnels and there was a story that, deep inside, a cave still existed which had been equipped by the Japanese as a work shop and which had still not been discovered. One solitary Chinaman was supposed to know of its whereabouts but he refused to share the information because he could not get hold of the salvage rights, and the value of the tools inside was so great he was reluctant to share the spoils.

Merpati Airline Hotel stood by the edge of the rocky, shallow sea bed, opposite the airport. Flying by the airline, and since there was no onward flight to New Guinea until the next day, we were supposed to get our accommodation and food free. It looked better than most Indonesian hotels, with a low, fairly modern wooden building stretching out in a wide L-shape, facing the sea and the dramatic sunset that now filled the sky with orange-pink waves of light against which palm trees and fishermen wading through the shallows with small nets were silhouetted in an imitation of a classic travel calendar photograph of a paradise island.

In the hotel, we met up with a party of miners who took us off for dinner at their camp base about a mile away (Gene, an exaggeratedly dressed Texan, who was their head, ticking off one of the Australians severely when he tried to secrete a half-empty can of beer into the Volkswagen mini-bus we drove in). After a plastic meal of frozen food, flown in from Australia, in a mess-room made icy cold by ultra-efficient air conditioning, we went back to the bar until the little Chinese girl, serving beer after beer and double measures of Scotch, firmly closed it up. Then we sat in the lounge, drinking a last round ordered on the excuse that it was 7 May and Robin's birthday.

Robin, Gene and a couple of the other men had a rather flighty, intellectual conversation about the state and the future of the world. I found myself sitting next to a large Dane who, steadily drinking vodka almost neat, was as 'pickled as a newt' and morose as well. Tears rolled down his cheeks as he told me about his lovely young Indonesian Batak wife (whom he'd like to be with at that moment) and how he had to fly a plane out at dawn the next morning.

'Nothing better than a Batak wife,' he slurred, his shoes off, sitting cross-legged on his chair, a rumpled shirt half open to expose a large belly overflowing over his belt. 'Marvellous way to live. I can have it off with anyone I like, but if she so much as looks at another man, her family will kill her. Really,' he insisted, pressing my hand with a large, sweaty paw, 'I mean that. In this day and age, they would kill her dead if she did the dirty on me.'

Skip, for that was his name, despite being totally inebriated, scattered pearls of valuable advice amongst the stories of his life and experiences as a pilot, especially when I told him I was half Swedish and have an uncle who rates as the best-known entertainer in Scandinavia. Povel Ramel, my uncle, happened to be one of Skip's heroes. His eyes crossed as he gazed at me in disbelief and finally took my word for it.

'Shrrup,' he slurred belligerently at the others. 'Shive shumthing 'portant t'tell yawl. Thris Ghirll's Povel Ramel's neisch. Shime going to do everything I can t'help shittle lady.'

If we wanted to get to the Dani tribe in central Irian and to the Asmat in the South, where the largest and most exciting groups of isolated tribes lived, we would have to enlist the help of the Roman Catholic mission in Jayapura. They were the only people likely to get us there. We would have to pay our way and be extremely tactful for, after the Wyn Sargent affair, anything to do with the word anthropology or isolated tribes was suspect as far as the Indonesian government was concerned.

Skip also gave us a note, scribbled on a piece of paper torn out of an ancient *Reader's Digest*, to his wife's uncle who was the head policeman in the Baliem Valley where the Dani tribe live. If we got into trouble there, he would help us.

We managed to escape from the party at around two in the morning and as Skip staggered towards the door, I wondered how on earth he could possibly hope to fly a plane a few hours later.

As we tumbled dazedly into bed, neither of us too steady after so much unaccustomed alcohol, I wondered also how we were ever to get up in time to get back to the airport to catch our flight at five-thirty.

The people from the mining camp had been dubious about our chances of the flight to Jayapura leaving that morning, but the seedy-looking Dakota was waiting there on the runway and only due to leave an hour behind schedule. As we boarded it, we saw Skip cross the runway and climb into the cockpit of a trim little jet, his clothes still as creased as ever but his step firm and his eyes clear.

'That man must have the constitution of an ox,' I remarked slightly bitterly as I eased myself gingerly into one of the uncomfortable canvas seats of our plane and cradled my aching head in my hands, my stomach heaving as we were offered the Merpati breakfast of cold lumps of sticky rice wrapped round a few grams of highly spiced meat.

The Dakota took off all right but once in the air it began behaving like a badly disjointed yoyo, bumping up and down and swinging crazily from side to side. Obviously, the pilot did not like it any more than I did, for after an hour and a half of this bucking progress, he announced we had bad engine trouble and would have to return to Biak. The other passengers, all Indonesians, sat stolidly, taking this hitch without comment, while both Robin and I groaned aloud. It looked as though the others had been right and we were not, after all, to reach Irian that day.

We sat in the now sweltering airport for another hour after coming down in a series of jolting bounds and then, to our amazement, were informed that another plane had been laid on and we would now leave for Irian in an hour's time. Merpati, on this occasion, had, thank heaven, come to our aid.

A few hours later, this time after a smooth flight, we landed at Sentani, the airport for Jayapura, and set foot on Irian Jaya where, according to all the information Robin had gathered, we were likely to see the most exciting isolated tribes of our whole expedition through Indonesia. If, that is, we were able to get to them.

Sentani airport is some distance from the city. To my surprise, it was considerably larger than the airports we had landed at during the last few weeks. It was also a bustling hive of activity and crowded with Europeans, mostly women and children, who looked as though they were dressed up for a garden party. I wondered if my hangover had affected my brain.

I had expected Irian to be wild, primitive and uncivilized, but our first impression of the country, at the airport, was totally opposite. In an 'Alice in Wonderland' sort of way, I felt thoroughly let down as we waited for our baggage, watching the groups of European ladies, missionaries and wives of FUNDWI, dressed in sleeveless, neatly pressed dresses or trouser suits, their hair immaculately groomed, scrabbling to get supplies, refrigerators and deep freezes off the fortnightly flight which had just come in from Australia. The white, white ladies, greatly outnumbered Indonesians, and the only dark-skinned, frizzy-haired, indigenous Papuans were a few shabby-dressed characters acting as porters.

'We'd better go to the hotel first and drop our luggage rather than arrive with it on the mission doorstep,' Robin decided, and yet again we made the mistake of telling the teenage lank-haired driver of a pick-up to take us to 'the best hotel'.

The drive from Sentani to Jayapura must be the most scenically beautiful route between any airport and capital city in the world. The city itself must surely have had its name changed (to what must have been quite some confusion for the people who live in it) more often than any other city in the world. Founded by the Dutch, it was first named Hollandia. When the Dutch were removed from West Irian by the Indonesians in 1962 and UNO took over the country, it was re-named Kota Baru (Newmarket); then Sukarno took over and dubbed it Sukarnopura and, when he was discredited, it was finally christened Jayapura, and Irian Barat was re-named Irian Jaya (Irian Victory).

The road to the city runs through open rolling country, past a series of deep, large and glassy-surfaced lakes, strangely northern-looking for a tropical country, open, grandiose and magnificent, surrounded by hills with small villages nestling beside the shores of the lakes and occasional patches of exotic jungle giving the scenery a romantic, fairy-tale look.

The road, originally built by the Dutch, had deteriorated badly and was in the process of being re-made under the auspices of a foreign-aid programme. Work seemed to be progressing slowly and at one point a queue of traffic was held up on both sides by a steam-roller that had slid sideways off the edge of the tarmac. Half the road was blocked by the steam-roller and the other half by a line of oil drums.

Everyone hooted their horns in a sort of nightmarish tattoo that did little for my head, but sat in their cars without attempting to do anything constructive.

Robin took over and jumped onto the road, heaved aside a couple of the barrels (they were empty), ran back to our taxi and told the driver to get on with it. The rest of the traffic stayed still, stunned by this exhibition, and we passed through first, on the wrong side of the road.

From then on the drive developed into a mad, careering race. The other taxis we had passed took exception at such cheeky behaviour and turned the route into a Monte Carlo rally, tooting their horns, passing us as we whizzed round hair-raising corners, and then being re-passed by our driver (the vehicle may have had good tyres but it certainly did not have good brakes) who was not going to be bettered.

There were jeers of derision from the boys in front as we passed numerous taxis stuck by the side of the road with flat tyres, and screams of success as, first again, we rounded the last upward corner and began descending the steep incline down to Jayapura.

I held my breath, not because of the hectic ride but because of the staggering panorama spread out before us; Rio de

Janeiro in miniature with the city sprawling down jungle-clad, steep, rounded hills towards a horseshoe bay dotted with lush green islands. As a situation, the city was in an almost paradisical position with the protection of the mountains behind and the shelter of a deep-water bay in front.

At the height of Dutch colonialism, Hollandia was said to be an attractive small city, with the finest yacht club in the world, built out on a pier in the centre of the harbour. The same could certainly not be said of Jayapura now. At the far side of the bay, a pathetic straggling row of waterfront slums spread in a line of pathetic rusted shacks built on rotting stilts spanning the water across to a small island. On the slopes behind, giant scars slashed through the tumbling jungle to make room for tiny prefabricated huts. Even the centre of the city had a shabby, jerry-built air and the few modern administrative buildings were seedy-looking and unattractive, centred round an ugly, three times life size, bronze statue of a sailor with grotesquely bulging muscles, elephantine hands and huge splayed feet.

The yacht club had gone as well, and in its place was a small rusty pier, and a ramshackle, scruffy-looking restaurant jutted out from the waterfront. The Dutch, we had been told, when they realized they would have to evacuate Hollandia, spent their last two days crowded into the club, drinking every drop of spirits in the place before setting fire to the building.

To me, Jayapura was a sad and sour place and not least because those who live in it have almost succeeded in hounding out the Papuans whose territory by right it is. Irian, rich in timber and minerals, was about to enter a boom era and everyone except the indigenous people of the country was rushing to jump on the bandwagon. People from Makassar, Sulawesi, Sumatra and Java arrived in their thousands to trade and, even in the market, the Papuans are ganged up against, with prices being controlled by the Indonesians. The few local sellers are pushed out of the centre of the market. The Chinese control the shops and even the lumber companies were using imported labour.

The Papuan, say the outsiders, has no room in a progressive nation. He is not used to regular hours and steady work and no-one has the time or the patience to teach him these lessons. Gradually he has been pushed further and further back from the city and, with the influx of foreigners, is subjected to the inevitability of poverty, prostitution and disease.

We were sitting on the verandah of our hotel when the surprising miracle of a harassed, rather plump Indonesian lady in Bermuda shorts and a short, loose smock appeared by our table.

'Are you Mr and Mrs Campbell?' she asked breathlessly, pushing damp strands of black hair out of her eyes and peering short-sightedly at us. When we said we were not, she looked rather as if she were going to burst into tears, flopped into a chair and introduced herself as Mrs Yani, the Head of Tourism in Irian Jaya.

The authorities in Jakarta had grandiose ideas about the future and the scale of tourism in Irian, but they saw it through heavily tinted, rose-coloured spectacles, and poor Mrs Yani was supposed to make their dreams come true virtually single-handed. Whatever her drawbacks, she was certainly heaven-sent as far as we were concerned and turned out to be our passport to both the Baliem Valley and the Asmat. Her eyes lit up when Robin talked of our travels and the cooperation of the tourist authorities in Jakarta, and she became practically goggle-eyed when she learnt we both wrote and were interested in the progress of tourism in Irian. I must admit we omitted to tell her the reasons for our interests in tourism (the effect it would have on the indigenous people of the country) but Robin was perfectly fair in explaining about his reasons for travelling in other parts of the world.

She clapped her hands delightedly and outpoured a torrent of ideas and suggestions in remarkably good English.

'My dear Mr Tenison and Mrs Tenison, you are very welcome here. Your trip will be terrifically successful and you will see what we are doing for tourism. A few days ago there were three German ladies on a similar mission and I arranged for them to go to Wamena in the Baliem and Agats and, as I need to go to both places myself in order to prepare for great numbers of American tourists coming soon, I can come with you and also make arrangements. We will share the cost of the flight and everything will be much cheaper.'

'First,' she said, 'you have to go to the mission and persuade Father Franz, who runs the flight schedules, to take us all to Wamena and Agats.' She had a car and driver there at the hotel (in order to meet an elusive couple called Campbell who she vaguely thought were American or English and who were meant to be going on a nature tour through Irian) so we got the driver to take us down into the town and drop us at the mission.

The Catholics, their fingers burnt twice, first over the death of young Michael Rockefeller and then over the whole Wyn Sargent affair, were understandably dubious about us at first and justifiably suspicious of anyone who might rock their already tenuous position in Irian. Fortunately, Robin was able to persuade them we were not out to cause a sensation in any way or liable to be an embarrassment to anyone and, after we finally caught up with Father Franz (which, after chasing hectically around the town all evening, did not eventually happen until the next morning) he managed to get our plans for visiting first the Dani and then the Asmat looking as though they might possibly come to fruition. It was a major achievement for few foreigners had been allowed to either place and no anthropological permits were being granted for the present or foreseeable future.

Roughly, the outline was that we should fly to Wamena, the airstrip in the Baliem Valley, by a scheduled Merpati flight, in two days' time. We would then spend six days with the Dani, be picked up by the missionary plane and be joined by Mrs Yani and then flown down to Agats for the six days we had left before Robin had to catch the plane he was to take on to Papua New Guinea where he was to take a brief look at the mining activities of Rio Tinto Zinc Corporation in Bougainville.

Once we left Indonesia, it was not possible to return without a new visa so I, on my existing visa which would have a few days left on it before it would expire, was to fly back alone to Jakarta, pick up the luggage we had left there with David Treffry and then re-join Robin in Singapore.

At the hotel that second evening, I had my first experience of that strange language known as pidgin English.

We were sitting on the verandah, having a beer, and were joined by a party of rather coarse, loud-mouthed Australians on a business fact-finding mission to Jayapura. They yelled rudely at the two Papuan waiters trying to do their best to cope with their requests: 'Hurry-up-then-you-damn-boys-quickey-chop-chop-you-fetchee-beer-proper-cold-lightning-fast,' they shouted; or something very like it. To me, it seemed an unpleasant and extraordinarily complicated way of asking for 'Two cold beers, please'. Later, I discovered it was indeed a long-winded language; imagine the word for a cross-saw, for instance, being 'You push him he come, you pull him he go'!

The mission seemed to have a most efficient radio control spread out between their stations in the Baliem Valley and the Asmat and, for the next day, we watched a pleasant Dutchman – wearing shorts with his shirt already stained with sweat, as even at that hour of the morning the heat was intense – twiddling with dials and knobs, trying to make contact with faint voices that came through a distorted crackle of static, in Dutch, English and Indonesian.

The babbling suddenly stopped completely and the Dutchman swung round on his chair to talk to us.

'The weather has closed down in the west,' he said, 'and I've got a plane somewhere up there. At this time of the year, the climate is so unstable, things get really difficult.'

The radio crackled again and the large, sandy-haired man turned back to the job of juggling with his knobs, trying to follow the vagaries of the weather, sudden storms and low clouds, immersed in the business of keeping in touch with the far outposts of the mission and protecting, as far as possible, the lives of the pilots who flew for it. Those pilots in Irian have a tough and dangerous life. Much of the flying they do is over high mountains or across hundreds of miles of virtually uncharted areas of swamp or jungle. The airstrips they land on are usually short stretches of grass hacked from the forest or mud banks built from the swamp. Crashes are frequent.

It was a plane crash which caused the discovery of the Baliem Valley in 1954, a huge fertile area of land, high in the mountains, surrounded by jagged peaks with virtually no access other than by air. After the discovery came a botanical expedition to the area and then the missionaries, both Catholic and Protestant, men whose aim it was to pacify and convert the wild Dani tribes, about 50 000 strong, living in the valley and the mountains around; tribes described as so warlike and dangerous that they prompted one of the first Protestant missionaries in the area to write a book called *Cannibal Valley* (actually a totally misleading title for, although the Dani were, and still are, a war-like people and life is considered of little value there is absolutely no evidence to show that they were ever, unlike the Asmat tribes, eaters of human flesh).

Since then, the valley has been opened up to a certain extent. Now there is a fairly large Catholic mission at Wamena and a small township has been built around a sizeable military and police post. There was even a tarmac airstrip large enough to take Army planes and a regular Merpati flight schedule.

We embarked on another battered DC4 and began our journey to the Dani in a rather subdued frame of mind, afraid that, from Mrs Yani's descriptions, we might be arriving too late to see the Dani in all their glory and that the Baliem, like so many places we had seen in Brazil, might be disintegrating under the controversial axe of 'civilization'.

'I will book you in at the hotel in Wamena,' (we had not even thought of there being a hotel there) the lady had told us gaily. 'You will love it there. Of course, it is simple, not like our wonderful hotel here in Jajapura; still, it is very comfortably pleasant and soon there will be a modern skyscraper built in the town for the thousands of tourists who will visit the valley.'

In Jayapura, we had also learnt of a project, put forward by the authorities in Jakarta, called 'Operation Koteka', a plan to civilize the Dani, which had as its patron the first lady of the land, Madame Suharto, the President's wife. Under the project, the Dani were to be clothed, learn to use modern tools and build hygienic, modern houses instead of their thatched huts.

It was something of a relief to find the Dakota carried only a handful of passengers besides ourselves, and those were all either Papuans or Indonesians, not a band of cut-price, all-in tourists.

After a two-hour flight, we swooped up and over a range of heavily forested mountain slopes and came down to the incredibly wide, intensively cultivated area of the Baliem Valley, split by a large river winding through the green lushness and ringed by a circle of high jagged peaks. We stepped out of the plane into strong aerated sunlight and a dramatic, romantic world on which civilization seemed to have made very little impact. Admittedly, there were signs of the twentieth century in the tarmacked runway and the small collection of prefabricated, tin-roofed huts which make up the tiny township of Wamena, but far more exciting to us was the sudden, startling impression of having gone back to the Stone Age as we stared with blatant amazement at the large crowd of Dani tribesmen who stood behind a flimsy wood barrier watching the arrival of the Dakota. At that first glance, they looked primitive, savage and totally alien against the background of tin shacks and asphalt.

The Dani stood silent and still, small people who, from a distance, looked larger because of the sturdiness of their build and the upright carriage of their bodies; the dark, almost black men dressed only in their kotekas, thin, twisted gourds attached to their penises, some with nets over their matted, kinky hair, others with headdresses of bright feathers, nearly all of them carrying long, wooden spears like ceremonial staves. Amongst the men were a smattering of women with string baskets hanging down their backs from bands across their foreheads, naked too, except for a strange mini sporran made from curves of stranded, woven reeds, hanging from below their hips to just above their knees and barely covering their pubic hairs. Like the men, they were dark-skinned and had tightly curled black hair, often hanging in matted kinks. They too were small, tough, wiry and sturdy.

They stared back at us, calmly, showing neither particular interest nor surprise in us. There was no evidence of 'Operation Koteka', of clothes or modern implements. The only evidence of supposed civilization was a piece of plastic covering one man's head in place of the 'Ena Sharples' type hairnets in woven string many of them wore; and a few pieces of plastic strung around the neck of another man instead of the strange collars looking slightly like false dickies made of white cowries, sewn onto strips of greasy leather, which most of the other men had.

In a daze, we looked around for the hotel and saw nothing but a dismal corrugated-iron shack by the runway. That was the hotel.

A couple of Dani boys – wearing kotekas of only eight inches instead of those sported by their elders which often reached up to shoulder height, held against their bodies by pieces of string tied around their chests – picked up our bags and led us through the barrier and the crowd of silent Dani towards this building. As we passed, they moved back to make a path for us and we got the first smell of the slightly sweet, acrid aroma of rancid pig's fat coming from their bodies. Unlike the rest of the tribes we saw in Indonesia, the Dani seldom wash, for the simple reason that, as we were soon to find out, it gets very cold at night in the Baliem Valley. For the naked Dani, a thick layer of pig's grease provides a welcome protection from the almost icy blasts sweeping down from the mountains (some of them are actually snow-capped). At first, the smell was almost overpowering. After a time, we got used to it although I never became totally immune to the almost shattering waves of stale, pungent, pigsty perfume which assailed us when we crawled into a confined space of about a hundred cubic feet and joined a dozen or more squatting Dani, around a chimneyless fire, in one of their village chiefs' huts.

Between the hotel and the outskirts of the little town a large, open, tin-roofed shed acted as a market. Without doubt, it was the strangest trading place I have ever seen, or will ever.

At the far end, Indonesians, mostly Makassarese, stood behind a group of small kiosks and some wooden stalls, selling cheap, shoddy articles of clothing, torches, plastic, rusty knives, cigarettes, salt, tobacco and tinned goods at vastly inflated prices. The other end was allotted to the Dani, and here, on rough benches along crude trestle tables, sat rows of Dani women (naked except for their strange reed skirts) side by side, close as they could get to each other, with pathetic piles of fresh vegetables heaped on the tables in front of them.

It was one of the most flagrant illustrations of racial discrimination I have ever experienced, with the Indonesians commandeering the most sheltered quarter and the Dani separated as though a physical barrier had been erected across the shed.

The women with babies curled up in the string baskets hanging down their backs were like rows of twittering brown sparrows; many of them were knitting new baskets with their fingers, knotting greasy string with the speed of light. They were all talking so that the air was filled with the quick patter of high-pitched voices, a chattering in a bird-like tonal language that finished sentences with a long-drawn-out staccato sound, on a rising scale, winding up in an 'eeeeee' almost high enough to smash a champagne glass, had there been one handy.

The Dani women are very small, with primitive, rather negroid features, thick lips and wide, splayed nostrils. Most of them had their hair cut short, covering their heads in a grease-matted tangled cap of tight kinks; their breasts hung long and heavy, tilting at the tits against their chests, and their stomachs bulged over the tight band of their curious semi-circular mini-skirts. They kept themselves very much to themselves.

The men, on the other hand, were marvellously disdainful about everything. Walking square-shouldered and erect, their penis-sheaths jutting out in front of them and their heads crowned with every form of headdress, from plastic bath caps to knitted string hair-nets and bands of glorious feathers that were coronets of vivid colour, fashioned in a variety of patterns and shapes. One sported just a single bird-of-paradise feather rising from a band of leather sewn with cowries and most wore long ties of grease-impregnated pig-skin hanging down their chests. Like the women, they had flat, spreading noses, often disfigured by a large hole through the septum, but their foreheads were high and their eyes arched by thick heavy brows. A thin coat of curly hair covered their bodies and, though they had no hair above their upper lip, their chins were rimmed with short, tightly curling beards. Many of them stood in front of the Indonesian stalls, not touching anything but staring intently at the cheap goods on sale.

There was still no sign of Operation Koteka and, indeed, both the men and women seemed quite happy with and even proud of their naked state.

It began to rain. A cold driving shower swept through the Dani area of the market and the women huddled together, crossing their arms and linking their hands behind their necks for warmth. The men did the same, hugging themselves as they continued to strut around like turkey cocks.

We walked along muddy tracks to the Catholic mission, the only reasonably attractive thing about the town, built of wood with a church standing near it.

One of the Fathers there told us he would radio Father Camps, with whom Robin had corresponded from England, and tell him we would be leaving for Yiweka at the northern part of the valley the next morning.

We also met a young Austrian, a layman, helping the Fathers with an agricultural programme. Later that evening, he came to the hotel to tell Robin about his experiences with the Dani.

'What the people need here is a "cash crop",' he told us. It was a theory we were to hear again and again.

The Dani, Carl said, were brilliant natural farmers. Their crops of sweet potatoes, tomatoes and other vegetables were superb and their husbandry of pigs was magnificent.

'They have everything they need to make themselves self-supporting – crops, meat and fish from the river. If they were left alone, they would be perfectly happy, but with the building of a town at Wamena and the pressures of schemes like Operation Koteka the situation inevitably alters.'

Vegetables from the Baliem, we gathered, used to be sent by plane down from the valley to Jayapura; now they were brought in from Makassar. The outsiders had successfully managed to boycott the produce from the Dani and few of the Wamena townspeople would buy their goods. If they did, they usually cheated them right and left.

Although the Dani had no particular desire for clothes, the men, in particular, longed to buy razors, torches and knives. For those their cowries were no longer of any use. They had to get money and they had virtually no way of obtaining it.

In our two narrow rooms that night it was freezing cold, the sort of cold we had not experienced since leaving England and for which we were totally ill-equipped. We lay shivering on either side of a corrugated-iron partition, listening to the wind moaning down from the mountains, to heavy rain beating on the tin roof and to the rats which seemed to be gnawing at the metal legs of the iron beds. The blankets smelt musty and dirty. I was still coughing, sneezing and aching from Ceram and it was impossible to get comfortable on the hard bed. The noise of the rats intensified once we had blown out the lamp and I began to have hallucinations about them actually attacking me as I lay there shivering, unable to get warm; however, I huddled my arms around my body, Dani fashion. I could see now why they covered themselves in pig's fat; in this climate, especially if one was naked, it was an obvious way to keep warm – and the same applied to not washing. I tried to do a cursory wash before going to bed but the water in the rusty barrel outside was about as cold as an Alpine stream and not nearly as clean, so I merely dabbed at my face and hands and left it at that.

Early next morning, while it was still chill and damp (raw as a February morning in England), a Dani, dressed in ragged clothes, barged into our room without knocking as we were getting dressed and plonked a rusty thermos of coffee down beside us.

At the Wamena mission, we had heard the rather disturbing news that three German ladies were due to fly into the Yiweka post that morning, having come by mission plane from Asmat. For Robin, Father Camps was vital to his search for information about the situation of the isolated tribes in Indonesia. The Dutch Father had been one of the first missionaries to enter the valley and he was reported to know more about the tribe than anyone else. German tourists or not, we could not wait to leave the hotel and set off up the valley.

Late as usual, accompanied by the hotel manager's son – a rather dashing young man, dressed in 'with-it' denim jeans and jacket and carrying a .22 rifle and taking along a friend of his for the trip – we set off for the walk to Yiweka which, if we made good time, should take us about four hours.

Obaharok, a Dani chieftain, the husband of Wyn Sargent

An Asmat carving on the
bow of a ceremonial
canoe

Asmat carvings against
the sunset

An attractive Dani girl
chops a banana tree in the
Baliem Valley

Dani men, wearing their
penis sheaths, in West
Irian

Asmat women balance on the frail plank walks at Agats

Chapter 20

Before we had gone far, we were joined by an unusually tall Dani, dressed in faded, torn shorts, who shouldered Robin's knapsack, leaving him with only the heavy camera case and me with my beastly plastic carrying bag. That bag, a cumbersome, rectangular-shaped affair of cheap, brown plastic, was the bane of my life during this part of the journey. It was not quite large enough to take everything I needed to carry in it and neither was it small enough to be easy to carry. It looked aesthetically unattractive, made no pretence of being waterproof and its strap broke with boring regularity. It had, however, been the only vaguely suitable thing I had been able to find in Ambon or since then and I was stuck with it. On the journey to Yiweka, it seemed to weigh a ton, it bumped uncomfortably against my hip and the narrow strap bit into my shoulder and I finally ended up hanging it, Dani style, down my back with the strap around my forehead.

Wamena is built at the eastern end of the Baliem, near where the valley narrows and the river begins its torrential, cascading, turbulent, twisting route through the mountains finally to wind its way in a series of curving loops across the mangrove swamps to the south coast of Irian. We walked west through the centre of the wide valley towards the mountains at the far end, and as the sun rose and the skies cleared, it soon became furnace-hot again, in total contrast to the cold of the night.

At first, we were on a wide, muddy track, scored with deep ruts from the tyres of the few tractors in Wamena, trudging through thick sludge between flat fields of sweet potatoes. We passed a few Indonesians, who politely raised their hands giving the Indonesian good morning, 'Salamat Pagi', and a lot of Dani walking towards the town. Our companions greeted the men with a pat on the shoulder or a shake of the left hand and a high-pitched nasal 'Nyak'. The women kept their eyes shyly to the ground and muttered a twittering 'Louk', words which apparently combined everything from 'Good morning' to 'How's your great-great-grandfather?'

All the men were naked except for their dried-gourd kotekas, and I never did discover quite why the Dani wore their strange penis-sheaths. Someone told me it was the obvious flaunting of the male organ in a permanent state of erection – the older and more important you are the bigger the sheath. Someone else said it was to protect them in battle and yet another person put forward the suggestion that the gourds were there merely to keep flies off their penises. Whatever the reason, the long, dried gourds gave the Dani men the most extraordinary appearance.

Not being a man, I am not really equipped to comment on such a question, but it appeared to me that the kotekas must be most uncomfortable – the penis and one ball were squeezed into the narrow opening and tightly tied there with narrow string and I found myself fascinated by such questions as: How did they pee? And when they made love, did they leave the koteka on or take it off? I never found out the answers to these questions either.

Whereas the Dani women were rather drab, the men, like the birds of paradise their country is so famous for, obviously liked to dress up, even on a normal day. They were like brilliant, exotic birds with often highly ornate feather head-dresses, wearing long cowrie collars or necklaces of huge, curved white shells round their necks. Black patterns of soot mixed with grease decorated the bodies of many of them or encircled their eyes. They were also extremely graceful, striding along with their heads high, walking on the balls of their feet with apparently effortless movements, strong and fit with muscles bulging. They were gay and cheerful, all of them breaking into a wide smile as they passed us, their white teeth unmarred by the chewing of betel nut.

There were Dani everywhere, groups of women, working in the fields, plodding towards Wamena, walking along a small path, single file, herding two or three enormous black, coarse-haired pigs in front of them; groups of men passing the time of day squatting in a circle under the shade of a solitary tree or striding purposefully towards the town.

We walked through a small patch of scrub jungle, passed by a short smidgen of welcome shade, and came out to the point at which we had to cross the river.

A narrow suspension bridge of wooden slats, swung on thin wires from poles on each bank, spanned the water. Recent storms had destroyed most of the flimsy handrail on either side and many of the slats, and in a slight breeze the bridge swung gently from side to side and bounded crazily up and down when anyone crossed it. The river was about 150 yards wide at this point and rain from the mountains had swelled it, with thickly muddied water swirling past at a horrific pace. If one fell in there, God help one.

I knew what the first man to cross Niagara on a tightrope must have felt. I held my breath, balanced gingerly on the two-foot-wide slats, and swayed giddily. Robin would have helped me but the bridge was not strong enough to take more than the weight of one person at a time. I had to make it on my own. Somehow I crossed to the far bank without falling into the foaming torrent of water and then, to my embarrassment, had to sit down, my legs shaking so much that I could not go on.

The manager's son, Ronnie, produced a plastic bottle of water flavoured with lemon and I took great welcome gulps. It was the first time I had done any real walking since Ceram, and I had not realized how much I still ached from that venture or how stiff every joint of my body had become. After a ten-minute stop, we were immediately joined by a party of three Dani men who shook our left hands heartily as though we were old friends, accepted cigarettes and grunted words none of us, except our Dani companions, could understand.

We trudged on through the valley, now on a narrow path that was baked iron hard by the sun in some places and squelchy with ankle-deep mud in others. Fields of sweet potatoes spread out all around us, devoid of trees or shade, bordered by neat irrigation channels. In patches of fallow ground, big black pigs rooted amongst high, coarse grass that was dotted with pale blue and white flowers. Butterflies fluttered lazily around our heads and, in the distance, the mountains rose hazy and purple-blue, many of their peaks wreathed in wisps of white mist. One, at least, was so high that even in this tropical belt, its jagged top was continually covered in snow. In the distance, we could see occasional patches of greenery indicating a Dani village.

At our next stop, Ronnie unpacked his gun from its canvas case and began popping off at a few small birds flying way beyond his range in a way that would horrify any British sportsman, and again Dani men appeared from nowhere to join us and squat on the ground. They touched our bodies to make contact, the reek of pig fat oozing over us like an odorous blanket in the heavy, humidified heat. We were also surrounded by a thick cloud of sharply biting mosquitoes that came from a clear sky and took stinging nips from any exposed flesh. They were such vicious creatures they even managed to bite successfully through the cotton tee-shirt and jeans I wore.

Our Dani bearer pointed proudly towards the glint of a tin roof, reflecting the sun from a tree-fringed village at the foot-hills of the ever-growing-closer mountains. Ronnie translated.

'That is the Protestant mission school near the village where Wyn Sargent lived,' he told us. The ricochet of the American woman's stay in Irian had bothered us throughout our expedition to Indonesia, from the moment we left England to this, the last island we were to visit and her particular area of interest. In the Baliem, we learnt more of the full story, why the Indonesian government had felt it necessary to extradite her, and why they were now so suspicious of any foreigners, especially anyone to do with anthropology, visiting their tribes. Certainly, there were faults on everyone's side, but both of us finally ended up by feeling that Wyn Sargent, however justifiable her motives, had gone about things the wrong way.

Wyn Sargent as well as being an anthropologist, was a journalist, and her original contact with Indonesia was when she travelled in Borneo a few years before and, through the help of the American Embassy, started a monetary appeal for the Dayak tribes. Then, late in 1972, she went to the Baliem to live in order to write a book about her experiences of co-habiting with a Stone Age tribe and while there married an Irian Chief.

In the Baliem, Wyn Sargent was accompanied by an Indonesian girl from a tourist agency in Jakarta. They obviously had conversational difficulties because very few people speak the Dani language and Obaharok does not speak Bahasi Indonesian.

Her marriage to Obaharok, the middle-aged Dani chief, had been arranged through the normal Papuan procedure of presenting the husband with a dowry of pigs. Obaharok already had three wives and some children but, as the Dani are polygamous, that was no deterrent to his having another wife; and, in any case, marriage amongst the tribes seems to be taken quite lightly all round, Divorce amongst the Dani appears to be an even more popular pursuit than it has become in this country; the only difference that instead of squabbling over settlements of hard cash they squabble over the repayment of their dowries of pigs and cowries.

The Indonesian authorities became alarmed when Wyn Sargent began to criticize the police administration of the Baliem Valley, and the Protestant missionaries there were concerned when she persuaded the women of Obaharok's village not to send their children to the missionary school. Dani children normally accompany their mothers to the fields from the moment they are born. The fields are their schoolrooms, with simple wooden implements replacing books and toys as they learn to weed and hoe.

Things finally came to a head in the valley when Obaharok began boasting of the power his marriage to the American woman would give him over the other tribes of the Baliem. Soon, it was rumoured, Obaharok said he would become 'the biggest chief in the world'. Other chiefs, who had made pacts of peace with Obaharok, didn't like this one bit, and inevitably the rumours spread to the police in Wamena. Wyn Sargent, whose visa had expired anyway, was asked to leave.

In America, this now world-famous lady has started an energetic campaign to expose ill-treatment being carried out on the Dani by the authorities.

While we were there – although we certainly saw and heard ample evidence that the situation was in no way ideal in the Baliem Valley and that the police had burnt down some villages, killed pigs in outbursts of Muslim fanaticism and had fired over the heads of some of the tribesmen – her reports seemed to be highly exaggerated and her husband, Obaharok, appeared, contrary to one of her outbursts, to be suffering from neither torture nor ill-treatment.

The Yiweka mission was made up of a school house, a simple wooden building with a tin roof, a school teacher's house and the mission house. After just under four hours, we walked up the grass runway past a screen of trees almost completely hiding the Dani village, crossed some shaky planks across a dyke and walked up the path to Father Camps' house, a two-storeyed building he had made himself which had a surprisingly Dutch air about it. A neat, cosy and snug-looking building of wood. All it needed, I thought, was a border of formal flowers (apparently it had originally had those too, but the Dani had cut and eaten them).

The front door opened onto a narrow room, bare except for a wooden table, two wooden benches and a cheap looking-glass hanging on the wall. It was full of Dani men and their smell was exceedingly strong. About a dozen of them sat on the benches, lounged against the walls or peered at themselves in the mirror, fingering their kotekas, knitting ceremonial bands with string and a bamboo needle, to tie tightly around their wrists, or rolling tobacco in thin twists of green leaves. At first, in this enclosed space, the crowd of Dani looked rather fearsome, their naked bodies, painted faces, pierced septa and feathered decoration suddenly making me remember their reputation as being some of the most warlike people of Indonesia. Any fear, however, was quickly dispelled by the shy smiles all of them gave us as they crowded round shaking our hands with their left ones and then went back to what they were doing.

A Dani girl, in a faded cotton skirt and blouse, carrying a child on her hip, viewed us suspiciously and then led us through to Father Camps' sitting room/dining room, with windows on two sides and the remaining walls cluttered with books and magazines overflowing from the shelves onto the floor. The wooden ceiling was covered with ornately decorated and viciously barbed carved spears about fifteen feet long, stretching nearly the length of the room. Against one of the bookshelves hung a collection of rather garish bible illustrations. Books lay open on the table at one end and on the coffee table at the other, between a comfortable sagging bamboo sofa and three armchairs. There was no sign of the Father.

Two of the Dani came into the room with us, one young and extremely virile, his jet black hair shining with grease; the second older, his forehead encircled by a coronet of dirt-stained cowries and a mask of black stretching around his eyes and across the bridge of his nose to intermingle with the side-burns of short, frizzy hair that continued in an unbroken line round his chin. He wore a necklet of dirt and grease-impregnated pig's leather from which a fringe of leather thongs fell down his chest. New bands of plaited golden reeds encircled his wrists and similar armbands of a different pattern were tight above his elbows, exaggerating the bulge of his biceps, and ornamented with the tufts of some animal hair. He grunted a greeting, accepted a cigarette and sat down, very much at home, in one of the chairs. I noticed that the top joint of the little finger of his right hand was missing.

This, we discovered, was the now world-famous Obaharok,

one-time husband of Wyn Sargent. He was, in a certain sort of way, good-looking with strong features and deep-set eyes that crinkled at the corners when he smiled. His body, covered with that coating of curling black hair, was strong and muscular and his koteka was of a long enough span to make him obviously fairly important. I supposed it was possible that anyone might have found him attractive, in an animal sort of way, but to a Westerner he seemed somewhat dirty and his body had an extremely pungent smell.

We found out, on one of many other occasions when Obaharok joined us in the Catholic mission home at Yiweka, that the Dani chief felt very much the same way about Westerners. In an hilarious conversation, with Father Camps translating the complicated Dani clicking and grunting, he described his brief life with 'Mama Wyn', as the Dani called her. I suppose Obaharok could only have been about five feet tall, and in photographs of them together she appeared to tower over him. Her neat Abercrombie-and-Fitch-type version of a safari suit and her wide brimmed Texan hat with a feather stuck in the band, made an extraordinary contrast with his shinnig dark-skinned nakedness.

Every now and then, as he spoke, he would accept a cigarette from us, holding it between fingers that were missing the top joint, dragging in the smoke and then exhaling it in small bursts. When he was not speaking, he flicked through a magazine (usually upside-down) or tapped on his koteka, his fingers drumming softly on the brittle gourd.

Father Camps arrived with another couple of Dani in tow whom he shooed gently from the already crowded room. Beside the Dani, he looked enormous, a man in about his forties, well-built with no spare flesh, a gingery beard and hair and with the end of a rolled cigarette poking out through his teeth. He did not seem in the least pleased to see us and his greeting was curt almost to the point of being rude as he looked from us to Ronnie and his friend who lounged on the bamboo sofa. He quickly cheered up and mellowed when Robin explained who we were, apologizing for his bad humour and saying that the arrival of the three German ladies at his bachelor establishment had rather thrown him.

Father Camps was an exceedingly busy man who, though extremely gregarious and very good company when he was relaxed, had little time to waste in mere social intercourse. His life was dedicated to the Dani, and visiting tourists were just not his thing

The priest introduced us formally to Obaharok, whom he called 'Mr Wyn Sargent' and the Dani grinned broadly jerking his head back with what could only be dexcribed as a suggestive leer, flashing white white teeth from a very black face that was thickly greased with pigs' fat and engrained with soot. It was hot in that small room, which overflowed with books, magazines, papers and people. Flies buzzed against the closed windows, and the air was soon thick with tobacco smoke and the sweetish, sickly smell of the Dani.

Having accepted us, Father Camps decided that he might as well get us settled in. 'I don't know why I am so popular all of a sudden,' he said, with a shy, disarming smile that lit up his face.

He showed us into the best of the three rooms; it was a palace compared to the hotels we had recently stayed in, cool and airy, yet protected from the cold at the same time, with two ship-like bunks of wood, the glory of a pair of clean sheets on each and the comfort of a couple of thick blankets for the chilly nights. The Germans were to sleep in the other two rooms.

'The last person to sleep in that bed,' Father Camps said proudly, pointing to the one I had already put my bag on, 'was ex-King Leopold of the Belgians' – a man who, like Robin, was deeply concerned about the future of primitive tribes and who was also an ardent botanist and a great traveller despite his advanced years and who had come to Wamena some few months before us.

If I did nothing else in the Dani, at least I slept in a bed last occupied by royalty. Anyway, regardless of who had slept there last, the delicious comfort of that bed, the cleanliness of the scrubbed, swept floorboards and the ecstasy of those coarse cotton sheets which *actually smelt of soap* was something I will never forget. Outside the two little mosquito-netted windows, huge spiders' webs swung gently in the afternoon breeze – expectant, large, black carnivores the size of a clenched fist in their centre; their prey moved around the sticky strands that interlaced from eave to eave. But they were safely outside and, for once, I was able to ignore them.

Such comfort made me soft and instead of spending the time writing up my notes, which I should have done, I indulged myself by reading about Michael Rockefeller's death in the Asmat in a new, sensation-packed, American publication the Father had on his shelves. As we were soon to go to the area he lost his life in, it made fascinating reading.

Outside, a row of Dani men and women queued up on the path, bringing fruit and vegetables to sell to the Father, because from him, at least, they knew they would get a fairer price than they could hope for in the market. Below, in the front room of the house, the goods were carefully weighed and paid for in money or in kind – a metal axe, a torch or knife being worth so many pounds of potatoes, tomatoes, pig meat or fruit.

In the late afternoon when the air was pleasantly cool and the valley flooded with soft gold light we climbed up the hills and walked to a Dani village, where we were invited by a tribesman into the central men's house. The Dani bent to crawl in through the entrance and then, squatting on his haunches, turned to beckon us inside. We ducked through after him and followed his example of squatting on the ground as the height of the roof made it impossible to stand up.

It took a moment or two to get accustomed to the gloom that was broken only by the light filtering through the doorway. Inside, the hut was about ten feet in diameter and four feet to the ceiling. Between four posts holding up the floor above, a fire smouldered on a stone hearth with the smoke spreading out through the room and finally floating out in wreaths through the open doorway. The floor was surprisingly clean and fresh, laid with a thick covering of sweet-smelling hay that helped to counteract the impregnated, rancid pong coming from our companion.

Unable to communicate with him in words, we grinned and he grinned back. He jerked his head in that cheeky, lecherous way and we both did the same. Grinning and jerking went on for some considerable time in total silence and it was all most companionable, our strange, geriatric gyrations broken only when we offered the Dani a cigarette and he gave a satisfied grunt. Every now and then, he leant forward and gave my hand or arm a friendly squeeze.

At the back of the room, a dark hole led to the upper sleeping quarters of the domed hut. Around the walls were neat stacks of bows, arrows and flint-stoned axes with their finely polished heads attached to handles hewn from hardwood at an angle, strapped on by lengths of narrow, string-like vines. These Dani were indeed 'Stone Age' men and, although they now bartered for metal axes, traditional, stone-headed implements were also used for cutting down trees, clearing the ground and hoeing. The blue-grey stones, as hard as metal, and finely honed to a sharp point, came from some secret place outside the valley and were, to the Dani, of considerable value both in a functional and a ritual way.

Gradually, more men came to join us, crawling in through the small entrance, shaking our left hands or patting our arms and then crawling across the floor to take up a squatting or cross-legged position. Touch was obviously an important form of communication to them for they touched us and each other frequently.

Robin had been nervous of taking any photographs. The last thing in the world we wanted to do was to give Father Camps the idea that we were only there to take sensational pictures, and neither, of course, did we want to upset the Dani. However, they seemed so friendly and so unconcerned by our presence that he took out his camera and attached the flash.

The first time it went off, there was a high-pitched squeal from all the men; one of the younger ones knelt on the ground and buried his head in the hay and the others chattered excitedly, filling the hut with a cacophony of sounds ending on a high-pitched 'eeeeee'.

Robin gave the camera to the oldest man in the room, whom we supposed to be the chief, since his koteka was long, his beard fringed with grey and his hair covered by a complicated string net. He looked wise and wrinkled and the others had cleared a small space for him despite almost every inch now being taken up by the blackened, dark, brown-skinned bodies. With a trembling hand, and extreme caution, the old man pressed the flash button and the hut was filled for a second with a blinding light and again the men squealed in unison. This time, however, instead of being frightened, they were excited and showed it by drumming light, fast tattoos on their gourd penis-sheaths with their fingernails. I noticed then that nearly all of them had at least one, and most of them four or five, top finger joints missing on their hands.

The camera was handed round and the flash button popped and popped to greater excitement until we decided it was time to leave. The film and the flash batteries had been used up and, as far as we knew, we had not succeeded in getting a single usable picture, but the sensation we had caused had been well worth the effort.

Our original companion escorted us to the gateway of the village and waved us in a lordly way towards the mission.

We did not go down immediately but sat for a time on the hillside watching the last of the sunset, the spirals of smoke coming from the villages dotted along the hills and the edges of the valleys. We looked upwards to the high, forest-topped mountains and across to the higher peaks in the west, drinking in the beauty of the Baliem Valley and listening to the sounds of the Dani as they called to each other in high voices that echoed in the stillness of the evening. On the bank around us grew little berries, plump and red, that tasted of a mixture between strawberries and raspberries. I imagined the fantastic impact this place, so near utopia, must have had on those first men who found it by chance.

Father Camps had lived in the Baliem for over twenty years, and I could understand his feelings when he said to me at one point:

'This valley is my home and my heart is here and with these people. Last time I went back to Holland on leave, I was hopelessly homesick for Yiweka after only two months. If I could have my wish, it would be to live the rest of my life here but that, I think, is not to be.'

His people, he felt, must learn to stand on their own feet. 'Now they begin to rely on me too much and often I think it would be better for them if I left them to struggle a little for themselves and not have everything handed to them on a plate by the missionaries.'

When we got back to the mission, we found the Father, looking rather uncomfortable, surrounded by the German ladies who, though certainly not fat, all seemed on the large size in that small living room; they had rather harsh, strident voices, plenty to say and opinions to voice. He was listening to them politely but said little himself.

Father Camps, who was a considerably efficient engineer as well as obviously being a first-class builder, had erected a system of water tanks that provided ample rain water for washing, drinking and cooking. In a spotlessly clean and airy wash house behind the main building, he had erected a lavatory that actually flushed (the first we had come across for some considerable time) and had an arrangement of taps from one of which rain water flowed straight into a large tub for washing and carefully filtered water flowed into another for drinking and cooking.

That evening, the Father cooked supper himself with the help of two Dani boys who seemed to be a regular part of the household, but from then on he let me either help him or prepare the meals myself. His kitchen, unlike the rest of the house which was extremely comfortable, was spartanly bachelor in style and had two small kerosene stoves for cooking and a strong smell of paraffin coming from the dish cloths which the two boys seemed to use for every conceivable purpose. It had been so long since I had even been in a kitchen that I thoroughly enjoyed giving it a good clean and reorganizing everything so that, although the Father was very flattering about it, I am sure neither he nor the boys could find anything for a week after.

Father Camps had a remarkable relationship with the Dani. Every day, men, women and children would come pouring into the mission to see him or to sell him things, crowding into the room inside the front door and overspilling into the living room or knocking on his study door and asking to consult him about some problem or other they had. Only in the evenings, when more than six tried to cram into the living room to join us and the room became hopelessly overcrowded, did he flap his hands at them and tell them kindly but firmly to clear off. Few of the Dani ever came in when we were eating and if they did they would sit quietly in one of the bamboo chairs, leafing through *Paris-Match* or some other six-month-old magazine, usually holding it upside down.

The Dani were his people, his flock and also his friends. He treated them with respect but also, when necessary, like children. He loved them but he was realistic about their faults.

'They are no fools, these people, and many of them are extremely shrewd,' the Dutchman told us, rolling yet another twist of strong Dutch tobacco deftly in a piece of thin paper. 'Often they come to me with heartbreaking stories about knives and axes they say have been stolen from them, expecting me to give them new ones for nothing. Another trick they have is playing off the Protestants against us Catholics; if one of us won't play their game, they go to the other side and try there and then come running back telling tales.'

I had been struck many times on our journey by the way in which isolated, wild and often savage tribes were prepared to accept missionaries in their midst and often even obey what they must surely have felt were extraordinary rules, especially those imposed by Protestants who forbade smoking, dancing, drinking and much of the adat of the tribe that was all-important to their way of life. I asked the Father why this was.

286

'Often,' he explained, 'a missionary is the first outsider to visit a tribe. He arrives as a friend, carries copious presents which he gives free and which are of tremendous excitement to the people. He is unique, has all the values of life like fire, knives and salt at his finger tips, and therefore he must be a man of great standing. Is it any wonder they are prepared to follow his ways in order to be like him and obey what he says to get the rewards he promises?'

The Catholic missions were going through something of a revolution in their attitude towards primitive, virtually uncontacted people. Conversion was no longer, they believed, of paramount importance. It was the people themselves, and not primarily their souls, which mattered and it was for the missionaries to try and help by easing them into civilization, by trying to teach them the ways of the modern world and by educating them in the ways that would help most. This is preferable to giving them a semi-academic training that would only equip them for jobs that would never be fulfilled because already there were few enough jobs for semi-educated Papuans on the island. At Yiweka they had, in fact, only baptized about twenty-three Dani, as baptism meant the acceptance of many things the tribes were totally incapable of accepting.

'Take marriage for instance,' Father Camps pointed out. 'Here in the Baliem, the divorce rate is probably higher than anywhere else in the world. A man gets bored or angry with his wife or she cooks him a poor meal and immediately he divorces her by returning a few pigs to her family.

'The Dani are polygamous and nearly every man has two or more wives; some have even ten. Part of this is due to the fact that, by custom, the wives seldom have more than two children and when a child is born a man is forbidden to sleep with her until that child is old enough to walk. Inevitably, he gets frustrated and takes another wife to fill in the intervening time.'

Father Camps expanded this custom, making us laugh by stories of Dani men who tried desperately to get their one-year-old babies to walk long before they were in fact able to.

'Then there is the problem of abortion, a total contradiction to the Roman Catholic beliefs. In order to keep the birth rate down, the women practise abortion, after the birth of the first child, by putting pressure on the head of the young foetus with their fingers.'

He led us to a window and pointed to a boy sitting strumming a guitar on the steps outside.

'There is one of the examples of that practice. Now the boy lives at the mission. He hates his mother and swears he will kill her if he ever finds her.'

The boy was totally blind. Where his eyes should have been were dark, gluey cavities, rimmed with flies clustering in a heavy rim round the sockets. In his case, the abortion had failed but fingers pressing against the foetus had done irreparable damage.

The next morning, we were to climb the mountain behind the mission to see the strange, natural pool from which the Dani get that all-vital commodity of life – salt.

We had a delicious breakfast of home-made bread and wild honey, before the German ladies surfaced, and began the long trek up the mountain whilst the morning air was still cool and sharp.

As Father Camps had said, it was not difficult to find our way. We were lucky and hit on a day when, for some unknown reason, large numbers of Dani had decided to climb for salt. Normally, it was usual for only half a dozen or so to climb up each day but, on this occasion, there were scores of little brown women, heading for the mountain path and the scrub jungle that cloaked it, half-trotting, their reed skirts swinging from below their hips and heavy bundles being carried on their backs or heads. We joined the procession, wondering why many balanced large banana trunks on top of their heavily laden nets and how their small bodies could bear such enormous weights.

I thought we were walking reasonably fast, considering the precipitous angle of the track and the twisting route we were following that crossed and recrossed a small, fast-flowing stream, but the women, who were carrying those amazing loads whilst we had nothing but our cameras and my bag, trotted past us up the steep incline at an amazing pace. They were shy creatures, covering their faces when we tried to photograph them through the trees, their children hiding behind their scanty skirts. As they passed, they merely mumbled a quiet greeting, 'luok', and then scuttled on, using their bare feet like monkeys' toes to grip the criss-crossed roots and slippery stones.

After an hour and a half of hard climbing, we heard a loud chattering of women above us and clambered up a last few yards of even steeper, narrow winding path and came out into a clearing where large, smooth-topped grey stones tumbled down a slope towards the salt pool. Already there were about twenty or thirty women in and around the pool and more were arriving every minute. It was an astonishing sight.

Some freak of nature had caused a spring of salt, forming a pool about three feet deep, to rise up just below the clear, natural stream which flowed in a rushing tumble down the rocks above. The pool, containing about 40 per cent of saline, was grey, thick and covered with a heavy scum. Most of the women were already standing in it with the water coming up to their thighs or waists.

To process the salt, the Dani women chew the inner pith of the banana trunks and then soak the porous pith in the saline solution. Then they wrap the salt-impregnated substance in the outer skin of the banana trunk and carry it down to their villages. The pulp is burnt in their fires, ending up as a black, charred, salty powder. Some also filled gourds with the salty water and these would be emptied onto the ground and left until the sun dried out the water, leaving a rim of salt. They kept most of it for their own use, but the salt was also used for trading with other tribes further down the valley and in the mountains beyond.

On the flat rocks around the pool, some of the women were stripping off the outer green layers of banana trunks that were often as much as eighteen inches in diameter, with sharp knives made from split bamboo. The others, standing waist deep in the pool, were dipping long strands of white pith into the grey water and then shoving it into their mouths, chewing away until the pith became a grey, soggy mush. Having soaked the resulting mush in the pond, pushing it backwards and forwards until it looked like a dirty floorcloth, they would scramble out of the pool and carefully wrap it up in the green fronds again. They worked with urgent determination, teeth masticating as though their lives depended on it, hands pounding and pulping all the time and, despite the muck in their mouths, keeping up a steady stream of twittering. With every minute, the pool got more crowded as yet more women stripped off the bark and jumped into the water with their pith. Soon they were standing shoulder to shoulder and others arriving had to sit on the rocks and wait their turn, rolling long cigarettes from green leaves, nursing babies at their hanging, avocado-shaped breasts or eating blackened baked sweet potatoes they pulled from string nets hanging down their backs.

The older women were not a very pretty bunch, with their brown skin wrinkled, their eyes set close together and their noses short and wide. Some of the younger ones were beautiful though, their kinky hair hanging in tightly curled strands around their faces, their teeth white when they smiled and their eyes clear and full of humour. At first, they were all shy of us; the older women scowled, looking tough and ferocious, and the young girls hid their faces. After a time, during which we just sat on the rocks above, they forgot we were there and ignored us, carrying on with the vital business of the day.

With the Dani, it is customary, up to the age of seven, when one of their family dies, to cut off a finger of one hand (at the first or second joint). The operation is performed by numbing the hand with a hard blow and then cutting off the finger with a quick slash of a bamboo knife. The stumps seldom become infected. I noticed now that nearly all the women working the pool, even the younger ones, were minus at least two, and more often four or five, fingers. This gave their hands a strange, clumsy, prehensile look, although it did not seem to impair them in any way and a few, waiting or resting on the rocks, knitting nets with their fingers, did so with a speed that made knitting needles seem ridiculous. After they are seven years old, the men cut off the top of their ears as well to show grief for a dead relative.

The men, infinitely more handsome to look at than the women, took no part whatsoever in the proceedings. About a dozen of them lazed on the smooth stones high above the pool, smoking, eating potatoes or chatting to each other. No Women's Lib here, this was not men's work; they basked in the sunshine like glorious, proud lizards and one, getting bored, pulled from his matted hair a Jew's harp made from a piece of bamboo, which he held to his mouth and played a soft, haunting tune with the same notes repeated again and again.

The way the Dani women wore the scanty, curving strands of reeds that were their skirts defied all the laws of gravity; they did not hang from the hips but below the curve of their bellies and from halfway down the curve of their buttocks and, although I noticed all the women had a curious way of walking with their knees turned in, almost touching, I could see no other reason for the skirts not to slip down. As it was, they all stayed in place, just, but only just, covering their pubic hairs in what would, had they been more beautiful, have been the most provocative and tantalizing way.

On two of the evenings at the mission, Father Camps showed us films he had taken of the Dani and some of their rituals. He had not been filming long but he was talented, had good equipment and, because of his relationship with the Dani, was able to take some staggering sequences of film. Crowded into the small living room with the Germans and a number of highly odiferous Dani, with the air thick with tobacco smoke, we watched in absorbed fascination. He first showed us a film he had taken of the opening ceremony of Operation Koteka.

At dawn on the great day when Ibutine (little mother), the President's wife, and an accompanying barrage of bountiful ladies, were to fly into Wamena to give clothes to the poor, naked savages, large numbers of Dani were made to stand outside the airport in rows. Unfortunately, she was late and a number of them fainted under the hot sun before she arrived. After the large military plane finally touched down, the ladies walked along the rows of children, trying to garb their offending nakedness with khaki shirts and skirts or shorts. Unfortunately, they had trouble all round. Getting the shorts over the little boys' kotekas caused a difficult and rather embarrassing problem. Because of the small size of the Dani, the size of the uniforms provided had been misjudged; they were miles too large and the skirts all slipped from the hips of the little girls.

I am afraid the well-meant but misguided charity of the beautifully groomed ladies from Jakarta in their graceful sarongs, tight lace jackets and bright, jewel-coloured sashes was so incongruous it made me giggle almost uncontrollably. The boys' kotekas made bulges far more obscene than the gourds themselves and the little girls' over-large skirts were a poor substitute for the grass skirts they normally wear from puberty to marriage, when they adopt the curving bands of reeds.

The other films were of Dani dances and rites. There was a staggering sequence of a war dance involving two tribes of Dani with the men dressed in all their glory in tall headdresses of fur and feathers, carrying long spears, their faces terrifying in black and white and with shining boars' tusks or shells through the holes in their noses. When these rites take place, they dance for hours in a clearing up in the hills, wheeling round and round in circles, charging each other, with spears raised high, in a great mass of bodies, rushing backwards and forwards in great waves. On the fringe of the mock battle, which within seconds could get out of control and become the real thing, the women jumped up and down in excitement, singing and encouraging their men, their skirts swinging and their naked breasts flapping from side to side as they grew more and more excited. Many of the faces of the men we now knew and some were in the room with us, grunting delightedly as they recognized themselves on the screen.

Despite all the efforts of the government officials, many of the Dani still continue to have intertribal battles that are not just rituals, with large numbers of men being killed and wounded. Single killings are also fairly frequent in the valley when an argument is resolved by killing or the reprisal of one killing by another.

Another film was of the ritual mud fights which take place at a girl's first menstruation when her naked body is clothed for the first time in layer upon layer of grass skirts, newly made for the occasion. Men and women, half in fun and half in earnest, roll and fight in a pit of mud until their bodies, heads and hair are caked with layers of the orange-yellow clay. They wallow in it, slide in it and throw great, spattering lumps at one another, then run down to the river to wash most of it off and return to the village to clothe the girl in her new skirts. It looked fun.

We saw films of their long funeral services where, like the Toraja, gifts are exchanged between families, pigs are sacrificed and feasting goes on for days. We watched pigs being held by two men and slaughtered by a third, running at it with a raised spear and plunging the point at its heart. We saw the ritual stones, decorated with feathers, belts woven from reeds and threaded with cowries, and large string nets laid down the centre of the village to be counted, admired and argued over. We saw the pigs being cut up and put into a pit of burning coals to cook for the feast. The dead man was brought out from his hut on a throne and set over another fire, his relations wailing and weeping as his body slowly curled and burnt over the flames.

Then there were shots of a curious rite the Father said he had only seen once during the many years he had been living amongst the Dani – a purification ceremony which took place following an episode of incest in one of the tribal families. It was strange and serious and for once the usually smiling Dani men were grim and tight-lipped. Shame blanketed the whole tribe although the crime had been committed by only two of their people. After a long pit had been dug, an arch erected over it and strange triangular symbols of greenery put up around the village, the people walked one by one through the pit of mud, water and pigs blood. At the far end, they were anointed on their bodies by an old man and the crime was absolved. It was a touching and moving ceremony.

Finally, the Father showed us a film he had made at the mission in an attempt to illustrate to the Dani the value of money and paper notes. The people, he said, could not tell a five-rupiah note from a one thousand one and were often convinced that ten pieces of paper money of an infinitesimal value must be worth more than one of a larger denomination. As a result, they were frequently cheated by the Indonesians to whom they sold goods or bought stuff from in the Wamena market. The film was very simplified, with the different coloured notes pinned to a board and short sketches of bad men cheating the Dani and good men giving correct change or value for money. It was extremely effective and both Robin and I were full of admiration for the way he had made it.

The more we saw of Father Camps, the more we came to respect him. He was full of energy and every bit of that energy seemed to be put towards improving the livelihood of his people. He was even compiling a dictionary of the Dani language and at odd moments would disappear with excitement into his study with one of the older Dani men or women who appeared shyly at his door. A little while later, he'd emerge waving bits of paper excitedly and announcing that he had just added the sixty-sixth alternative form of the word sweet potato to his list of meanings that denoted the vegetable in flower, in bud, or of this or that variety.

In his church too, Father Camps was a figure to be respected, and the service we went to on the Sunday morning we were at Yiweka was an exhilarating experience. It took place in a simple, wooden hut with straw matting on the floor, furnished only with a crude altar and a few benches. Most of the Dani sat cross-legged on the ground, men at the back and the women and children in the front, packed in so tightly the building almost bulged at the joints. Even the smallest baby was as quiet as a mouse and the only movement occurred when a small boy would get up and silently pee with great accuracy into a square inch of clear space. The women's nets covered their heads and shoulders like shawls and they listened intently to the Father as he intoned in the Dani language, occasionally rocking to and fro as they sang back the replies.

The main part of the service was short and totally incomprehensible to us. Then a young, neatly dressed Dani, one of the few baptized, took the floor and proceeded to tell the story of the Good Shepherd with the help of an ornate picture with all the trappings of long, flowing beards and golden haloes. He was extremely eloquent and worked up his audience to a fever pitch of excitement as he waved his arms and his voice rose and fell into climaxes of thunder and gentleness. The Dani men and women watched him, totally immersed in the story, leaning forward eagerly, their eyes on his face and their mouths open, the only sound coming from a greedy baby hungrily sucking at his mother's breast.

Our time at Yiweka went all too fast, the hours sped by on winged feet as we climbed the hills, wandered into more villages and listened to Father Camps.

On one occasion, we entered a village and were greeted by one of the old warrior chiefs of the valley who held a spear in his hand and shook it menacingly at us, jumping up and down. Not knowing what to do, we stood still; a rather frighteningly large, snorting boar made advances at us from the back and the small man at the end made equally frightening gestures in front. Eventually, fear of the pig overcame fear of the man and we went forward to be led once again into the men's hut, the largest hut in the village. The small area inside was packed with warriors and it was clear they were holding some sort of a conference. We crouched in a corner, keeping quiet, and they ignored us as the meeting went on with one man talking after another, all excited and obviously angry about something, the old chief having most of the say and the other grunting or nodding in agreement. It went on for what seemed like hours while we sat there not daring to move, unable to make out anything except the occasional Indonesian word for police and references to various villages and Wamena.

At last, they wound it up with a final, impassioned speech from the chief. They all shook hands and turned their attention to us. Now that the meeting was adjourned, we became the centre of attraction, as Robin handed round tobacco and cigarettes and I, after some eloquent miming from the chief, gathered he wanted his beard trimmed and was able to produce a pair of nail scissors from my bag and perform barber services. We stayed there a long time as every one of the men wanted the same treatment. I knelt on the hay-covered floor, trying not to wrinkle my nose as I leant over them, terrified of nicking the skin, and snipped away at the fuzzy rim of hair around their chins.

I was rewarded by a present of two kotekas. What I was supposed to do with them I was not quite sure and when I mimed the suggestion Robin should wear one the Dani collapsed into howls of infectious giggling.

Most of the time they were the most friendly people but there were, nevertheless, times when it was possible to be extremely frightened of their strength, their often savage looks, and quicksilver change of mood from friendship to anger.

One morning, feeling that Father Camps was obviously busy and would be glad to be away from us for the day, we decided to go for a long tramp up and over the mountains to a collection of villages further up an offshoot of the main valley. When we reached the top of the first hill, having climbed to a dizzy height up an almost sheer cliff, on a slippery tortuous path where one step forward often meant two or three slithering back again, up slopes of coarse grass and thorny bushes and through patches of tulgy woods, I gave up. The almost sheer drop to the valley below made my head spin; my breath came in short, painful gasps, and I knew I would never make it higher up the next range of mountains, along the top, down again and then the long trek back to the mission along the valley.

'I'll stay here and write up my notes,' I told Robin, assuring him that I was perfectly all right, just tired, and he should go on with the Dani and his son who had come up with us. I settled myself in a rounded hollow of soft grass by the side of the path, pleasantly warm in the sun, alternately writing and dozing until a cold, dark cloud brought me to my feet. Within minutes, it began to rain and a heavy, sweeping mist of grey vapour swept across the hillside, totally obscuring the valley. Slipping and sliding, mostly on my bottom, I reached a wood below and took shelter under the thick, spreading branches of a tall tree with wide club roots. Up above in the sun, butter-flies of blue and orange had floated around me and the air was full of bird song. Here in the wood, the only sound was rain dripping from long, hanging streamers of ghostly strands of Spanish moss and the mist distorted the tree trunks around, turning them into sinister shapes and blanking out the rest of the world.

It needed only the appearance of a tough, stocky Dani to set my imagination racing. He carried an axe in his hand and appeared in front of me with no warning whatsoever, the sound of his bare feet muffled by the mist and the rain. Two feet away he stopped and stared at me, totally still and without the suspicion of a smile on his face. I stood equally still from an almost paralysing fear and my brain turned somersaults as I considered whether he planned to rob me, kill me, rape me or carry me down the hill. As far as I was concerned, there was nothing to stop him doing either or all four of the alternatives. After what seemed eternity, he took my hand in a large paw from which four of the fingers were missing, patted my shoulder, grunted and then squatted on the ground beside me where he stayed for the next half hour, whereupon the mist rolled away as suddenly as it had come and the full glory of the Baliem Valley lay stretched out below me once more. Then he grunted again and disappeared back into the wood, swinging his axe and taking a slice out of a tree trunk or two as he went past.

My only sadness about our time at Yiweka was that my aches,

pains and stiffness seemed to grow worse instead of better. I had a hacking, painful cough and I felt stupidly, feebly tired almost all the time. I was also agonizingly irritated at night by swelling, slightly poisoned mosquito and other insect bites that dotted my arms and legs like smallpox. In fact, we were both in rather a mess, the wound in Robin's foot was swelling more each day and his toe nail had become as black as any Dani's. He was beginning to limp slightly and, though he made light of it, I think the pain was considerable.

Next morning, together with the Germans, we left for Wamena. We had heard nothing on Father Camps' radio about our onward flight to the south in the missionary plane and we could only hope it would appear the following day to take us to the Asmat as planned.

Chapter 21

The trek back seemed endless. The sun blazed down un-
mercifully until, for once, I longed for it to rain. The ladies,
and the six bearers they needed to carry their enormous
suitcases, needed endless stops along the way. In the state I
was in, I was quite happy about this but, after a few miles,
Robin could not stand the relaxed and rather slow pace.
While we plodded on and the ladies frequently paused to
take more and more pictures of women working in the fields
(the men, I had discovered, also worked on the land but only
to prepare the soil and dig the irrigation ditches), he went
trotting off to visit the village where 'Mama' Sargent had lived
with her 'head hunter' husband.

'Nothing but ghoulish curiosity,' I said, churlishly, as he
left us, jealous of him but knowing quite well I could never
keep up for the extra six or seven miles it meant travelling.
'I thought it was I who was supposed to have the "woman's
magazine mentality".'

'You never know,' he retorted, 'I just might find myself a
Dani woman there.'

He arranged to join us at a village near Wamena where there
was reported to be an interesting mummified figure which the
Germans wanted to see.

Our destination was about an hour's walk from the Yiweka
side of the town. We had to turn off the main track and follow
a narrow path across fields and dykes to get to it. Around

the huts was a kind of moat, about fifteen feet wide and filled with muddy, stagnant water, spanned by a narrow branch to which two curves gave a serpentine effect.

Inside the village, the elders were waiting for us, informed by Dani bush telegraph that we were on our way. The chief demanded we should all pay 5000 rupiahs each to see the mummified figure. It was the first evidence of lust for money we had seen amongst the Dani and it was both rather pathetic and unattractive. It ended in a settlement for 1500 rupiahs, plus some leftover gifts for the natives that the Germans still carried with them, razor blades, hairpins and a packet of tobacco. These and the money, carefully fingered, were laid out on a large banana leaf in front of the men's house and the chief disappeared inside, bobbing a head tightly covered with a string net and pulling aside his extra long koteka as he ducked through the entrance.

Robin arrived, panting, as the chief emerged again, carrying in his arms a distorted, blackened, skeletal figure whose head was bent over raised knees. The body, some fifty years old, had been slowly smoked over the embers of a fire and the flesh had shrunk over his bones. It was a macabre sight, a woman's net bag hung from its head down its back and a long, blackened koteka stuck grotesquely up in front of it. Reverently, it was set on the banana leaf with the offerings we had paid spread out in front of it. The empty black sockets where eyes had once been stared blankly at us and the trash before him. I found the whole thing rather sickening – the clawlike bones and curving fingers were horrific – and was glad when we left.

Far more fascinating to me in that village was the koteka garden flourishing outside the walls. Over a small scaffolding of bamboo poles, rampaging gourd vines grew in profusion and from the flat leaves and narrow stems hung the green fruit that would eventually be made into kotekas. Some of them hung down, narrow and straight, but many were trained, with string or over stakes, into the twisted shapes that make each penis-sheath an individual ornament. If we had been unimpressed by the Wamena Hotel, the Germans were horrified by conditions there, especially by the rats who spent a busy night as, outside, a really fearsome gale built up with rolls of thunder, electrified streaks of lightning and wind howling through the valley.

Mrs Yani, full of bounce and vigour and gushing with clichés, stepped off a Merpati plane the next morning, resplendent in a shocking-pink check shirt and a pair of brand new denim jeans.

Weren't we amazed by all the naked, primitive Dani? Didn't we find it unbelievable that such people could still exist in Indonesia? Had Yiweka been amusing? 'And what about the hotel here? Isn't it fantastic, considering the difficulties they have to contend with? Have you been comfortable?' she asked gaily as we walked along the Wamena airstrip towards the unity mission Cessna that was to fly us to the Asmat.

For a time we followed the course of the Baliem river and it was easy to see now why the valley had remained undiscovered for so long. The mountains that ringed it were of an amazing height and steepness and the only way through them was the narrow gorge through which the river raced in a series of foaming rapids.

Robin and Jim shouted at each other, discussing the possibilities of negotiating the river by rubber raft as they do in the Grand Canyon.

'I'll try and fly you over the course of the river on the way back,' Jim yelled, 'but we'd better make straight for Agats now.'

We could see more Dani villages, clinging to the steep mountain slopes at what seemed incredible heights; the huts were surrounded by circular walls of stone, fanning out to make narrow terraces for planting. The villages were virtually inaccessible and most, despite their comparative proximity to Wamena, had never had any contact with the outside world or missionaries. The harsh, jagged spurs were dotted with them, though the life up there must have been unbelievably tough, and many of the stone-fenced terraces looked from the air as though they were built on almost perpendicular ground. Occasionally, we saw little brown dots working on the land or people running from the huts as we flew over.

Then we climbed even higher, our ears popped, and the air inside the little aircraft was thin and cold. Below, nature had defeated man and the slopes were empty of human life. Thick jungle forests were only broken by high, jagged peaks or silver ribbons of water falling hundreds of feet down grey-white walls to narrow ravines only a few yards wide. Clouds closed in again and, for a time, we flew through a pale grey fog and I was as scared as hell. The mountain peaks were all around us, we did not have the power to fly above them and, at any moment, I expected the tearing impact as we hit the side of a hidden mountain. Jim seemed totally unconcerned – this was a country that had claimed many pilots – yet he chatted away cheerfully and often, to my horror, actually turned his head sideways to shout something at Robin as the Cessna bumped and lurched through pockets of air. Jim, as they say, knew this route like the back of his hand.

Below us stretched a vast, uninhabited area of jungle wilderness, a sea of dark green, through which widely spaced, sluggish-looking, curving, winding rivers – tinted café au lait by the waters of the heights behind us – made their way towards the sea. Thick jungle covered the lower, gently unfolding slopes and then flattened out to fill the whole world, stretching to the sea and Asmat; a world that was so different from the Baliem Valley it was hard to believe they existed in the same universe.

There was no airstrip at the major settlement of Agats so we landed at a place called Ewer, a few miles up a river estuary north of the river flowing past the mission. We came down to a short, narrow runway, built of mud in a small area carved out of the jungle. The runway looked waterlogged, and the first time we made the approach Jim pulled back at the last minute and we rose again steeply into the air.

'It's darn wet down there,' he said unnecessarily. 'I hope we'll be able to make it. Well, we'll have another bash.'

He did make it, sliding for a moment sideways across the runway but righting the little plane and ending in a neat stop beside a long, wooden bungalow on one side and uniform rows of about forty little wooden huts perched on high stilts on the other. Outside the bungalow, also built on piles, a few rotting canoes, filled with earth, acted as gardens propped up above the water line, planted with trailing vines of some sort and a ragged line of maize.

In the Asmat, there is virtually no dry land; everything is swamp, covered for part of each day by brackish tidal water that slips silently up the banks and then retreats to leave behind a sea of mud covered by a nightmare interlacing of roots. We had been asked to bring fresh vegetables from the fertile, productive Baliem Valley and I was proud of my Dani net bundle.

The priest from Ewer was away but an Indonesian there, in charge of the radio, took us into the bungalow and gave us coffee – a strong, delicious brew sitting ready in a thermos. The Bishop of Asmat was also away that day, he told us, and as we were not expected until twenty-four hours later, no boat had been sent from Agats to meet us. However, he had a canoe with a motor waiting outside that would take us round the coast to the mission.

Outside, through the window, we could see tall, black men, lean and thin as bean poles, darker and more negroid-looking than the Dani, with their heads shorn almost to the skin, accentuating the shape of their skulls, unloading our baggage and refilling the plane for Jim's return journey. A group of children watched them; the smallest ones were naked, the older girls wore faded and torn cotton frocks or an infinitesimally small triangle of ragged cloth tied into a kind of bikini from a piece of string round their hips, and the boys were in tattered shorts. Compared to the Dani, they looked under-nourished and almost at starvation level; many were covered with ringworm or scabies and a few were pale-skinned and red-haired as a result of some mineral deficiency.

Inside the radio crackled and Jayapura made contact. The static was bad and the Indonesian repeated over and over again:

'Please send cigarettes with the next consignment. Cigarettes urgently needed. Repeat, send cigarettes.'

The tide was out. We clambered into a long, narrow canoe of wood, hewn from a tree trunk with a Johnson motor at one end; Mrs Yani was in the back with the boatman, the baggage in the middle and Robin and I in the front.

My ears had become totally blocked after the aeroplane and no amount of holding my nose or coughing would clear them, so I lived in a world of my own as the canoe chugged slowly down the outflowing turgid river, with the smell of the swamp all around us and the weird network of twisted black roots, like a million spiders' legs, reaching down into the thick mud on the banks. Crabs scuttled across the wide areas of chocolate-brown mud, white herons and other birds poked long beaks into its depths and the imprints of unknown animals were indented into its surface. We rode with the flow of water, entered the sea and turned left along the coast, in choppy water, towards Agats.

This was the area where Michael Rockefeller had died, a death that was still open to speculation, conjecture and argument. Had he been eaten by crocodiles? Drowned whilst trying to swim to the shore? Slaughtered and consumed by one of the still-cannibal tribes in the district? Or captured and kept alive as a hostage or God figure by an Asmat or other tribe of people? No-one really knew and until we saw some of the many aspects of Asmat art which we were shown during the next few days, I found it hard to see why he had come to this seemingly God-forsaken place.

He had visited the Asmat on two occasions and, on his expedition there in 1961, had written: 'The key to my fascination with the Asmat is the wood carving. The sculpture which the people here produce is the most extraordinary work in the primitive world. And equally as remarkable as the art is the fact that the culture which produces it is still intact; some remote areas are still headhunting; and only five years ago almost the whole area was headhunting. The Asmat is a land of jungle, winding rivers and mud. You wouldn't believe it, but there are no hills and no stone in the entire area.'

On his last expedition, he had set off, with one companion and two Asmatters, to round the coast and explore one of the more remote rivers. Out at sea they had been struck by one of the bad storms and high seas which frequently hit this area. The craft, a form of catamaran of canoes, had overturned. Soon they began drifting out to sea on the strong current coming from the coast. Michael Rockefeller (a young man who seemed to have been loved by everyone who had come across him), an Olympic-class swimmer, decided to swim to the shore. He attached two empty plastic jerry cans to his arms, jumped into the water and began to strike out strongly for the coastline, and that was the last seen of him. The second man stayed sitting astride the boat and was later rescued by the enormous search party which had gone out to look for them as soon as the Asmatters raised the alarm. Of the young American, Michael Rockefeller, there was never any trace, though a jerry can, believed to be one he had worn on his arm, was later discovered in the swamps.

Not long before the accident, Michael Rockefeller had bought a huge, ornately carved 'bis' pole from an Asmat tribe, a totem fashioned into a complicated pattern of phallic symbols, interlaced together. These poles are made when a tribe is about to kill someone outside their group in order to fulfil the requirements of some of their ritual ceremonies. There is a theory that they may have been the very people who discovered the young American, killed and ate him, to honour the bis pole he had bought from them.

No-one knows and, despite the rumours that he was

living captive on a desert island, having been picked up by a nomad tribe wandering around the coast in their boats, it seems, sadly, that no-one will ever know the full truth of the story.

From where I sat in the front of that canoe – as we rounded the point and forged our way through slightly choppy water, out round shallow water towards the mouth of the next river – the sea looked as unfriendly as the mangrove coastline. One could even see the strong cross-currents which swept through it and the thought of trying to swim through that sea, crawl through the root-entangled barrier of mud to reach even a faint resemblance to dry land, seemed inconceivable.

It took us about an hour to get to Agats, fighting the water on the way up the river for about a couple of miles from the estuary, passing the small Asmat village of wooden huts and then drawing into a jetty beside the township of wood-slatted buildings, all on stilts, that made up the centre of the area. From the jetty, a catwalk of planks, about ten feet above mud level, led to others branching out in all directions dissecting the town like narrow roads.

A collection of Asmatters watched us silently and sullenly. They were a total contrast to the chubby, cheeky and grinning Dani and, although Mrs Yani shouted at them cheerfully to take our luggage, they made no move to help us. They were dressed in dirty, ragged, shabby and tattered clothing, all had closely shaven heads and most of them had skin diseases that covered their exposed, dark bitter-chocolate flesh in scabs and weals. Most of the men had distorted septa, hanging below their nostrils and disfigured by holes that were often the size of a half-crown. They were considerably taller than the Dani and as thin as rakes though their carriage was as proud and upright as that of the little people of the valley in the mountains.

One of the American Fathers from the mission arrived on the jetty, surprised to see us arriving a day early, and we walked, in a straggling line, along the catwalk that was about four planks wide at this point, past a shop from which honkytonk music was coming in a loud distorted wail but which seemed to have few goods for sale, and onto the spreading wooden building which was the home of the nuns living in Agats, where Mrs Yani was to stay.

Mrs Yani had told us she had come to the Asmat to get things ready for a group of about a hundred tourists who were expected to arrive there by sea, on a cruise ship, in a few days' time.

No-one, it seemed, knew quite where they were. Nothing had been heard of the imminent arrival of the cruise ship for some weeks now and nothing had been done to prepare Agats for their one-night stopover. The thought of a hundred probably blue-rinsed ladies teetering in high-heeled shoes along those nightmare catwalks (often a plank or two would be loose or even missing and the chances of falling off into the mud below were odds on), carrying an equally blue-rinsed pekinese in their arms, had me giggling almost uncontrollably as we followed the small, black-bearded young American priest to the Agats monastery.

I had not been in a monastery before and I suppose I had imagined finding a prison-like construction full of cells at the end of that walk through Agats instead of the solid, calm and beautiful building we finally entered.

It was built of local hardwood, deep red, and made to last for a long time, a four-sided building surrounding a mound of carefully irrigated earth planted with orange and lemon trees and crowned by a magnificently carved bis pole towering above the roofs of the building. Around it bent, curved coconut palms had been planted in the swamp, fibrous roots showing over the mud and their tenuous anchorage making them lean over so far that their leaves almost touched the ground.

A covered passageway ran around the inner side of the courtyard with doors on all sides, and the Father led us first to two guest rooms on the left. The rooms were large, clean, pleasantly airy and furnished comfortably with a desk, armchair and four-poster bed swathed in a garland of mosquito netting.

There were no double rooms, of course, but there was something pleasantly old-fashioned about them and a great air of peace hung gently over the whole place. The monastery also had an extremely efficient and blissfully clean row of lavatories and, what is more, *showers*, actual showers from which clear water ran, and every room was closely screened against the hordes of mosquitoes flourishing on swamp life.

The Fathers, and the Bishop, who had returned from his trip up river, were having lunch in a light dining room, food that was cooked by the nuns and brought across to the mission. It was a simple meal and our sack of provisions was greeted with great delight.

The Fathers at the Agats mission are from a denomination called the Crosiers, a small order that started in Holland and later made America its base. I do not know quite what I expected a group of monks to look like but it certainly was not the group of relaxed, relatively young men sitting round the table, dressed in jeans or shorts and open-necked shirts, spreading home-made bread rolls thickly with strawberry jam or peanut butter. Except for one older brother who was Dutch, they were all Americans; one was plump and moon-faced; the Bishop himself had a kind, amazingly young face and blue eyes that showed signs of the strain he had undertaken with the job, and the youngest was a jolly 'Billy Bunter' looking character. Not one of them, rather to my disappointment, wore a coarse brown habit with a cowl and, to me, they could have been a group of American club men getting together for a stag session. Even their conversation was totally relaxed and untheological.

They all greeted us warmly (should I, I wondered, have knelt to kiss the Bishop's large purple ring?), but with definite restraint. Robin had corresponded at some length with one of their order, a Father Trenkenshuh, but he was at one of the mission posts way upriver and the others trod warily, sounding Robin out politely but cautiously on his motives for coming to the Asmat.

The position of missionaries in Indonesia was a sticky one

and they had to be permanently on their guard against upsetting the authorities or appearing to be interfering too much
with government policy. As the mission in Wamena had
suffered from the Wyn Sargent affair, so those in Agats had
suffered from the drama and sensation which had accompanied the death of Michael Rockefeller.

It was obvious that, at first glance, Robin looked too young
to the Crosier Bishop, Fathers and the lay brothers, to be
running Survival International and the last thing they wanted
was someone coming into the area and stirring up trouble
in any way.

After lunch, they outlined their plan of living for us. Then
they had a two-hour siesta, followed by a cup of tea and then
worked until seven-thirty when there was a break for supper
followed by more work until ten when they all met for 'rest
and recreation' in a large airy living room. In the morning
they had early service, breakfast at 7.30 and then work until
lunch. Each had his appointed job of teaching, running a
lumber co-operative, overseeing the hospital or supervising
the many projects they were involved in.

My first suspicion that the Crosiers lived a comparatively
easy life was soon dispelled. While we were there, we quickly
came to realize how much was involved in running the mission,
how hard they worked and how extremely pious they were.

After the siesta, during which I had slept soundly on the
comfortable bed despite the almost overwhelming heat and
humidity, we were taken round the town by the small,
intense, dark-bearded Brother Mark who had met us at the
jetty. We visited the high, impressive cathedral – a conception
of modern architecture made entirely from local materials
and carved with the complex interlinking figures of Asmat
art. We looked in at the nuns' house and shook hands with
smiling, dark-skinned nuns in blue cotton dresses, gay,
laughing women who came mostly from an island off the
coast of Irian. We walked to the banks of the river to see the
co-operative lumber mill, where the Crosiers had set up
modern machines for cutting the local hard- and ironwood

into planks. There was a delicious smell of fresh sawdust and the valuable deep-red ironwood lay in mammoth piles of gigantic trunks (that had been floated downriver from deep in the heart of the jungle), or was stacked neatly in already-sawn planks.

Father Mark had told us they had been successful in teaching Asmatters to work the machines and cut the planks to perfect symmetry. The only trouble was that the men were often pressed into working for the government mills, for which they worked at the price of practically slave labour, and there was now competition from foreign lumber companies moving fast into the area.

Like the Dani, the Asmatters, it seemed, had been quite self-supporting when left to their own devices – gathering sago, which grew wild along the river banks, hunting wild pig and deer in the jungle, fishing and sorting out their problems by killing when necessary to protect themselves or provide offerings for their gods. Now, with the coming of civilization to the area, they were being pushed into a position where they had practically no place in a land which, by the right of generation upon generation, was theirs.

Makassarese and Indonesians from other parts of the continent were moving in quickly. Jobs that could slowly have been taught to the Asmatters were being done by cheap outside labour who were used to working fast. To the police and military who run the region, the half-naked, dark-skinned, lean people were little more than an embarrassment.

We visited the government-run art centre, set up when the gleam of tourism entered the government's eye. It was dusty, the plankway that led to it was badly in need of repair and the palm roof was rotting. A bis pole had half fallen outside, and inside the often thirty-feet-tall, weirdly carved poles of figures crouched one on top of another, distorted giant penises curved into exaggerated erections, were stacked higgledy-piggledy in a darkened room. Ceremonial shields and paddles lay in heaps on the floor, knives carved from the bones of cassowaries overflowed from a termite-eaten box. As an inducement to prospective tourists it was not impressive, but if they wanted to buy Asmat art this was where they would have to come. A recent order had stated that all Asmat art was to be sold through official channels. Neither the village carvers nor the mission could sell artifacts except through the government and the art centre.

As we walked through the town, we were passed by the strange Asmatters with their closely shorn heads almost showing the skin of their skulls. Often, the plank walkways were so narrow it was difficult to pass and they stood aside politely with a muffled 'Salamat Pagi'. Most of the men wore dirty, tattered clothing and, although a few of the women had equally filthy, ragged cotton dresses that hung like sacks over their thin bodies, most of them were naked except for a soiled brown sarong tied around their waists, or a straw skirt, even more mini than those worn by the Dani, slung around their hips. Apart from their clothes, the men and women were almost as hard to tell apart as their children. The women's breasts were narrow, hanging almost flat against their chests, and their bodies had a high, protruding but tightly muscled shape to their buttocks that was far more masculine than feminine. Their legs were long and boyish, stretching from narrow hips – as models they would have been a couturier's dream.

Few Asmatters lived in the town, most of them keeping to the native village lower downstream, connected by a terrifying two-plank walkway that sagged and often had huge gaps in it. When Father Mark left us to return to his duties, we tried to negotiate the quarter-of-a-mile-long bridge between but gave up after only about a hundred yards because, even for Robin, the problem of getting across the walkway needed the skill of an experienced tightrope performer.

In the town itself, Indonesians, Chinese and a cross between the two shouted at each other from house to house, radios blared from unshuttered windows and small children played on the walkways or fished with string and bent pins into the now fast-filling gullies below. Small, soft-shelled and prehensile black crabs jerked sideways across the oozing, grey-brown mud below. Even worse were small, only two- or three-inch-long, transparent newt-like creatures, the same colour as the mud, that flopped around with gills working hard, occasionally disappearing into the water and then appearing again by taking another plopping leap. I watched them, one evening, from the window of my bedroom when the mud around the mission was almost daylight bright under the light of a full moon. The splashing thuds they made as they landed made a strange kind of music, and sex, too, seemed to be 'rearing its ugly head' amongst these creatures for they appeared to be trying to land on each other's backs and chasing each other through the irrigation channels that bordered the coconut groves. There was something very nasty and sinister about them.

That first evening, we were summoned to go and have a talk with the Bishop in his 'palace', a house built off a pier at the end of the mission. The Bishop was a worldly and very erudite man despite his youth. The questions he asked Robin were sharp, very much to the point and extremely penetrating although they were gently and politely put.

Robin was, for about an hour, painlessly but very efficiently 'grilled' and he obviously came through the test with flying colours for, from then on, we seemed to be accepted by the Crosiers and no-one could have done more than they did to make us feel at home, impart as much knowledge as they could in the short time available and move us, like pawns, as widely as possible around the chessboard of the Asmat that came under their auspices.

Like Father Camps, he told us that they too were concentrating far more on the welfare and the future of the lives of the Asmatters than on converting them for a quick baptism. At least his people, the Bishop said, were in a slightly better way than those to the west of the area, the Mimeka people, who had been completely exploited by lumber and mining companies and had now sunk to a state of degeneration that had become a social and depressingly insoluble problem.

To us, the state of the Asmatters, through no fault of the indefatigable efforts of the mission, appeared far worse than that of the Dani. But then the Asmat had been in contact with the rest of the world for a far greater length of time than the Baliem, and it horrified us to think what might so soon happen to those tough little dark men of the highlands, if these swamp coasts were anything to go by.

In Agats, the indigenous people we saw looked confused and, as the Cornish would say, 'mazed'. They had every reason to do so. One minute they were told to destroy every factor and facet of their adat, the next they were ordered to resurrect these customs – as they had in the old days, in order to entice tourism – especially, of course, their valuable carvings, which had been formerly forbidden because they were part and parcel of the paraphernalia that incited warlike behaviour.

How were these people, labelled as primitive tribes, to be expected to know whether they were coming or going? So far, civilization had brought them few perks. The tattered clothing they wore could not be washed because they had no soap, so they got lice, scabies and other skin diseases. They had shops in Agats but the things on sale cost far more than they could afford. Above all, they had to watch while strangers took over their land for the enrichment of others and not themselves.

Because of the Bishop's belief in Robin's integrity, plans had been made for us to leave next morning to go up another tributary, visiting various outlying mission posts in the interior. On that first trip, we would be away from the mission for a night and so we repacked the knapsack at first light the next morning, taking with us only what would be needed for an overnight stop.

Full of my fairy-tale ideas, I thought that a Bishop's barge should have been ringed by gaily striped awnings, equipped with every comfort and flying a Bishop's pennant from a flag pole. It was not at all like that. The craft was a battered and dented metal hulk, with a small, incredibly dirty cabin up in the bows and the back covered with metal soon hot to the touch.

313

Two Asmatters sat on high stools in the front, one steering solidly, the large hole in his nose showing plainly when he turned his head sideways, and the other staring into space ahead. Both had ringworm or some other skin disease that showed through the holes in their dirt and grease stained, once-white, singlets.

For hour after hour, we chugged slowly up the muddy river with black smoke pouring from a thin funnel and the smell of diesel fumes over everything, passing by never-ending scenery that was flat, monotonous and, except for the birds, coloured only by green and mud tones.

There was little sign of human life. Evidence was there in the fish traps spanning every sidestream and tributary – V-shaped lines of sticks that would be covered when the tide was high and exposed with fish flopping around behind them when the water receded back to the sea. Occasionally, too, we had glimpses of camps on the bank, made by sago gatherers, that were small settlements of domed huts, temporary shelters of branches and sago palms. Fires still smoked but, at this time of the day, the shelters were totally deserted.

Once or twice, we passed a solitary long canoe from which a couple of naked men or women were fishing with spears or nets. From a distance, we could see them standing in and propelling the narrow craft forward with long paddles; the silhouettes of their figures made strange shapes with their long legs, and their stomachs and bottoms stuck out forming S-bends in their bodies. But when we got near they sat down and hid in the long wooden boats that often had carvings of strange, intertwined, pornographic figures on the prow. They shouted something at the Asmatters driving our boat and got an echoing shout in return.

Our companion, the boisterous Brother Jim, told us these shouts were a form of telegraphic communication used by all the river people. Often the driver and his mate would make them at an apparently empty stretch of mangrove and get a ringing answer that could clearly be heard above the noise of the engine but which seemed to come from nowhere. Those few shouts, apparently, would, in a kind of morse code language, provide a wealth of information about what was going on in this or that village. The information would then be passed to the next people higher up the river and so on, shouted across great distances in voices trained to carry and express a lot in only a few words.

Before noon, we arrived at a small settlement called Jamasj where an outpost of the mission was run by a Father Dale, another young American. Here we left the Bishop's boat for some repairs to be made on it by the mission mechanic, Brother Clarence, and we changed onto another equally smelly but larger metal boat. It chugged more slowly but had the comfort of a flat foredeck which, providing one could stand the heat and insects, at least gave an opportunity to sunbathe and get away from the fumes of the engine. Another couple of hours or so brought us to a larger village, built on both sides of the river, where we were met by another Crosier Father, this time a Dutchman, who lent heavily on a stick as he waited for us to moor alongside a solid wooden jetty.

Compared to the other villages we had seen, Erma, at first glance, looked attractive. Outside the mission house, where Father Jamas lived by himself, large bushes of hibiscus had been planted, and redundant canoes, filled with earth, were used as colourful gardens for tropical flowers. The main high-plank walkway around the mission house was well-maintained and, in most places, had the sophistication of a stout handrail which made walking on it much less hazardous.

The Father, however, was depressing, and at least some of this, I felt, was caused by his isolated life. Except for the tenuous contact he made by radio to the mission centre each day, he often spent weeks alone, seeing only the villagers. He was pessimistic about the future, the backwardness and the inability to grasp the basic essentials of twentieth-century life of the people with whom he lived.

After lunching with him and drinking gallons of iced

lemonade, he took us along the plank catwalks through the village and, as we approached the mission, we could see that it was neat and tidy. The Asmat huts and the people sitting around outside them had an all-pervading air of squalor and dejection about them. Once the Asmatters in this region had lived in long, communal huts; now they lived in small, almost identical little wooden boxes, and many of these had tattered walls, rotting piles and large open gaps in the palm thatching.

At the far end of the village, a small area of raised ground formed a bit of relatively dry land and here we were able to leave the ramps and trudge through six inches of black, sucking mud to the community boat-building centre. There a couple of men stood hacking at enormous tree trunks and a third was beginning to carve a traditional symbol on what would eventually be the prow of the canoe. Women and children watched them; their bullet-shaped heads were virtually bald, accentuating large ears and high foreheads, wide, thick-lipped mouths unsmiling and deep hollows furrowed into the bones around their necks and shoulders. They were silent and rather grim and most of the men had long, puckered scars around their chests and backs as evidence of former accidents, knife or spear wounds.

Outside one hut, in a small, thatched wigwam on the ground, the village master carver was working on a three-foot-high sculpture of the Virgin and Child; Mary in the process of giving birth, a haloed Mary with an Asmatter's face and the child half protruding from between her legs with its arms outstretched. It was crude yet compelling, cut from ironwood with the deep red grain of the wood following the outline of the woman's figure. The old man who had carved it showed it off with pride and led us up a notched log to his house to where about a dozen other similar figures looked rather weird and out of place inside the single bare room. The floor was uneven with many of the boards broken or rotten. There was no furniture and at one end an old woman squatted over a sultry fire, stirring something in a metal pot. Otherwise, the room was empty except for a pile of spears in one corner and some fish nets spread out on one of the walls to dry.

Father Jamas was reluctant for us to leave and it was late in the afternoon when we set off again to return to Jamasj where we were to spend the night.

The boat, when we got back on board, was crowded with Asmat men and boys who apparently wanted a lift downriver. They argued when Jim told them to get off, for a moment looking ugly, their usually rather flat eyes menacing, giving a fleeting insight into how close these people still were to killing for the slightest excuse. Jim gave in, after an argument, to the extent of taking some of them to the houses on the other shore, but once there he insisted they all leave. He had trouble making them understand and neither of the boatmen made any effort to help him so that finally he had to force his usually smiling face into a parody of fierceness and shout until they cleared off and the last remaining couple of boys leapt from the roof into the water, swimming like fish to the shore.

The three of us sat on the foredeck, leaning against a rubber tyre, swatting at mosquitoes, all of us red and burning from the trip upstream.

'We have a mission rule not to give any rides on the boats, except in emergencies,' Jim told us. 'It sounds a bit hard but usually they only want to go for the trip and if you agreed to take one, a hundred others would want to go too.' From the crowd of people now gathered on the bank, I could see the sense of this. For a chance to ride downstream on one of the tin boats, men would leave their work and women their children, dropping everything for a quick trip to another village where they might have relatives or friends.

Just before it got dark and light still came from one of those sunsets that was by far the most beautiful thing to me about the Asmat, we saw a couple of canoes way out in the main-stream of the river; a man stood in each, silhouetted against muted streaks of dove grey, pink and gold. Shouts echoed across the water and we slowed down. They came alongside us with amazing speed, with their paddles flailing the water, balancing in the rolling canoes like ballet dancers as they crossed our wake and grabbed hold of the tyres hanging down the side. They had been fishing, were naked except for small G-strings of cloth, and their catch had been good. In the bottom of one canoe were a collection of large, sinister black crabs and a couple of two-foot-long fish and in the other were not only fish but a couple of haunches of wild boar that must have come from an extraordinarily large animal. The boatmen showed great excitement at the catch and Jim bought all the crabs and fish for a thin flat slab of tobacco.

'What do you say we buy one of the legs to take to Father Dale?' he suggested. Then added rather nervously, 'I suppose it's fresh and hasn't been sitting in that boat for days; perhaps it's not such a good idea after all, though one sure longs for a bit of fresh meat here and Dale's got a fantastic cook.'

'Marika's the expert,' Robin offered. 'Ask them to hold it up and she'll take a professional sniff.' With the canoes almost rolling over as the fishermen, desperately eager for another sale, held up the huge leg, its coarse hairs with matted blood and covered with flies, I, eager to be of some use, leant as far as I dared over the side of the deck, lying on my stomach, sniffing hard. Except for the obvious strong odour of wild pig and an all-pervading smell of swamp, the meat was as fresh as a daisy, the hacked-off end showing fatless, rich red and bloody meat.

We paid for it with another slab of dried-up tobacco, one of the stock we had bought in Agats before leaving – about twelve pounds of flesh for the price of about 10p and certainly the cheapest piece of meat I have ever found. The fishermen looked delighted and raced away, their paddles flicking in and out of the water, with smooth, powerful strokes, making for one of the sago encampments along the shore and shouting excitedly to some dark figures on the bank.

'It seems awfully little to pay for all that meat,' I said to Jim, worried we had been cheating them, but he assured me it was a fair price.

'Tobacco's like gold dust to these people; they'll do anything for it and the worst thing the missionaries ever did was to bring it into Asmat. You bought that tobacco from the mission so it was relatively cheap, but the Chinese in the stores charge outrageous prices for the stuff and if you give the people money they'll only be cheated when they go to buy something. Unless they go to the mission, they haven't the chance of paying a fair price for anything and a piece of tobacco like that will last them about a month.'

As the sky clouded and night closed in over the swamps, it became cool for the first time. It was still extremely humid but at least it was possible to lean against the tyre on the deck without rivulets of sweat running down one's back.

How the boatmen saw in the dark without any form of light was incomprehensible to me, as I could not even make out the outline of the bank, but we continued downstream with the engine going, chugging loudly, and the boat moving quite fast now that the tide had turned again and the current was with us.

We were proud of our boar's-leg prize and the boatmen were happy with their fish. They sang in harsh, off-key voices, shouted to the bank and got echoing replies from the darkness. For the first time, they began to smile at us, grunting in a friendly way as they accepted cigarettes and giggling when the fat, jolly Brother Jim gave them a playful punch in the ribs.

It was a happy, relaxed meal, elegantly served by Tim, Father Dale's Asmat cook, who could well have been the maître d'hôtel of the Savoy Grill. After it, we sat drinking strong, delicious coffee, cup after cup from a seemingly bottomless thermos until we were all yawning with such regularity that bed became inevitable despite the most stimulating conversation with Father Dale, Father Dave and the mechanic, Brother Clarence.

During the many and varied conversations, we learnt about

the extraordinary cargo cult-worship which, now and then, sweeps through the New Guinea tribes. It had started with a plane, loaded with supplies for food, crashing in the jungle; the crew were killed and to the Papuans it was as though a parcel of goodies had been sent to them from the sky. The people stopped working and concentrated on building high bamboo towers towards the skies to encourage more white birds to land.

At intervals, hysterical forms of this cargo cult-worship broke out in various tribes. One group, believing all Americans were rich, had saved money in order to buy the President of America. Another group, seeing an advertisement in an Australian paper showing a picture of money 'growing on trees', had begged, borrowed or stolen a store of small notes which they buried in the ground and then, refusing to work, fish or hunt, waited for it to grow. Usually, the leader of these cults was a man with some deformity and, while the craze went on, many of the tribes would become ill almost to the point of starvation.

That night, we slept in the same room for the last time until we reached Singapore and, as we made a pretence of washing and crawled sleepily between heavenly clean sheets, I remarked, yawning yet again:

'I can't possibly imagine how we can be so tired, having done virtually nothing except sit on a boat all day long.'

We were both to say the same thing many times again during the days we spent in the Asmat and I think neither of us had any idea just how tired we both were or how much of a beating our constitutions had taken during three months of almost continual, exhausting, non-stop travelling.

We left Jamasj the next morning, visited a few villages on the way down the river and got back to the mission well after the sun had set. The following day, we left at the crack of dawn again and, once more accompanied by Brother Jim, chugged slowly up yet another river, reaching Father Trenkenshuh's village by mid-day, after another long, monotonous voyage past never-ending banks of mud and twisted roots with the flat dense jungle spreading out behind. I could not believe that men could hunt through that untamed, waterlogged maze of twisted roots, shifting mud and giant, tangled undergrowth. Yet they did, edging their narrow canoes up almost invisible streams and running bare-footed through the hostile undergrowth.

The major excitement of the trip was seeing a crocodile, at least fifteen feet long, basking on a mud bank, the colour of its horny scales almost melting into the background but its pale, yellow belly catching the sun. It was reptilian, revolting and, even from the safe distance of about fifty yards, full of menace.

The meeting with Father Trenkenshuh was a rather nervous one. He and Robin had exchanged numerous letters from a distance of thousands of miles and now they were to meet for the first time. They held many of the same ideas but also, inevitably, had many points they argued over and, whereas Robin is a layman with a philosophy degree, Father Trenkenshuh is an ordained Catholic priest with a first-class degree in anthropology.

The Father was on the jetty to meet us and he looked totally opposite to everything I had expected. For one thing I had imagined him, from the amount of writing he had done and the fantastic stories we had heard about his exploits and achievements in the Asmat, as a man of middle age or more. In fact, despite having crew-cut hair that was almost snow white, he was only thirty-five, the same age as I am, with an unlined face and humorous blue eyes behind large glasses. He was also enormously tall, towering a good foot above me and as lean and lanky as one of the Asmatters themselves.

It was a slight case of Stanley and Livingstone suddenly confronting each other, and I mentally kept my fingers crossed as 'Trenk', as we were quickly to call him, and Robin shook hands in a rather reserved way and sized each other up. They could not have been more different to look at but, fortunately, after a grilling by Trenk that was just as intense and astute as the Bishop's had been, Robin was accepted, any tension was totally dispelled, and in what sadly was only a visit of the best part of a day, they became firm friends.

As we walked beside this intelligent, humorous, gangling man, who wore pink shorts and tee-shirt and who walked bare-footed, we paced the length and breadth of his village, Ayam, the largest in the area. The people here were far more friendly, women waved from the doors or the steps of their houses, men smiled as we walked through a communal hut of thatched palm, stepping over their legs and an old, intricately carved bis pole lying across one end.

The houses were built on either side of a wide track, irrigated by deep ditches filled with brackish, swamp-smelling water. Behind us, as we walked, a band of black, curly-haired children with dark, round eyes followed, shouting and giggling, and then shrieking with excitement, as Brother Jim, in his element, chased them, waving a plastic toy snake he produced from his pocket.

It may have been the fact that Ayam, one of the more remote of the mission outposts, was built on an island of virtually dry land so one could walk round with a wonderful sense of freedom, and there were even some real gardens outside some of the houses; perhaps it was the fact of being in the invigorating company of Trenk, or maybe we were now accustomed to Asmatters; in any case, they had relaxed in their attitude towards us. But whatever was the cause, these people seemed almost gay and looked more healthy than any others we had seen. In many ways, they appeared more primitive with fewer clothes and more evidence of adat about, yet they looked far more intelligent and alive, without that glazed, dull look in the eyes of the people further down the river. The women, especially, were tall and graceful and one girl, at least, was positively beautiful to look at. But, despite the peaceful air surrounding the village, there were plenty of signs of the articles of war in the spears propped against the walls of some of the houses and the numerous phallic bis poles dotted around; their intertwined figure-carvings were strangely sophisticated against the simplicity of the dwellings.

Although, by nature, more of an optimist than Father Jamas, Father Trenk was very aware of the problems facing the Asmatters. He disapproved of the custom of trading in tobacco and was trying to teach his people the true value of money in rather the same manner as Father Camps but without the aid of films. He was concerned about the corruption of the Indonesians in the area and their bad relationship with the people. He was worried about the problems of finding a cash crop the tribes could deal in now that their main resources of lumber, crocodile skins and much of the fishing had been taken from them by outsiders.

He talked enthusiastically about the museum of Asmat art being built in Agats under his auspices, of the plans he hoped for farming buffalo in the area and of the idea of getting a team of tropical agricultural experts into Asmat to make a survey of the possibilities which might exist in the region.

We were late setting off again and glad that Father Trenk would be coming down to Agats the next day to spend our last evening in the Asmat with us at the mission.

Once again, there was a sensational sunset and as parakeets, hornbills and egrets flew home to their nesting places in the jungle, the darkening sky became the province of truly enormous bats, flitting and wheeling against a pale, almost circular moon or dipping down to skim across the silver-sheened water. It was another long voyage and once again, by the time we returned to Agats, we were almost painfully tired though at the most we could only have walked a couple of miles during the whole day. The heat and the humidity seemed to drain one of every ounce of energy and, again, I ached and scratched as I climbed under my mosquito netting in one of those maddening roundabouts of being too tired to sleep. I was also lonely for Robin. As soon as we got back to Jayapura, he was leaving for New Guinea and I would head back to Jakarta and Singapore alone.

On our last evening in Agats, one of the Fathers took us to the hospital to see a man who had recently been brought in from the jungle with a leg badly bitten by a crocodile.

He had been hunting, half paddling his canoe and half pushing it with a foot along the sludge of a stream bed in the swamp. A large crocodile had snapped through the leg outside the canoe and, although the pain must have been unbearable, he had somehow managed to get back to the river where some fishermen found him and brought him to Agats. He was one of the best hunters and warriors of the area.

Walking along the planks at night was even more scary than it was in the daytime but we reached the hospital without falling off, were met by one of the nuns and led under a covered passage to a room at the end where the man lay.

The horror on my face must have been obvious as I looked around at the dirt and squalor of the whole place. It was drab, dingy and appeared to be half falling down. The wounded man was lying on a filthy mound of brown rags with an equally dirty strip of netting hanging above him. The pallor of his face under the blackness of his skin was frightening and a stink of rotting flesh came strongly from the filthy bandaging around his wounded leg.

The Father with us spread out his hands in a sad gesture that was almost one of defeat.

'What can we do?' he asked. 'This is a government hospital with a badly paid government doctor. He does his best but he has none of the equipment or medicine needed to cope with almost the simplest of problems. The nuns help as much as they can and the maternity wing works quite well but in these wards a fight without money is a losing one.

'This man,' he said, 'has obviously got gangrene and I imagine we will have to fly him to Jayapura to have the leg amputated or he will die. With the proper medical care, he would probably have ended up with nothing but a limp and a scar; as it is . . . ' His words trailed off and, after giving the hunter some tobacco (the only thing we could do for him) and taking his offered hand which, to my shame, I found very difficult to touch in that all-pervading smell of suppurating, rotting humanity, we left the hospital.

This was an appalling experience, particularly as we knew

we were powerless to help. But supper and the late-night rest and recreation period were a welcome relief. Everyone was very gay and the arrival of Father Trenkenshuh seemed to put new life into all the residents at the mission, although it seemed there were many points on which some of the other Fathers crossed swords with him, though gently and almost always with a touch of humour.

Even Grace made me giggle (I had at last got used to standing and waiting for it before sitting down to a meal). 'Lord bless you for these thy gifts of food and drink but please try and make it a better meal than the last one I had here. Amen.'

In just a few days, we seemed to have made many friends and that evening there was a wonderful sense of harmony as we sat and talked, drinking whisky and beer, during the rest and recreation period after the generators had stopped and work was over for the day. Our leave-taking next day was sad, full of genuine friendship on all sides and, from the Bishop, very moving. Despite looking extremely drawn and tired, he insisted on coming down to the jetty to see us off and I had a hard time preventing myself from kissing him on the cheek as a token of my thanks. (I do not think one does kiss Bishops – unless, of course, one happens to be closely related to them.) He was a truly marvellous man and the service we'd been to, in the cathedral, which was packed to full capacity with Asmatters, had impressed us both. He conducted it in Asmat and made a short sermon which brought smiles and nods of agreement from the people.

We left on the morning of the day after Mrs Yani had expected to greet her hundred tourists. She was still convinced they would arrive despite there having been no news whatsoever of the cruise ship on either the military or the mission radios.

To bid them welcome about a hundred Asmat men had been press-ganged into service and made to dress up for a ceremonial canoe display. Ritual canoes, painted along the sides, decked with leaves and with their prows carved with crouching, phallic figures, were lined up along the banks of the river.

In them, groups of men had been standing since dawn, holding carved paddles and waiting for the ship as they had waited all day the day before. To us, they looked pathetic beside spears that were meant for killing and were finely garlanded with feathers. Their skin was painted, giving their faces a frightening outward appearance that was further increased by large nosebones, of curving boar's tusks sticking from their noses, and headdresses of long, false hair or feathers. The effect should have been a good one, but it was totally ruined by the tattered, filthy shorts and singlets they all wore and the way many of them had caps or hats on under their headdresses. Also, they looked miserable and as though they were hating every moment of the whole thing.

As we ploughed round the estuary and along the coastline towards the airstrip at Ewer and could see for miles across the ocean, there was still no sign of the ship and, on that occasion at any rate, Mrs Yani and Agats waited in vain for their tourists.

Tom landed at eleven and flew us to Jayapura; he followed the sensational course of the Baliem river as first it meandered through swamps and jungle and then began its series of dramatic waterfalls and rapids as we rose higher and higher to cross the huge central range of mountains that dissects Irian Jaya.

Chapter 22

Robin left Jayapura to fly to New Guinea early the next morning and I sat at the airport, sweltering in a temperature of about 120 degrees, squashing flies, swatting bugs and drinking can after can of local beer. (One of the best things about Indonesia – apart from its beaches and beauty, many of its people, the hospitality, sunsets and vastness of it all – is the lack of coca-cola and coca-cola advertisements.)

I sat there for over seven hours, waiting for an inevitably delayed flight to Biak where I would have to spend another night. I was hot, miserable and dejected, and convinced I was going to miss the announcement of the plane's departure when it did leave.

By the time I was on the point of suicidal hysteria, the garbled message blared through a loudspeaker and within hours I was back in Biak and drinking with the mining boys again in the bar, filling in time until my next flight left thirty-six hours later.

Due to Peep the pilot, the time went quickly. The first evening he drove me to the other hotel in the town and introduced me to its owner, Mrs Engles, and her family. The hotel looked much more fun than the Merpati one, very shambolic and full of grottos covered with tropical shells, cascades of water and trees that housed numerous, cuddly, furry cus cus, funny little creatures with velcrome hands for climbing up tree trunks, long tails and huge myopic eyes.

Mrs Engles was a magnificent lady, larger than anyone

I have ever seen, encased in great rolls of comfortable fat and a deep rumbling, very frequent, infectious giggle. She had been married twice and had three daughters in their early twenties and late teens who were the most beautiful girls in Indonesia.

As a friend of Peep's and also as a friend of the good Father Rutyes in Ambon whom she knew well, I was greeted like a long-lost child, told to treat her crowded, cramped living room as my home and introduced to the teenaged daughter whose heart-shaped face, limpid dark eyes, clear pale coffee skin and incredible cascades of hair quite took my breath away. The other, elder, daughters were away so I was shown album after album of photographs of them winning beauty competitions and starring in Indonesian films. Each one was more beautiful than the other and when she asked me to say which I found the best I was unable to make up my mind.

I dined with them that night and lunched there the next day. Mrs Engles said that I looked like a plucked chicken, and she tried to feed me up with hundreds of tempting dishes and endless plates of cakes and sweets, but sadly something had happened to my stomach and I could not do more than nibble her excellent food. When I said goodbye she gave me a present of a fantastic shell, smooth, magical and gracefully curled, and a pair of early Chinese funeral pots from her collection of Chinese porcelain which Peep and Father Rutyes had told me was worth well over a million pounds. I was completely overwhelmed and cried yet again as she clasped me to her fabulously generous and more than ample bosom (I disappeared completely into its folds), kissing me goodbye as though I had been one of her beautiful daughters.

That evening many of my nightmare problems of travelling were miraculously solved by the arrival of David Treffry at the Merpati Hotel. I could not believe my eyes and suffered from a fleeting pang of embarrassment at being found in the bar surrounded by about a dozen men from the mining camp, and then greeted him with almost Engles-like enthusiasm. I was to stay with him for a night in Jakarta but I had had no thought of meeting him in Biak on his way back from a mission to Irian.

After what seemed more like three years than three months I set foot once more in the palatial splendour of a Singapore hotel, and in one hot, sticky hand I clutched a sheaf of letters that I had read and re-read since picking them up from the Embassy in Jakarta (where the consul had looked at me as though I was a ghost raised from the grave) and over which I had shed many more tears of joy because everything was, really and truly, honestly and deliriously, wonderfully right at home. I had shed tears as I read them and I felt better than I had for weeks despite this uncontrollable cascade of water which I seemed totally unable to prevent.

I knew I had lost weight, but when I zipped up my dress the sight I faced in the first full-length mirror I had seen for over a couple of months was ridiculous. The size ten knitted cotton number looked as though it was a joke hand-me-down from a large maiden aunt.

Wearing it, because there was nothing else, I braved the cocktail lounge, fortified myself with a vodka martini in which I demanded treble the normal ration of ice cubes and then strolled into the restaurant, renowned for its steaks, with what I hoped was a nonchalant air.

Despite being a woman on her own (not at all the thing in smart Singapore restaurants) and despite the dress, I was reluctantly shown a table – the smallest in the room, tucked far away in a corner and almost totally obscured by a serving trolley. When a waiter finally condescended to pass a menu to me from as great a distance as he was able to reach, the prices on it made me gasp. I had expected it to be expensive, but £1.50 for a cupful of consommé was grotesque. But nothing, not even such crazy figures, was going to stop me now. I joined the big spenders (it was all on credit cards anyway, so who cared?) and firmly ordered my consommé and the most expensive cut of meat they offered, 'flown in fresh daily from Australia'. To impress the waiter I also ordered half a bottle of the second most expensive claret on the wine list. He may not have known that I had just spent three months exploring the wildest parts of Indonesia, I told myself, but at least he will not be able to overlook the fact that I have a nose for a good bouquet.

It was a fiasco. To start with, I strongly suspected the consommé came straight from the tin of a gentleman called Campbell and neither lemon juice, seasoning nor sherry had wafted anywhere near it; to finish with, one look at the two-inch-thick, blood-oozing hunk of meat on my plate (the meat I had been licking my lips at the thought of for so long) had me begging the nearest waiter for the bill and rushing from the restaurant before I chucked up on the tartan carpet of the restaurant.

So many things are an anti-climax when you look forward to them, but getting home was everything and more than Robin or I had ever dreamed of. He arrived on time in Singapore and we flew back on the last eighteen-hour leg of our journey together, holding hands like a couple of lovesick teenagers.

Except that the children had grown, a foal had been born, there were twice as many cows as there had been when we left and our bedroom had been repainted, nothing much had changed. It just all seemed bigger, better and infinitely more precious and beautiful.

From an expedition such as we had undertaken there must be an end product. In this case there are two, Robin's book and mine, both on the same subject but one thoughtful and informative and the other an attempt to paint a picture in words of an experience we both felt was something of such immense breadth that we despaired of being able to relate it in more than a mere portion of its million facets.

I, after an overdose of painful tests and examinations by doctors specializing in tropical medicine, was found not to have picked up some glamorous Eastern disease but to be suffering from common or garden malnutrition which had begun in Ceram and escalated at a frightening rate since then, until I ended up with anorexia and was unable to eat at all.

At least that explained the crying and bones which stuck out at ugly angles through my skin. Personally, I was rather delighted with the Twiggy effect and the joy of, for the first time in my life, being a 'skinny Lizzie', but Robin and everyone else used words like 'Belsen' and went round with such long faces that gradually I began to nibble again and the tears ceased.

Now all that is over and Indonesia seems a long way away. But the contact is there and the ties are strong. Both of our lives were touched by the lives and the problems of the tribes we had travelled so far to see and by the lives of those people whose role it is to try and protect their interests. All of us will try to do what we can to help but in the end it is in the hands of these people's governments that their fate – people so often beautiful and in their own way highly cultured – ultimately lies.